HEATHER E. HEYING

ANTIPODE

Seasons

with the

Extraordinary

Wildlife and

Culture of

Madagascar

ST. MARTIN'S PRESS
NEW YORK

ANTIPODE: SEASONS WITH THE EXTRAORDINARY WILDLIFE AND
CULTURE OF MADAGASCAR. Copyright © 2002 by Heather E. Heying.
All rights reserved. Printed in the United States of America. No part of
this book may be used or reproduced in any manner whatsoever without
written permission except in the case of brief quotations embodied in
critical articles or reviews. For information, address St. Martin's Press,
175 Fifth Avenue, New York, N.Y. 10010.

www.stmartins.com

Design by Kathryn Parise

All photographs, except those credited to Bret Weinstein, are by
Heather E. Heying.

Map by Brad Wood

LIBRARY OF CONGRESS CATALOGING-IN-PUBLICATION DATA

Heying, Heather E.
Antipode : seasons with the extraordinary wildlife and culture of
Madagascar / Heather E. Heying.—1st ed.
p. cm.
ISBN 0-312-28152-8
1. Natural history—Madagascar. 2. Golden frogs. 3. Wildlife
conservation—Madagascar. 4. Madagascar—Description and travel. 5.
Madagascar—Social life and customs. 6. Heying, Heather E.—Journeys—
Madagascar. 7. Women biologists—United States—Biography. I. Title.

  QH195.M2 H48 2002
  508.691—dc21

                                                 2001059185

First Edition: July 2002

  10 9 8 7 6 5 4 3 2 1

TO THE PEOPLE OF MADAGASCAR

CONTENTS

PART 3

ACKNOWLEDGMENTS

This book would not have been possible without the generosity, humor, and goodwill of the many Malagasy with whom I was lucky enough to interact. I cannot hope to list all, or even most, of them here, so I will restrict myself to those few whose insight and integrity truly stand out. Rosalie Razafindrasoa was consistently brimming with wit and charm. All of the naturalist guides of the Maroantsetra Guide Association were extraordinary; individually, many acted as my teacher, though few knew it at the time. In particular, the joy that Felix carried with him through his days was contagious. In addition, Emile, Paul, Augustin, and Armand added intelligence and levity to many days.

Angeluc Razafimanantsoa and Benjamin Andriamihaja were each utterly unique and amazing personalities in the Malagasy landscape. I want to thank the many members of the support staff at Projet Masoala, especially Pascal, Solo, and the five conservation agents with whom I shared Nosy Mangabe while I was there, who invited me into their lives. Several agencies of the Malagasy government, especially DEF and ANGAP, granted me access to the lands of Madagascar. The fisherman who gave me mangoes, the man who supplied me a raffia mat on which to sit, the curious children and rice vendors—all contributed to my experiences, this book, and my life. For allowing me to live among them, and observe their frogs, this book is therefore dedicated to the people of Madagascar.

There were, of course, many *vazaha* whose roles in the creation of this book, sometimes unwitting, were critical. Because my raison d'être in Madagascar was field research, the members of my doctoral committee at the University of Michigan played an important role in helping me be prepared for and inspired by my several trips. I therefore thank professors Arnold Kluge (my adviser), Ron Nussbaum, Dick Alexander, and Barb Smuts. All were wonderfully supportive when I told them that I was putting my research aside for a short time to focus on *Antipode* (and a bit relieved when I got back to writing the dissertation).

Among the many additional scientists to whom I owe debts of gratitude are Franco Andreone, Isabel Constable, Claire Kremen, Chris Raxworthy, and Bob Trivers. In addition, the Wildlife Conservation Society, and especially Matthew Hatchwell, were extremely helpful during my time in Madagascar.

I was blessed with two outstanding research assistants, Jessica Metcalf and Glenn Fox, who were indispensable in the field, enduring no end of indignities while working under often harsh conditions, and who also did not cringe when informed that I was writing about our experiences. In addition to providing keen observational skills, clever analysis, and great humor, Jessica did me the great service of introducing me to her parents, Ros and Peter Metcalf. Without their warmth and spirit, my time in Madagascar in 1997 would have been far more difficult, dreary, and less chocolaty.

Several dear friends and family members worked to keep me sane while I was in Madagascar, via frequent letters. Of these, Dyan Haspel-Johnson, my mother Jessie Heying, Laura Howard, and Nancy Peters also engaged in the mind-boggling effort to help me get the manuscript into shape once I was home. In my stubbornness, I often resisted their suggestions, which made their continuing, unflagging persistence yet more admirable.

I want to thank my literary agent, Ed Knappman, for seeing promise in a proposal from an unpublished author. My editor, Brad Wood, who remained a dogged and enthusiastic proponent of this work, although he sometimes may have wished it were heavier on the herps. Elizabeth Royte, for her many helpful comments.

Most especially, I thank Bret Weinstein, now my husband. He has been a consistent advocate for both my scientific work and this book, and he has worked long hours on both with me, his own enthusiasm often surpassing my own. Indeed, he has provided not only intellectual and scientific support but, as should be apparent from the text of *Antipode*, philosophical, moral, mechanical, technical, field, medical, emotional, and even physical support as well. For all this, and so much more, I thank him from the bottom of my heart.

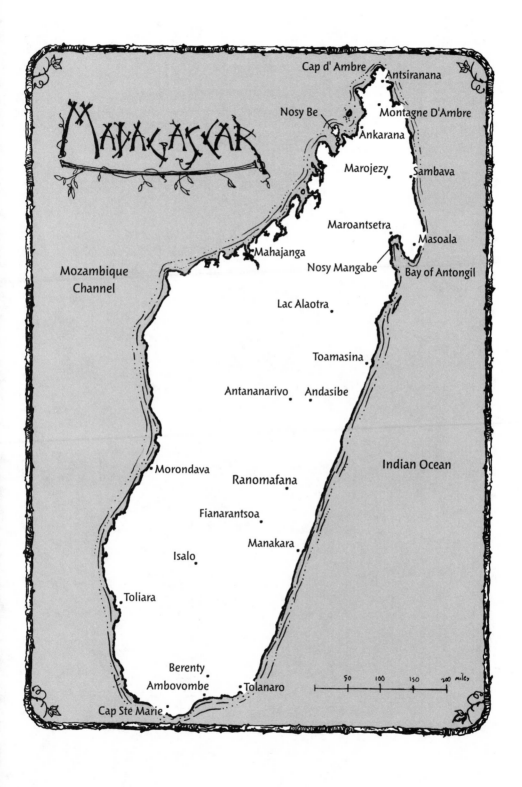

ANTIPODE (n):

1. the opposite side of the world
2. a person from the far side of the Earth
3. diametrically opposite or contrary

ANTIPODAL (adj):

(humorously) having everything upside down

PROLOGUE

Many years ago, Madagascar beckoned me. It was 1993, and my boyfriend, Bret, and I had recently finished college. We thought, briefly, about going to Europe. Instead, we headed to the great red island, so called for the mineral deposits that turn its soil a deep rust. Our heads were full of strange ideas regarding the number of tribal chiefs we might meet, and how many cats we would be expected to consume. At the time, our home was Santa Cruz, California, where we made a habit of dashing around on our mountain bikes, soaking up the scent of redwoods and Pacific salt air. Scrutinizing a globe before our trip, we discovered that we were heading about as far away from home as was possible. If we dug a hole straight down from Santa Cruz, we would end up not in China, but in a spot in the southern Indian Ocean, from which the nearest landmass was Madagascar. We were heading to our antipode.

Near the end of that trip, we found ourselves in the north of Madagascar. We stood at the edge of a sacred lake, surrounded by dripping rain forest.

"Do not use or touch the water," our guide advised us. "It is *fady*. The ancestors would not approve."

With that warning of *fady*—taboo—echoing in our heads, he left. We were finally alone in the wilderness of Madagascar. We dropped our packs and pitched our little tent, then spent a long time getting a fire started as the temperature began to drop. Overhead, a troop of crowned lemurs leapt through the trees, chattering and grunting. Already Bret had learned their calls, and he spoke to them. They paused long enough to investigate the strange primates on the ground. As dusk fell, they moved on, and we followed them into the darkening forest.

Soon we lost the lemurs, outpaced on foot by their antics high in the trees. A tenrec scuttled by, nose to the ground, its spiny shrewlike body seeming to dare would-be predators to try to take a bite. Then it, too, disappeared into a sea of green. We stood utterly still in a rain forest now devoid of obvious animals, with only the otherworldly plants for company.

"What is that?" I hissed at Bret, hearing faint rustling on the ground. It was all around us, as if the Earth was preparing to open up and swallow us whole.

"I have no idea," he admitted. We looked at each other wide-eyed as the rustling grew louder, and closer. Leaves of understory plants began to bend around us. I squatted to investigate. Now at eye level, the source of the rustling became clear. An army of terrestrial leeches was on the march, attracted to our heat. As the big warm-blooded mammals in their midst, we must have looked like the source of a hearty blood meal, and leeches from all over were convening on the place where we stood.

"Let's move," Bret suggested with a grin. "I'm sure we can outrun them." And so we moved farther into the forest, away from our tent. There were no recognizable trails, but we stayed on a constant westerly bearing, so that it would be easy to find our way back.

"Haven't we been here before?" I asked as we passed a giant gnarled tree.

"Can't be," Bret answered; "we're still going west." He tapped the compass for emphasis, then added, "Always trust the compass before your own intuition." We had invoked these words often during backpacking trips in the High Sierra.

It was now very dark. I felt as if we'd made several turns. We were wandering far from the shores of the sacred lake, with no trail back. Ahead of us, through the trees, we saw eyes.

"Mouse lemurs?" I whispered, breathless. There seemed to be many of them, writhing in a frantic dance. Bright eye-shine capered low to the ground, the sounds of hissing and popping—was that snarling?—confusing our interpretation of the fantastic scene.

"Perhaps," Bret agreed slowly. "Or snakes. Maybe a mating ball. Turn off your headlamp," he urged. We turned off our lights, but the eyes did not disappear.

"What the hell?" we both asked aloud, now truly scared. If they had been eyes, they, too, would have blinked off when our headlamps no longer shone into them. We flipped our headlamps on again and went slowly toward the lights. Within a few yards, the mystery was solved. Emerging onto the embers of our own fire, glowing red and popping, we were relieved, but deeply confused. Nothing in this forest was as, or where, we thought it was.

We looked again at our compass, and it now read north. Cursing, Bret stuffed it into an out-of-way pocket and vowed not to use it again. Back home, it had worked perfectly. We later learned that magnetic idiosyncrasies in the Earth mean that you need a specially calibrated compass in most of the southern hemisphere. We had been thwarted by our assumptions that Madagascar was, in this small way, just like home.

Over several years, I would discover that, except to the Malagasy themselves—the people who are from and of Madagascar—there are few ways in which Madagascar is like home. In the name of science, I would repeatedly visit that wondrous place, to better understand natural systems that are disappearing. The lives of the brightly colored poisonous frogs I went to study were essentially unknown before I began my research, and I had to start at the beginning to answer basic questions of their biology. How do males and females differ, and how many offspring do they have at one time? As I began to put the puzzle pieces into place, everything about those tiny frogs made more sense—the decisions they seemed to be making about mates, and where to make their homes. My knowledge of that biological system paralleled an increasing understanding of the people and cultural traditions of Madagascar.

The unique cultures of Madagascar, in concert with an economy that precludes most people from ever leaving the place of their birth, make the lives and expectations of the Malagasy utterly distinct from my own. It is this difference in perception and daily experience, in part, that I hope to share in this book. How does it feel to be a nature lover and biologist from the land of right angles and artificially white spaces, suddenly living in a tent and planning every activity around the weather and the phase of the moon? How does one integrate ideas of conservation in a forest you live in and come to love, while surrounded by warning signs that the forest will not last? This, too, shall fall to the global grab for land and natural resources. And how to reconcile the simple facts that human experience is in many ways universal—there are heroes and villians everywhere—but my particular expectations are not? I am so strange to these wonderful people in their homeland that I will never feel wholly at home there myself.

During four trips to Madagascar, these issues came in and out of focus many times. My trips were separated by months or years, from 1993 to 1999, and they represent very different stages of my personal and professional development. I begin the book by orienting the reader to Madagascar and explaining how I came to be there, but the true narrative begins in chapter two, and follows, in three parts, a broad spectrum of adventures and revelations the likes of which only Madagascar could generate.

PART I

1

You Are Here

Madagascar is an immense island. It is the fourth-largest in the world, after Greenland, New Guinea, and Borneo. All told, it is slightly smaller than Texas. This great red island lies off the east coast of Africa, in the Indian Ocean, not two hundred miles from Mozambique, but has less in common with Africa than one might expect, given its close proximity. Madagascar has been separated from all other landmasses for at least 80 million years, and in that time, the biota has become extraordinary and unique. Ninety percent of its plant and animal species are endemic—found nowhere else on the planet. There are neon-spotted frogs, and fully grown chameleons the size of pocket change. Enormous baobab trees looking as if they've been planted upside down. Bats with built-in suction cups on their wrists and ankles. Carnivorous pitcher plants. Leaf-tailed geckos that flatten against and blend in so perfectly with tree trunks that you can look one in the eye at six inches and think you're admiring bark. Every time you take a step in what remains of the wilderness of Madagascar, new surprises meet your eyes. And then there are the lemurs.

More monkey than ape in character, but not actually either, prosimians are among the most primitive primates. All Madagascan prosimians are commonly called lemurs, although some, technically, are not. Living species include the black-and-white indri, which look like giant teddy bears; they sing duets with their mates at first light, and again as the sun sets; their mournful song carries miles across the forest, and often across deforested land where they can no longer live, evoking haunting memories of their bygone presence. The island is also still home to the tiniest of primates, the mouse lemur, a big-eyed fur ball that scurries about in the trees with the aid of its opposable thumbs, the whole package smaller than a human fist. And there's the aye-aye, a scruffy, mangy-looking beast with bat ears and a long, wispy tail. This otherworldly creature uses an elongated middle finger to pull sap and insect larvae out of trees, filling the woodpecker niche in a place with no woodpeckers. Local legend suggests that if you see an aye-aye, you must kill it, else bad luck will fall upon your village. Aye-ayes are, understandably, a bit shy of people nowadays.

Aside from the aye-aye, the Malagasy myths that have risen up around the lemurs are mostly ones of exaltation. The indri is believed to have saved a man who, having broken a critical branch, was stranded high up in a tree. It is *fady* to hurt an indri. Other lemurs are hunted for food, but they are admired for their dexterity and skill in the trees. Tales are told of their social habits—one Malagasy friend told me that female lemurs seek out and eat the leaves of a toxic plant when they want abortions. And they are even, sometimes, valued for their beauty in this country at the bottom of the world's economic ladder, where aesthetic concerns are rarely a priority.

It is still a matter of some debate how both the landmass of Madagascar and the people living on it came to be there. Madagascar probably split from Africa early in the breakup of Gondwanaland, but remained attached to what would become the Indian subcontinent to the north, Australia and the Southeast Asian islands to the east, and Antarctica to the south and west. The last landmass with which Madagascar rifted was India, which ultimately broke away and moved north toward a collision with Asia that would raise the Himalayas.

Were the first Malagasy people Africans, Indians, Southeast Asians (present-day Indonesians), or Pacific Islanders? Perhaps Polynesians, with a bit of Southeast Asian, and some Arab blood, picked up during what must have been a long journey by boat. Few anthropologists agree on when people began arriving on Madagascar. But it is clear that neither the people nor the wildlife bear much resemblance to those on the African continent, and a sure way to insult a Malagasy is to refer to him as African. Although Africa and Madagascar are physically quite close, strong water currents in the Mozambique Channel make it difficult for anything to cross between the two.

Madagascar was a stopping point on trade routes throughout the age of colonial Europe—indeed, the oldest map of the region where I work was made by Dutch pirates. There are more than twenty distinct tribal groups, several variations on a theme of animist religion, and very little industrial or technological development. The French colonized Madagascar in the late nineteenth century, but they were ousted in a democratic vote in 1958. Lingering French influence explains both the prevalence of the French language across the country and the surreal appearance of fresh baguettes in even rural markets every morning. Due to widespread corruption, the new government gradually began provoking protests, and in 1975, it was replaced by the socialists. From then until 1992, during the socialist era in Madagascar, outsiders were particularly distrusted, and foreigners who hadn't managed to stay behind when the French left were not often let in during this period. The socialists had come in with grand ideals and plans, but they soon fell into disrepute. In 1992, after years of increasingly vocal protests from the people, a multiparty democracy was formed, and Dr. Albert Zafy was elected president. His administration, too, soon lost popularity, and in 1997, in a democratic vote, Didier Ratziraka, the former socialist head of state, became the president of Madagascar. By early 2002, Madagascar was again in a state of uproar, and the future of the Malagasy government was unclear.

Were I telling stories about modern American suburbanites, it might be safe to assume that the time not chronicled is spent watching television, talking on the telephone, shopping, and commuting between home and work. At night, our neighbors retreat to their walled-off homes, turn on the lights, and make themselves comfortable among their things.

In Madagascar, except in the capital, Antananarivo, there are essentially no televisions or phones in anyone's private home. Even in Tana—the more manageable name for Antananarivo—these luxuries are rare. When present, phones seldom work. In northeastern Madagascar, where I work, people commute, but it is not a commute most Americans would recognize. The locals walk daily between their palm-roofed homes and the outdoor market—the *zoma*—which reliably has baskets and rice for sale. Communal pit toilets and open charcoal fires are the bathrooms and kitchens, respectively. Electricity exists only sporadically in the one sizable town in the region. Twice a week, a turboprop lands on the local runway, there being no reliable roads that connect this part of the island to the rest, and all children and some adults within a certain radius come to watch the spectacular event. There are no print media, no books available. A single radio station exists, though few private homes—which are primarily open-air shacks—have radios. There is no privacy, and few precious things.

In Madagascar, time is so abundant as to be unmeasured, such that a request for a boat or a meal or a person to show up at a particular time, even on a particular day, makes no sense. If something else comes up, maybe that gets priority. Maybe not. Who can predict these things, and why would anyone want to? If it doesn't come today, maybe it will come tomorrow. Maybe tomorrow. *Peut-être demain. Ongomba rapitso.* In English, French, or Malagasy, it is perhaps the most often-used phrase in Madagascar. Meanwhile, in the United States, services are advertised based on their ability to get things *there*, wherever *there* may be, more quickly than anyone else. "When it absolutely, positively, has to be there overnight," you would do well to be in the developed world. In the States, time is measured constantly: Time is slipping away; time is of the essence; time is money. In Madagascar, no amount of coercion can cause things to move more quickly.

At the sites where I actually live and work for the majority of the time, there is no commerce, nothing to buy but an occasional fish from a fisherman pulled up onshore. A boat ride away is Maroantsetra, a town of flat, hazy tropical scenes, coconut palms on plains of sandy grasses, a town where you can sometimes buy vegetables, but where there are no appliances, no good shoes, no sunglasses for sale. This town is a flight away from Tana, where for a price you can obtain hydrochloric acid (as advertised in the local newspaper), a television, a Land Rover (only on the black market), an *International Herald Tribune* from a week ago, a good Indonesian or French meal, and even potted plants.

Tana is itself a long series of flights away from machine-washed and dried clothes, new hiking boots, delis, flourless chocolate cake with raspberry sauce, the *New York Times, Harper's Magazine,* Thorlo socks, alkaline batteries, duct tape, Krazy Glue, contact lenses, a blood transfusion, skiing, Snickers bars, maple trees and rhododendrons, box springs and mattresses, sulfa-free antibiotics, or anything new and improved. My most remote field site is five miles by foot from a village, which is a few hours by boat from a town, which is several hours by plane from Tana, which itself is several flights away from box springs, or transfusions. At this most remote site, all you can get is emergent trees thrust from the canopy, robed in flowers; lemurs clucking, peering; a parade of both colorful and cryptic frogs; cool breezes, with a stunning view from a tent platform; a vast forest rich with unknown life; and clean, clean air.

The great Pacific was just a mile from our house when I was a child, and when I needed to be reminded of my own insignificance, I would head down to the beach to stare across the vast ocean. In the spring, my father would drive us out of Los Angeles and into the desert, where my brother and I ran through endless fields of erupting wildflowers. The golden-orange California poppies, so garish and delicate, were my favorite. Other than those few weeks each year when sporadic rain caused flowers to actually grow wild, little grew without tending in L.A. The daughter of an Iowa farm boy turned computer engineer, I grew up believing that things don't grow unless people make them do so. My mother made our garden grow, carefully doling out water and nutrients, and if she stopped, everything died. Behind, under, and between her plants, animals from the hills scurried, reveling in this unexpected bounty. My fierce, loyal cat brought me alligator lizards. She would bite off their tails on my bed, where she would leave the tail, twitching, for me to find. It was a clue that somewhere in my bedroom a lizard with a bloody stump was hiding, terrified. This was our game, hers and mine.

Every fall, scorching Santa Ana winds would come in from the east, pummeling our already-parched city. If the winds coincided with a spark in the hills, brush fires erupted, sweeping across chaparral and houses with similar abandon. I remember one fire coming over the mountains toward our house, four, maybe five blocks away. A little girl, I stood on the roof with my father, with all the neighborhood fathers on their roofs, hoses in hand, wetting down the tinder of our lives. The fire, which we could not yet see, kissed our faces with raw heat. Finally, my father ordered me down, back to the room where my mother had put my little brother and our two cats. We were ready to escape to a car packed with family photos as soon as my father yelled "Go."

I fell asleep curled on a pile of blankets. The next morning, I woke confused, sweating, my sinuses filled with ash. The winds had turned, and the danger was past. My parents were haunted by our closest call yet, while the children and animals clamored for breakfast.

Days later, I walked through those hills while the ground was still hot, chasing lizards and snakes left uncharred. Gone were the scrubby desert plants, the only natives left in L.A. Most gardens remained, though, filled with foreign plants like agapantha and bougainvillea and night-blooming jasmine, and with yet more exotic plants, from places I could only imagine—from Brazil, and from Madagascar.

The walls of books that lined our house helped me conjure these faraway places. Many of my favorite memories from childhood are of being curled up alone with a book, hiding from social obligations. I read voraciously, developing early on a passion for fantasy and science fiction and, later, classic literature. A well-told story was the best escape, and until I could start generating my own adventurous narratives, I immersed myself wholly in those created by others.

Captivated by great literature all of my life, I was frustrated, in college, to find the opinions of literary theorists dictating which stories were valid and which were not. I left literature for science then, enticed by the promise of distinguishing between plausible and implausible stories by using the scientific method. Initiating my turn toward biology was Bret Weinstein, a friend since high school who, in the summer of 1989, handed me a book by the evolutionary biologist Richard Dawkins, suggesting that I might find some meaning therein. I found *The Selfish Gene* first daunting, then provocative, and finally inspiring.

Bret has now been my best friend and lover for many years, and his enthusiasm for evolutionary biology contributed to my own desire to be a field biologist. In 1991, before either of us ever saw Madagascar, we backpacked together through Central America, where we discovered firsthand the wonder of tropical ecosystems, the sheer pleasure of finding animals in the wild, and the privilege of being allowed to watch them do what they do. It's nothing like being at the zoo and finding the monkeys in their enclosures. When you're out in their world, in a vibrant, breathing forest, their real lives are arrayed in front of you in all their complexity. Filled with hunger, predators, and tree falls, those lives can change and grow as you watch.

In a way, literature and science are as different as they could be, one seeming to celebrate all the possible alternatives, the other trying to pinpoint which is most likely to be true. But in another way, literature and science are similar, as both aim to construct good stories from real life. Scientific inquiry takes the process a little further—it takes the possible narratives and assesses if they make sense, puts them to rigorous tests. Students of literature know that blood is thicker than water. Science offers us the opportunity to understand precisely why this is so. In science, we rely on hypothesis generation and falsification to assess the validity of our stories. But still, stories are what we're generating, and the most interesting stories will always have intrigue and drama, and discovering a story previously untold will forever be exciting.

During the middle of my first long field season on Nosy Mangabe, a remote island three miles off the east coast of Madagascar, my mother wrote me a letter. In it, she described a conversation she'd had with an old family friend. After she had explained to him, as best she could, what I was doing in Madagascar, he was still left with the nagging, and most basic, question: Why do it? She knew that I was, in her words, "studying something about evolution in poison frogs . . . but why?"

I answered her this way.

Science is, at its most basic level, the process of discovering "what is." There is an objective reality out there, and scientists seek to discover that reality in spite of the subjective lens of our perceptions. We are looking for pattern amid chaos.

The patterns in the universe are not necessarily useful to humans, however. As such, much of science—the sort we modestly call "basic research"—does not tend to be applicable to the curing of human disease, or to the problems of global warming. But basic research, knowledge for knowledge sake, is still the bedrock of scientific inquiry.

The particular quest I'm on has a lot to do with understanding how evolution—in particular, selection—guides the appearance and behavior of everything around us. Natural selection, and its lesser-known cousin, sexual selection, are responsible for much of the complexity of the natural world, so questions about that complexity necessarily come back to questions about selection. Understanding selection, then, is a goal worthy unto itself.

But if selection accounts for complexity—such as the specialized kidneys of desert-dwelling rodents in the American Southwest, or the bright red color of male cardinals during the breeding season—why not study some of the complexity that's closer to home? Why drag myself halfway around the world to do so? And why look at the sex lives of frogs?

Madagascar, the place to which I drag myself for my research, is utterly unlike any other spot on the planet. More than 90 percent of its mammals and lizards are endemic; for the frogs, that number is close to 100 percent. Part of the reason for the high rate of endemism is that Madagascar is an island. By definition, islands are isolated, and isolation is a catalyst to evolutionary divergence. Divergence means speciation, and new species on an island mean unique, endemic species.

Speciation is only half of the equation, though, in terms of species numbers. Extinction is the other half. While Madagascar, through its isolation, has generated massive numbers of new species, it also suffers, as does so much of the tropical, developing world, from massive deforestation. In places where populations are exploding, forests are cut down so that people can farm the land and eat. But when forests disappear, so, too, do the organisms that were in them. Only 10 percent of the original rain forest is left in Madagascar, and other Malagasy ecosystems, like the spiny desert in the south, are disappearing, too. And since Madagascar's biota—its myriad animals and plants—are so unstudied, species are surely disappearing that humans have never known, and never will. The little piece of the puzzle that I can discern in the time I have in Madagascar adds something to human knowledge that might otherwise go unknown.

That said, the work I'm doing is not going to save rain forests. The particular frogs that I study don't seem to have broad ecological importance. They don't pollinate flowers or disperse seeds. They eat ants and mites, of which there are plenty, and many other animals have the same diet. They're not important prey for any known predators, probably because they're poisonous. They don't disperse seeds. If you completely removed them from the forests in which they live, those forests would probably continue to be just fine, if a lot less colorful and musical.

Why, then, do I care to study them? Again, I'm basically trying to understand how evolution works. But that doesn't explain why I'm looking at behavior, or asking particular questions, such as: How do female frogs choose their mates, and how are territorial disputes settled among males?

These questions are what spark my interest. Scientist or no, we all have to follow our passions. Anyone who has ever watched as their pet cat chattered at birds outside the window, or seen a dog excitedly investigate a strange new smell, knows that what animals do is curious, and worthy of explanation. I take it a step further in my research: I sit and watch animals do what they do, all day long, for months on end, and try to unravel their stories. *Treachery* and *cooperation* are words invented for human behavior, but they occur among animals as well. One of the highest compliments that can be paid a piece of literature is to call it "timeless." The story of what animals do is necessarily timeless. The natural histories that weren't good have disappeared, continually replaced by classics. Every bit of animal behavior is rich with history and possibility.

Nature is filled with con artists and freeloaders, with courtships and shell games. If you can entertain yourself talking with friends about human interactions, it's not much of a leap to find nonhuman behavior fascinating, as well. It's a bit simpler, maybe, but no less important to the animals involved. For them, it's a matter of life and death: Do they get to mate or don't they? Where can they hide from the weather? Who wants to eat them, and whom will they eat?

I remember clearly the first time I walked into a rain forest as a would-be scientist. It was a vast wall of green, wet and impenetrable. We were in Costa Rica, and the professor I was with turned to me and said, "Look at all the questions waiting to be asked." I gaped at him. I didn't see any questions; all I saw were leaves. But over the years, that has changed, and when I walk through this rain forest now, I still see leaves, to be sure, but through those, under them, and beyond, I see a vast array of questions. Many are yet unanswered, even more still unasked. It is the opportunity to stumble upon questions, upon stories in progress, and to sit down and try to figure out what it all means—that is what motivates me, and my research, here on the far edge of remote.

2

Waiting for *Brousse*

During my first trip to Madagascar, my college graduation trip, very little went smoothly. Smooth, in my Western opinion, suggested efficiency, timeliness, and a world that bore some resemblance to that promised. Smooth was not part of the culture that we found.

In the decrepit coastal town of Manakara, where it seemed it would rain forever, Bret and I befriended several young men who talked excitedly about crocodiles that lived nearby. I had never seen a crocodile in the wild, but not for lack of desire. The men said heartily that the crocodiles were easy to get to and that they would take us there by canoe the next day. With promises of an adventure the following day, they slipped away, leaving us standing on a tropical beach, coconut palms overhead, the Indian Ocean slate and emerald, by turns, in the wind.

"We could swim," I suggested, as it had finally stopped raining. A woman with a basket on her head walked by. I stopped her.

"Is it safe to swim here?" I asked in French. She appeared to understand perfectly, and nodded yes. She was off, a smile playing at her lips. I stopped another woman, and received the same answer. She walked away, balancing an improbable basket full of ducks on her head. Still, we sat, not quite certain, waiting for something to develop. A gaggle of schoolchildren arrived, boisterous and loud, leading two teachers, pulling them toward the water. The children were reprimanded in rapid Malagasy, which I didn't understand. They immediately quieted down and sat on the sand.

"Is it safe to swim here?" I asked one of the teachers. She, too, laughed.

"Oh no," she said, "not at all. Last year, a woman was in only to her ankles, and a shark came up and dragged her out to sea. She never came back."

My eyes bugged out. "Her ankles?" I repeated, gesturing low on my legs to make sure I had understood.

"Yes, her ankles."

This, I did not find smooth at all.

The following day, we set off with the three young men to find crocodiles. The five of us sat low in the unstable canoe, while they took turns paddling down a wide freshwater canal.

"It is very important that we stay in the middle," they said over and over again as we hugged the shore, where tall grasses obscured undefined dangers.

"But . . ." I began, then stopped, resigned. We were, after all, looking for crocodiles, from a little rickety boat. Tasty morsels, easily capsized. What risks from the reeds could possibly outweigh the ones we had designed ourselves?

In the end, we found no crocodiles. The fierce reptiles were too far away, the men admitted, arms exhausted from rowing. We had been on the water since shortly after dawn, and the sun was now past its peak. We pulled up instead on a small beach, with the promise of a shark skull awaiting us there. Bleached in the sun, its teeth in razor rows along the inside of its massive jaw, here were the remains of an immense shark. Soon locals from an invisible village appeared, and they stood with us as we admired the shark jaw.

"Do you want to eat?" they asked us, and when we agreed, they led us to a few small dwellings, the yards immaculately taken care of, with glossy-leaved plants growing in small clumps. They were grilling a large fish on an open fire. We were to sit around the fire, and to make us comfortable, they began tearing apart their plants, to give us leaves to sit on.

"No, no, that's not necessary," we objected, startled to see them destroying their beautiful foliage. "We don't need leaves. We can sit on the sand." They looked at us, then at the artfully arrayed leaves, and nodded.

"Bad leaves!" they said, kicking them away. "Our guests do not want leaves!" They smiled at us, pleased that they had understood our intense dislike of leaves.

We had a delicious meal of fish and rice, and afterward we broke out an object that quickly provoked giggles all around—a Frisbee. Nobody had ever seen one before, so we demonstrated, and soon all the little boys of the village were trying their hand at it. The girls hung around the edges, curious and shy. We threw to them persistently, and when the girls grew bold enough to try, the boys, now ten minutes into their careers as Frisbee throwers, laughed at them mockingly.

When the fire died down and the breeze off the ocean began to feel cool, we got in the canoe and headed back to Manakara.

"It is very important that we stay in the middle," the men echoed, a mantra destined to be disobeyed. The sharp grasses at the edge of the canal glanced against our faces as the moon came up, and we began seeing the predatory eye shine of crocodiles, if only in our imaginations.

Back in Manakara, we became mired in a waiting game that was not of our own devising. We wanted so to escape, to explore other parts of the great red island, but we were not in control of our destiny. Waiting is an art form unknown in the developed world, though its many mundane shapes are familiar. In Madagascar, one waits for the official bearing the appropriate stamp. One waits for food while children are sent to find eggs. One waits for rivers to recede. For any task at all worth accomplishing, to wait is imperative. If it is possible to perform a task without waiting, it is either a banal task not worth mentioning, or so critical to the everyday functioning of the vast majority of people that the laws of supply and demand have actually become evident, even in a place where demand cannot always be followed by payment.

To buy the uncooked rice that keeps the Malagasy people alive, there is no need to wait. For everything else, one waits. The people do not raise their voices or weapons in anger. When faced with increasingly humiliating reasons to wait, and delays that stretch interminably, they do not threaten to abandon the system. There are no other options. The vast majority of the population has never been more than twenty miles from their birthplace, and for them, the system that exists is the only one conceivable. To abandon it would be a lonely and purely symbolic act.

Having finally escaped Manakara by train, Bret and I needed, on several more occasions, to get places. Madagascar is a large country, and we hoped to see a lot of it. Over the next several years, I began to realize that the pace of life in Madagascar *could* be beautiful and *is* strangely effective. On that first trip, I merely engaged in banging my head against the bars of Malagasy life. The act of trying to get elsewhere, overland, was a particular quagmire.

Taxi-brousse means "bush taxi," but I came to regard it as a constant, willful adversary. In my mind, ground transportation in Madagascar is overseen by the minor deity (Taxi) Bruce. Bruce is a god of many things, among them prolonged discomfort and fictitious departure and arrival times. Though he makes sporadic appearances in airports throughout the world, his expertise lies on the roads of Madagascar.

Taxi-brousse is the blanket term for public ground transportation between towns in Madagascar. *Taxis-brousses* come in many forms. There are putt-putt Renaults, vehicles designed for private transport, perhaps for a cozy family of four, into which Bruce will cram nine or so passengers and their baggage. At the other size extreme are *Eléphants de la Piste* ("elephants of the trail"), large trucks designed to transport cattle long distances, which have been fitted with wooden benches. Probably the most common morph of *taxi-brousse* is an old Peugeot pickup truck with a wooden frame on the back that is covered in thick green canvas. In the bed of the truck are deposited upward of twenty-five people, sitting on the wheel wells if lucky, on the floor if slightly less lucky, or on another person if utterly luckless. Regardless, there is never enough room to move in any way when the *taxi-brousse* is properly packed. Whole portions of your body are covered by other people, limbs fall asleep from being twisted into positions they were never designed to be in, and it is possible to forget that you even have a lower half. We have all experienced the discomfort of having a leg fall asleep, but having one remain asleep for an hour or more is an entirely different experience. It takes the issue of waiting from the realm of the philosophical and emotional and catapults it to the physiological. Waiting for something to start is nothing like waiting for something to end.

There are usually at least a third as many children as adults on a *taxi-brousse*, and though extraordinarily well-behaved, given the circumstances, one of them will generally be excreting fluids from some orifice. The children who are not suffering thusly from stomach flu or a mere runny nose are frequently treated by their satisfied parents to a whole fried fish, available from roadside vendors. Children everywhere play with their food rather than eat it, and in a space crammed with bodies, playing with whole fried fish usually involves gripping its body tightly in one's little palm while the combination of an unpaved road and poor shocks does the rest. The head of the fish inevitably ends up being thrust into the other travelers' faces, causing much merriment to the little keeper of the fish. After an hour or so has passed, in which the child is in possession of an increasingly grimy fish, mom or another relative will unarm the child, take a few bites, and finally toss the thing out one of many holes in the canvas tarp. Soon the cycle begins anew, when the next fish is bought.

As gasoline is hard to come by in Madagascar, some *taxis-brousses* carry their own supply. When the hose is threaded above the passengers, residual fuel often leaks onto their heads. To make a few extra Malagasy francs, the *taxi-brousse* often doubles as cargo transport, so the travelers may find themselves sitting on bags of tire irons, cement, or rice, and taken several hours off the "direct" route in order to make a delivery. As in much of the developing world, the baggage of many Malagasy travelers includes at least one live animal, most often a chicken or a goose, and it is the rare animal that has been secured inside a basket for the journey. Quick stops produce a flurry of squawks and feathers from the avian passengers, which quickly find that flight is beyond their capabilities and settle down on whatever is near.

There is the theoretical ability to control the climate on a *taxi-brousse*, but Bruce prevents this. When the world is hot and dustless, in the usually arid south after a rain, the windows are whole but inoperable. Then the heat of everyone's bodies, the exudate of sick children, and the disintegrating fried fish wielded jubilantly by healthy children combine in a thick fog that can almost be seen. When, on the other hand, the world is cold, dusty, wet, or dark, the windows are typically broken, absent, or intact but permanently open. This is true on the high plateau when the air is cold; it is true in the dry south when it has not rained, and copious amounts of dust blow in and stick to all surfaces; it is true on the east coast, where it is usually raining; and it is true at night, when, despite extreme physical discomfort, you are exhausted from the inaction of the day, and from attempts to avoid unidentified fluids and foods and to wrench your foot from between a bag of rice and the (flat) spare tire. It is then that the windows are down, or the green canvas develops a mortal wound, causing air to rush in with a high-pitched squeal, making sleep ever more distant. At night, too, the "dome light"—a naked bulb hanging from a wire—is turned on. The drivers are often in possession of a single tape of bad American music, which is played at high volume over and over and over again.

The final defining character of *taxi-brousse* is the rate of progress. The

Western mind strains against the endless delays and false starts, but the Western body, finding itself on a *taxi-brousse* in the middle of a vast wasteland, has no choice but to succumb. Succumbing gracefully to the sorts of insults Bruce offers is a strength of the Malagasy people. It was not, during my first trip to Madagascar, a trait I yet had in my arsenal.

Huddled on a rickety wooden bench, our backpacks lying in the dirt, we were waiting for a ride across the southern half of Madagascar. At two in the morning, flimsy tickets for our journey grasped in our cold hands, we were ready to leave.

"What on earth is that noise?" Bret asked, referring to the chattering, gurgling sounds emanating from a nearby tree. *Ackity grackity prack!* Slowly, he reached his hand up through the tangled branches, looking for he knew not what. Then—an explosion of wings and screams. Flying foxes sprayed out of the tree, filling the sky, fox faces masking their bat heritage. Malagasy in the vicinity looked at the two white people in disbelief, laughing at us as we cringed.

We were trying to go across the southern half of Madagascar by *taxi-brousse*. While chasing mudskippers in a mangrove swamp outside of Tuléar, Bret had cut himself open, requiring stitches from the local nuns. We took this as a sign to move on. The resultant *taxi-brousse* ride between Tuléar and Fort Dauphin, a distance of less than four hundred miles, took sixty-one hours. Before heading out, we were told to expect two days of solid travel, with one night of sleep in some unspecified village in between—about thirty-six hours from start to finish. In a country with deadlines not marked in hours or days, but in seasons, estimates of time should never be taken seriously.

We had by this time become well acquainted with *taxi-brousse*, having already traveled several hundred miles in its various guises. In this case, we were told the day before to arrive at the station at 2:00 A.M., and we did so. The *brousse* was packed and moving by 7:00 A.M.—a very auspicious start. Three hours later, we stopped for a large plate of rice—breakfast—in a small town. Later, we would reminisce about that first morning. Oh, those three hours, how blissful and uninterrupted—the longest stretch of time on the entire trip during which we were actually moving, during which time we made such rapid and unceasing progress that it was startling, truly, to discover that we had gone but fifty miles.

Within an hour of leaving the town where we'd had breakfast, we stopped again. The *taxi-brousse* had run into what appeared to be a totally unprecedented situation: a flat tire. The road was deeply rutted dirt, mostly dry because of the season, with occasional sharply spined plants growing unexpectedly in the middle. A flat tire had everyone stumped. We had neither a jack nor an inflated spare tire. The only useful tool we had on board was a cross-shaped lug-nut wrench. That, and the ingenuity of a lot of Malagasy men.

I sat in a nearby field that was dotted with cactus and cattle, the latter bearing the single large hump identifying them as zebu. Children nearby made music with found objects—pieces of bone and horn, dried cactus, or simply their palms on the ground. Zebu with rope through their noses nibbled at corn husks. Bleating goats were dragged past by local villagers. Nearby, there was a walled tomb with several wooden stelae—carved totems celebrating the dead—and zebu skulls placed around it, proclaiming the wealth of the dead man it marked.

Twenty-five hours into the journey, I had accepted that we would not be stopping anywhere to sleep. I was numb from the waist down. The *brousse* stopped often, at the whim of the driver—to greet old friends, new women, pigs by the side of the road. We had several breakdowns, during which local men appeared out of nowhere to help fiddle the engine back into working condition. Sometimes the stops were brief—barely long enough to crawl out the windows and stand on tingling feet, brains numb, while the locals pooled around the foreigners, whispering among themselves. Sometimes they lasted an hour, long enough to find a *hotely*, where we could buy a plate of rice.

In a town called Betioky, people began spilling from the windows of the *brousse* as soon as it stopped, which suggested to us that we would have at least a few minutes here, and that it might be a good town in which to find a place to pee. Peeing in a land without holes dug in the ground for that purpose, much less toilets, is hard enough without being white, and thus the object of endless fascination. There is no place to hide. The stealth pee is not possible. The sexes are roughly segregated for this activity—one side of the road for each. All of the locals, who swarm out to meet the *brousse*, selling fried fish and brightly colored liquids in plastic bags, are immediately drawn to the foreigner. The Malagasy women, not themselves desirous of an audience, try to escape from the lumbering white woman who follows them, looking only for an appropriate place to drop her pants, not wishing for the crowd that surrounds her. The only solution is to focus on the task at hand—squat with my pants around my ankles and pee, and not give the locals more reason to laugh by losing my balance or peeing on my shoes. Make no eye contact. Gales of laughter will erupt from the Malagasy in attendance, and concentration will be broken. Let them see you piss, but never let them see you piss on yourself.

The trip continued. I became ill, and vomited out the *taxi-brousse*, afterward realizing that a gaping hole in its side meant I had thrown up on my own leg. The gas line running overhead began leaking, which eventually burned holes in our synthetic jackets. Someone's chicken landed on my shoulder, and decided to stay. We stopped in a landscape with a single shack. The driver hurried away. Forty-five minutes later, he emerged, zipping up his pants, a pert young woman waving good-bye from the open doorway. Leaning against the *brousse*, he paused for a cigarette before resuming our trip.

The many bags of concrete were unloaded, and we were able to position ourselves such that our ankles were not bent back at odd angles. Fifteen minutes later, bags of rice replaced those of concrete, and we were back to starting position. Throughout this journey, the Malagasy around us chatted among themselves. Nothing that happened surprised them. I schemed constantly, through my helpless, hopeless anger. The poorest in Madagascar cannot afford to go anywhere beyond the village in which they were born, even by *taxi-brousse*, so we were surrounded by middle-class folk. I wanted to yell at someone that this must be changed. But this is what is, what is known.

Finally, we reached Ambovombe, the last town before the dirt road became paved for the final forty miles. It was evening, and as we came into town, I grew increasingly excited at the almost palpable proximity of Fort Dauphin, town of my dreams, renowned in my own head for its comfortable beds and cooling showers. The *taxi-brousse* stopped in an empty field. Fires glowed through the open doorways of shacks. Most of the passengers crawled out the windows and drifted away. I stayed near the *brousse*, waiting for us to be on our way, in the same way a child waits until dawn before waking her parents on Christmas morning. This is not waiting, but an irrational attempt to force time forward.

Then the driver and his assistant began unloading our bags from the roof of the *brousse*. I panicked.

"What are you doing?" I demanded in French, verging on tears.

"Tonight, we stay here. Tomorrow, we go." He had lost two passengers and would force the remaining fifty of us to wait until morning, when he might pick up replacements. If I had offered to pay the extra fares, he would have accepted the money but forced us to wait anyway. As long as there was space that could conceivably be filled with more people, more money could be made.

I snapped. My French was poor, but my meaning clear: How can you be doing this to me, to us? I realized, in my furious, exhausted, miserable daze, that I was speaking with the voice of someone accustomed to privilege. I was here, a new college graduate, believing myself an explorer, a sympathizer with the poor and downtrodden of the world, demanding for myself something different from what most of the world even knows exists. I needed a shower, a change of clothes, a bed. Ambovombe offered none of this. It seemed, in that moment, that the man responsible for bringing these things to me was the driver of the *taxi-brousse*. I couldn't tolerate his selfishness, but I was demanding that he tolerate mine. Of course, he refused.

His rejection of my First World demands brought us experience we never could have had otherwise. Two young Malagasy insisted that we accompany them to their grandmother's house. It was well past midnight by then, but the entire household was awakened for the coming of the foreigners. A bucket of rainwater—precious in the scorched south of Madagascar—was brought for us to shower with. A twin-size hay-lined bed was, despite our protests, taken from Uncle Edward and provided to us. Edward proved a fascinating man, well versed in the dangers of overpopulation, and the particular concerns of conservation in Madagascar. Grandma—always referred to only as such—was a cultured, southern rural Malagasy, and she insisted that we sit and have *ranon' ampàngo* (pronounced *ranopango*), which is effectively the national drink of Madagascar. After the rice is cooked for every meal, and is burned to the bottom of the pot, water is thrown in the pot and heated, unsticking the burned bits of rice on the bottom. The liquid is infused with the taste of burned rice, and little bits of rice often sink to the bottom of glasses of *ranon' ampàngo*.

While we sipped our burned rice water, all the members of the family filed through, shook our hands, and introduced themselves to us, explaining their relationships to everyone else. Cousin Hadj wanted to know about life in America—did we live in towns or on farms? Did we, like them, eat rice three times a day? Was it a very big place, like Madagascar?

Soon we went to bed, so comfortable sharing that tiny hay pallet after days in a *taxi-brousse* that it seemed just moments later that Jean-Claude, one of our rescuers, woke us. We must have breakfast, then go. We were included in the morning meal as honored guests, and it was arranged that when we got to Fort Dauphin, we would dine with the rest of the family there. In this way, we met a female judge and her family, and learned one Malagasy family's take on the place of their country in the world and the role of religion in changing times. On Western time, with the success of my Western demands and expectations, we would have rushed through, unseeing, missing life as it was lived.

3

Inescapably *Vazaha*

Madagascar, it is true, is more isolated than most countries. Being an island, people do not flow over its borders, introducing food, custom, dress, or language. As a place that is historically difficult to access, people in the West have not spent great amounts of money or long periods of time fighting over it. The people of Madagascar have thus had few prolonged periods of contact with cultures beyond their own, though Madagascar itself has several distinct tribes, which have fought among themselves sporadically. All of which is an attempt to justify the unique feeling that the foreigner gets when attempting to do anything, including simply exist, in Madagascar. Eyes are constantly watching. Hands stray, too, but less often, as some of the tribes believe that monsters who steal children's hearts come disguised as white people. It's better not to touch such monsters. It would be best, of course, to avoid them altogether, but such a rarity, such a thing of strange make and color, how can one avoid staring? So they do stare, usually from within a group—for there is safety in numbers—and watch as the foreigners do whatever it is that we do.

Today in Madagascar there are still few enough foreigners—*vazaha*, in Malagasy (pronounced *vaza*)—that the appearance of one inevitably prompts cries of "*Vazaha!*" from all children and many of the adults in the vicinity. Why the urge to vocalize what we all know to be true—that the white person in our midst is a _vazaha_? Why point and yell _vazaha_? Usually, it is tempered with the word _salama_ before it, making the phrase, yelled from the street and shops, from windows and moving vehicles, "Hello, foreigner." If any response by the _vazaha_ is made, the Malagasy who provoked it will often burst into laughter.

There is a guide at Perinet, the first-developed and easiest-to-access nature reserve in Madagascar, who was forever taking tourists, and occasional researchers, through the forest. This was most definitely his home. He felt comfortable in this forest and knew the people who lived around it. Seeing all the tourists come and, inevitably, go back to their homes, he had to wonder what the rest of the world was about. He began asking people about their countries of origin, which is not a common practice among the Malagasy, who are generally very insular, almost as if they don't really believe there is another world out there. One tourist asked him if he wouldn't like to go to France, or somewhere else in Europe, to see how other people live. His response was quick, direct, and unflinching.

"Oh, no, I never want to leave Madagascar."

"But why? Not even for a visit?"

"No, no" he repeated, then gave his reason. "I do not want to be followed around everywhere I go, while people yell, 'Malagasy Malagasy' at me."

This guide had two misconceptions, both of which I find telling. First, he imagined that the rest of the world is just as insular as Madagascar and thus responds to all foreigners the way the Malagasy do. Second, he thought the rest of the world would identify him as specifically Malagasy, rather than doing what is done in Madagascar, simply using the word _vazaha_ for all foreigners. The implication is that Madagascar is so well-known a place that people from the rest of the world will surely recognize a Malagasy as such, even if people in Madagascar cannot tell a Swede from an Italian.

In 1996, I planned a scouting trip to Madagascar, during which time I would visit several possible research sites, looking for evidence of the frogs I would study and assessing the viability of working in these places. Localities where the frogs had been seen and collected were known, but a spot with five or ten frogs wouldn't be sufficient to undertake a behavioral study, so I had to go evaluate the sites myself. Bret was coming along to help.

This was to be a short trip—only two months—and I wouldn't be collecting data, only finding a place to work the following year. Memories of that first trip as a backpacking tourist several years earlier haunted me as I prepared for this one. Most of what I remembered about Madagascar, now that I was going there with my biologist's hat on, rather than my adventure traveler's hat, was that it was incredibly difficult. The few guidebooks had assured us that the Malagasy were open, welcoming, and always wore a smile. I found, instead, a tremendous amount of suspicion, open wariness sometimes ceding into thinly veiled hostility, my white skin the subject of both fascination and intense distrust. As a traveler, rather than a researcher, when I would be staying in one place for a long period of time and getting to know the local people, I hadn't been able to convince many people that I wasn't like the French colonials they remembered with such ire. Nor should I have been able to—I was young and used to privilege, and though my inclinations were to the left, believing that everyone deserved equal opportunity, I didn't know what that meant for a people with no options.

Before I left for this scouting trip, I consulted with Ron Nussbaum, a professor at the University of Michigan, where I was a graduate student. Preparations for Madagascar include a fair amount of paperwork before ever leaving. Ron has an ongoing scientific relationship with Madagascar, and the research accord he had worked out with them applied to me, as well. The accord, of course, was never quite in perfect shape, as he never gave them *enough* Land Rovers or computers in exchange for the privilege of working in Madagascar, so there were some hurt feelings from those not yet in possession of expensive "gifts." I planned to go bearing several copies of the accord, letters to various bureaucrats who would be pleased to be addressed by name, my research proposal, curriculum vitae, passport, and vaccination record. The rules, Ron told me, changed almost every time he had tried to get permits there, so it was best to be armed with everything. He suggested that I load up on bottles of Johnnie Walker and plenty of T-shirts, as well. Such is the advantage of being a graduate student: The professor may have to dole out vehicles and computers to be allowed to conduct his research; the student must only discreetly supply small amounts of liquor and clothing to a few outstretched hands.

In addition to these small tokens, I had to stuff everything I would need for two months of travel to a variety of sites and climates into a backpack. How do you prioritize a second pair of shoes (the first is bound to get wet and rot) versus a rain jacket? Since research equipment was minimal for this trip, we mostly limited our gear to a tent, sleeping paraphernalia, and clothes. We were also careful to pack our new, specially calibrated compass, rather than our old one, along with various pharmaceuticals appropriate for the tropics. A tropical biologist must make sure all of her vaccinations, for diseases ranging from tetanus to rabies, are up to date and that all appropriate prescriptions to counter any number of eventualities have been filled. There had been plague outbreaks in northern Madagascar, so I took enough doxycycline, an antibiotic that happens to double as an antimalarial, to kill off plague should I get it. I took antimalarials as prophylaxis but also carried quinine as treatment, should it come to that. I carried several courses each of at least four kinds of antibiotic, each intended for a specific part of the body. Self-diagnosis and self-medication are critical skills in the field. I took Flagyl, a nasty drug that kills most things flagellated (microscopic organisms with tails), and isn't too kind on the human body, either. Still, it's what you need if you come down with giardia. I took topical and oral fungicides—for the creeping skin fungus that infects regularly—and topical bactericides, like Neosporin, for those small cuts which in the Western world would heal quickly but in the eternal hot wet environment of the rain forest tend to fester. I carried sterile medical syringes, fervently hoping I wouldn't need to dispense them to any doctor attending me. And of course, there was plenty of gauze, tape, and bandages. This was our medical kit—and though bulky and heavy, it couldn't be exchanged for another pair of pants or boots.

Finally, we were off. There were only two international flights per week going into Madagascar at that time. Ivato, the international airport outside of Tana, rarely bustled, except when one of these two flights was coming in or going out. Our necessarily roundabout itinerary took us through New York, Paris, Munich, Djibouti, and Nairobi before finally depositing us, almost forty hours later, at Ivato. We arrived at 4:00 A.M. I was jet-lagged, sleep-deprived, and generally unhappy with the prospect of dealing with permits and bureaucrats for several days before I had a chance of seeing the forest, and I wondered idly what in the hell they were thinking when they scheduled the twice-weekly international flight to arrive at such a preposterous hour. At that point, I was decidedly unskilled at hiding my irritation under such conditions. Compound that with my poor French, and situations—several days, weeks, and months of awkward situations—were waiting to happen.

The rules of movement and etiquette for obtaining visas, baggage, and official stamps from various airport bureaucrats are obscure, archaic, and often redundant. Furthermore, my name makes no sense to the Malagasy. None at all.

"Name?" The man asked in French after he flipped through my passport in disbelief. He looked up at me as if I'd handed him a grocery list in Serbo-Croatian, rather than an American passport.

"Heying," I said, already weary. "Heather Heying." If only I had a simple, eloquent name like James Bond. Even one with a hard consonant thrown in to the middle. But no. This ridiculous mix of vowels and *H*'s rolled off this man's tongue and onto the floor, where he promptly kicked it under a desk for later disposal.

"Eh?" he grunted. Apparently, he was feeling generous. I reached over the glass partition to point to my name, knowing that any effort to spell it in French would fail. He recoiled, then barked at me to do the same. I sighed. This went back and forth for a while, until he finally gave up and wrote down as my name some random word he found on the passport. Now I remembered my first trip to Madagascar. Because of my interaction with a similar man in this very airport, I'd had to travel through Madagascar as "California," the name given me by the authoritative bureaucrat, who had pulled it off my passport under "State of birth." This time, I was labeled "Los Angeles," handed two well-stamped pieces of paper, and summarily pushed ahead to the next trial.

I had had enough experience working in Latin America to realize that nobody there can pronounce my given name, either. Once I was through with the bureaucracy and on to interacting with people in Madagascar, I wouldn't have to stand by my given name and continue to confuse everyone I interacted with. The plants called "heathers," which appear in various Brontë novels and Monty Python skits, are in the Erika family (Ericaceae). This prompted one of the botanists on the faculty at the University of Michigan to say to me, upon our first meeting, "So, how do you like being an Erika?" Erika has a nice crunch to it—a hard sound you can attach your tongue to and stop at, knowing decisively where to parse the word. The Malagasy I know can pronounce it—and, more importantly, remember it—just fine. So in Madagascar, I am Erika.

From the first uniformed guard, I got passed on to several more, each asking for some unique combination of passport, stamped pieces of paper, and money. I didn't have any Malagasy money yet. It was illegal at the time to take Malagasy money out of the country, so you couldn't exchange dollars for it overseas, and therefore couldn't enter the country with any. There hadn't yet been an opportunity to change money in the airport. Still, the men I interacted with all showed surprise when I explained that all I had were dollars. Surprise, but not upset. Sure, they would take my dollars. They wouldn't give me change, but they would take the bills. They feigned ignorance of the exchange rate and managed to take twice the amount of money I should have paid. My annoyance at the entire procedure was clearly showing, and it just egged them on.

We escaped the bureaucrats and fell in among masses of ragged men with bent spines who were eager to carry our bags to a taxi for a pittance. I could barely hear, over the ruckus, the yelling of another sort of entrepreneur that graces the exit of Ivato—the money changers. As the practice is technically illegal, I didn't intend to change much money with these men, but I knew that we needed some Malagasy francs (FMG) for the taxi ride into the city and our first night in a hotel. I was sure they wanted to take advantage of me, knew it in my exhausted, bitter heart, and so fought them from the beginning. Walking into an interaction distrustful, hackles already raised, rarely works. Nothing went smoothly. When I emerged from that seething crowd—a money-changing event always draws layers of people as spectators—I had a thick wad of FMG, and slightly fewer dollars. The exchange rate was a bit under 4,000 FMG to the dollar, and the largest bill in circulation in Madagascar was a 25,000 FMG note—about six dollars. And as it turned out, the money changers' rate was almost identical to the one I received in a bank the next day. Via the government, or a man on the street, change $250, and you're a millionaire in Madagascar.

Tana may once have been a beautiful city. Set on the *haut plateau*, its elevation makes it cool, its hills keep one neighborhood hidden from the next, and the rice paddies in the middle of the capital hardly seem incongruous, so focused is the culture on rice. There are stalls selling food along most streets, as well as children in nothing but tattered shorts playing in the black swill that runs through them. Electric reds, oranges, and purples greet visitors to the lower town during the flower market; adjacent are stalls selling small pieces of twine and lengths of rubber, and men offering to repair and refill Bic lighters, which were designed, in the developed world, to be discarded when empty. Everything is recycled, used in all possible ways, yet the trash in the streets grows, trash already sifted through infinite times. Plastics, paper, string—no such things are thrown out, so what mounts in the streets are banana peels, chicken bones, the sludge from engines, human and animal waste, dead rats. The lake in the middle of town, still retaining a superficial air of peace and beauty, is reputed to be the receptacle into which the hospital dumps medical waste.

There are few *vazaha* in Madagascar, but the highest density is in Tana. The most obvious and pervasive *vazaha* is the aging French male expat. He comes in many shapes, sizes, and reasons for being there, but almost without exception, he will have acquired, usually through payment, a beautiful young Malagasy. Sometimes the slinky young things are girls, sometimes women, but what is always true is that once they have been rented by their parents, or sold by themselves, to a white man, they will never fully reenter normal Malagasy social life. It is difficult to go into a restaurant in Tana without observing yet another odious white man with his slinky young thing.

Walking through Tana, snapshots of a city simultaneously rotting and proud present themselves. In the lower town, near Avenue de l'Indépen-dance, a long, broad avenue with the train station at one end and the showy outdoor flower market at the other, is the shell of the Rex. It was once the only movie theater in Madagascar. Now there are none. A thin man with an intact shirt but no shoes carries a large wooden crate on his head. It is stuffed to overflowing with fresh baguettes. He weaves his way through the crowds, through sidewalk vegetable vendors, piles of trash far higher than he, and cars with relative ease. He has carried hundreds of baguettes on his head before.

In the upper town, land of the *vazaha*, where embassies and nongovern-mental organizations (NGOs) vie for space on the steep, narrow streets, men with flat, open baskets of orange mushrooms or startlingly red straw-berries approach cars, especially those containing *vazaha*, calling out their wares in French. Women vendors sell roses, lilies, lemons, and larger fruit back on the sidewalk. Just steps away, suddenly, the items for sale are no longer edible, or aesthetic, but seem as if they represent a stolen delivery. One man offers pruning shears and car mats. Several men proffer shiny new scissors. Another peers into a car with fingers full of sunglasses, sure that the white faces inside need dark glasses to hide their eyes.

Descending from the upper town toward the once-majestic lake, some-one, genderless behind swaths of rags, back turned to the road, has made a home of a cliff overhang beside a road on the lake. A fence, perhaps one foot high, two long, has been erected, as if to say, "This is mine, and none shall tread here but me." I wonder—does the fence attract people who otherwise would never think to crawl into that cold and muddy place?

Throughout Tana, old women, toothless, wander the streets, perhaps knowing where they go, perhaps not. Their hands are always out when *vazaha* or well-dressed Malagasy pass by, but fewer people give coins to them than to the children. What has been their life? Always begging on the streets? Recent ill fortune? What do they think to themselves as a *vazaha* in Western clothes passes? What do they think when their pleading is met with a steely gaze in another direction, no eye contact, no recognition of their presence, or even their humanity?

We stayed in a dank, cramped hotel in Tana at first, then, when it became clear that we would be stuck in Tana for a while, moved to a communal house established for researchers by some American universities. There was no escaping the suffocating masses of people. I almost pepper-sprayed a gang of little boys who were attempting to steal my wallet. Their tactic was clever: Most of the children surrounded me with their hands outstretched, covering the myriad little hands below, which were unzipping the bag I had secured at my waist and neck. There seemed no end to the misery and fumes that Tana offered, and very little to be at peace with. The poverty was unmatched by what I had seen previously in Central America. Even in the interior of Guatemala and Honduras, people usually seemed to have enough food to eat, and families seemed to take care of one another.

We relied on taxis to get us where we needed to go—to the government ministries for resident visas, to administration buildings for research permits. The Tana taxis are tiny, tinny little cars, usually French, mostly rusted out, engines barely able to mount the hilly streets of Tana with two passengers inside. The taxi drivers are so close to poverty that one time in three, when we got in a taxi, the driver promptly maneuvered to a gas station, requesting payment from us in advance so he could put a quarter's worth of gas in his car.

Acquiring research permits usually takes a tremendous amount of time. A frustrated *vazaha* researcher such as myself, who saw nothing but corruption and inefficiency in the system, was exactly what the bureaucrats expected. As such, they treated me the way they treated everyone else. "Come back tomorrow, with four copies of your research proposal, two in French. . . . No, we don't have any copy machines." Upon returning the next day: "We need two more copies in French. Come back in two days, between three and five in the afternoon." Attempts at reasoning with the bureaucrats were perceived as argument only, and treated as games. "You want to come back sooner? How about in two weeks? Yes, by then we might have your permits ready for you." I would backpedal, then gain a slight feeling of triumph when I was able to win back the original proposition: Return in two days.

All of this made me desperately unhappy, only exacerbated by the fact that I didn't yet have a research plan. I knew the kinds of questions I wanted to ask, and what group of species I intended to work on, but the whole point of this trip was to find a research site, and hopefully make some preliminary observations on animals so that I could return the following year with more carefully crafted hypotheses about the system. Now the bureaucrats demanded details from me.

"Exactly how long will you be in Ankarana? Why are you going? What will you learn?" What will I learn? If I knew that, I could have stayed home. My disgust with the system annoyed them further, and they kept me a while longer, seeming to toy with me like a cat does with a battered mouse, ripping into the prey more fiercely at weak signs of life.

As time wore on, our planned departure date from Tana repeatedly moved back, and I became dark and bitter. I was transported back to a conversation I had had with two friends, also graduate students in biology, just before leaving the States. Neither of them worked in the tropics, and they wondered aloud what my motivations were. At this point, I had to wonder myself if there was any good, solid, constant reason to be attempting whatever it was I was attempting. If only I could be back home, with the long summer days and the predictable and well-fed people and the accessibility of everything, and the comfort. Instead, I found myself in a land so foreign it brought me to tears many nights. The people would smile, but there was a feeling of underlying hostility—they were so unknown to my world, and my world wholly unknown to them. Most of the other *vazaha* I saw separated themselves completely from the scenes around them, not taking in the hostile stares, the pleading eyes, the depth of poverty of people who regard us as potential saviors, even as we are acting callous.

Walking through the streets, children begged money off *vazaha*, as did women with babies. The poorest on the street, with black grit for teeth and holes for eyes, deep expanses that perhaps could see, perhaps not, held their hands out, hoping. Sometimes I tried to communicate, but was left alone, empty, without recourse. Walking up a street, biding our time, waiting for the current permit deadline established by the bureaucrats to elapse, two women with children demanded money from us. Usually, such women faded into the background after we passed, erased. These women spat at us, called us dogs—*chiens*. Later, we walked back the same route, and these same women demanded money again. They didn't recognize us. We were anonymous in their country, but never invisible.

On an empty street, little girls with big heads carried woven handbaskets and looked startlingly like grizzled old women. Their siblings had already grown to lankiness, all legs and arms, scarcely covered in torn skirts and T-shirts. Prepubescent boys eyed the *vazaha* languidly. The eyes of adults flitted rapidly from the engine of a broken vehicle to the street garbage and the women and old men picking through it, then to the *vazaha* and their jeans. Some children smiled broadly at the *vazaha* and shouted "*Salama!*" Others were wary and scurried off, hiding behind trash or their siblings as we approached. Oh, to be gone from Tana, city of trash and anonymity.

4

Peut-être, Ongomba, Maybe

Our first stop out of Tana was the town of Antsiranana, also known as Diégo Suarez, named for a pirate who once frequented the area. The northernmost city in Madagascar, it is a mixture of tropical ease and whitewash, with a pace reminiscent of the Caribbean. Sky blue mosques decorate many corners. Rickshaws—called *pousse-pousse* in Madagascar—ferry brightly dressed women from mosque to market. The strikingly bold colors on clothes and buildings alike seem to match the tropical sentiment.

In Diégo, we found Angeluc Razafimanantsoa, a young man we had hired as a guide three years earlier, when we had come as tourists. He and his identical twin brother, Angelin, had been trained as naturalists, herpetologists, and research assistants by Ron Nussbaum and Chris Raxworthy, who was at the time Ron's post-doctoral researcher at Michigan. Herpetology is the study of creepy-crawly things—so named by the Greeks. More precisely, it is the study of amphibians and reptiles. The twins preferred their work as herpetologists to their usual role as tourist guides.

On our first trip, Angeluc and Angelin had played a trick on us early on, before we knew there were two of them. As we were coming out of the forest with Angeluc behind us, Angelin, dressed identically, appeared in front of us, lounging on a stoop. We turned, to see Angeluc just appearing around a bend behind us, but when we turned back to see Angelin, he had disappeared.

"How did you do that?" we asked Angeluc, laughing.

"Do what?" He smiled, bashful but a bit devious, knowing he had us going. As we continued through town, tired from our trek and wondering if we were hallucinating, Angelin again appeared before us, an apparition. Turning back, Angeluc had disappeared. We had already been treated to Angeluc's fantastic ability to whistle two distinct harmonies at one time, creating the eerie feeling that there were two men in a single body. Now he was separating before our eyes, splitting into his two voices.

Angelin, whom we thought was the singular Angeluc, excused himself, and shortly both of them began appearing in increasingly improbable places. Finally, they revealed themselves at the same moment and admitted that they were two. Such was the lighthearted joy of games that Angeluc brought to our ten days together, as he guided us first through the national park Montagne d'Ambre, and then through the special reserve of Ankarana.

Montagne d'Ambre—Amber Mountain—is a midelevation wet forest on a hill just south of Diégo. For logistic reasons, I was hoping that this would be my research site. Diégo is a large town, with a lot of resources, and is close enough to Montagne d'Ambre to visit once or twice a month, if not more. In the park itself, a new research building had just been completed, and it was gorgeous. There were rooms for imagined, future researchers to sleep in, a large common space, and an immaculate kitchen with running water, all framed beautifully in wood. The level of luxury, for field accommodations in Madagascar, was unbelievable. Angeluc led us to this spot with a mixture of excitement and hesitation, and let me absorb the implications of such a wondrous field station. He himself had never lived in such a place, with wood floors and screened windows. We had found him in his home, where he had lived since birth, a one-room shack without running water.

"How close are the *Mantella*? Can we go there now?" I asked him, hopeful. I was referring to the genus name for the tiny, brightly colored, poisonous frogs I had come here to study. Since Angeluc had previously worked with herpetologists, he understood somewhat my passion for frogs. Most people do not. Sometimes, people want an explanation, something that justifies why a person would study these little wet-skinned creatures. Some people study frogs because they are indicator species for failing ecosystems. Frogs are disappearing the world over, and though some localized processes have been identified, we are a long way from identifying a single, global explanation, perhaps because there is none. In the upper Midwest, frogs are suffering mutations on a massive scale, and other animals in the system are not. In Central America and Australia, a fungus is decimating frog populations. It is true that frogs often fail first in an ecosystem full of organisms. In part, this is due to their reliance on both aquatic and terrestrial ecosystems—pollutants in the water can get at eggs and tadpoles, and if the frogs survive to adulthood, they have to contend with airborne pollutants. Although all of this is true, it has nothing to do with why I study frogs.

I originally began studying frogs by accident. It was sheer good fortune, having nothing to do with good planning or predictive powers on my part. I had gone to Costa Rica for my first field season as a young graduate student, with a hypothesis about white-faced monkeys and their predilection for fruit planted by people rather than that native to their forests. Problem was, there weren't any white-faced monkeys where I was. I didn't have much time in that first field season to travel around and find a better site. But the forest I was in, at a tiny field station in the Sarapiquí, provided me with a beautiful, natural field experiment. Someone at a nearby ecotourist lodge had decided that the native poison-dart frog, a tiny red species, wasn't sufficiently exciting to lure tourists. So they imported a non-native species, a related animal, but much larger, neon green with black spots. Introduced species are a problem across the planet. Gypsy moth caterpillars are defoliating the trees of much of the eastern half of the United States, many of Hawaii's native species are disappearing under myriad introduced ones, and honeybees are displacing native pollinators throughout much of the Americas. Humans are the most widespread of the invasive species, having moved into all land areas except the Antarctic.

In Costa Rica, I had a perfect setup to study the effect of the introduction of a non-native species on a native one. It was then that I began studying frogs. I could say that tropical field biology regularly offers such opportunities for flexibility, but in truth, it's the other way around. Flexibility about what questions you want to address is a requirement, because it is extremely rare that everything goes as you planned it back home.

I got lucky. Those frogs turned out to be fascinating, and easy to stay excited about. The term *charismatic megafauna* refers to all those beasts that show up on nature shows and in pleas for money from conservation organizations—primates and big cats and wolves, and elephants and whales and ostriches. The term is used derisively by people who study important but ugly or uninspiring things. They're right: Those things *are* charismatic, and I like watching charismatic things more than I like watching fungus. I plead guilty to having sought out the most charismatic, unstudied thing around. I have dubbed these frogs, both in the neotropics and in Madagascar, the "charismatic *meso*fauna," small but not microscopic, and captivating. And while those in Central America are well studied, the ones in Madagascar were still waiting for someone to unravel their secrets.

After months of preparation, I had finally reached the forest in which the charismatic mesofauna lived, but now I had to rely on Angeluc to interpret it for me. For it was June in Madagascar: the dead of winter. In the tropics, winter doesn't get particularly cold—barely even cool in most places—but it is the drier season. Amphibians need water to reproduce, and though I thought the frogs I was looking for—the *Mantella*—were likely to reproduce all year round in wetter climes, they were sure to be less active, and harder to find, in the winter. Because of the schedule of the academic year back in the States, though, I had to make my scouting trip to Madagascar in their winter, our summer. Here I had my first moment of truth. I hadn't seen any *Mantella* yet, but absence is a hard thing to assess. Were the frogs absent because it was winter and they were estivating—hidden underground to protect themselves against desiccation—or because they simply didn't exist there, ever? Local ranges of these species seemed to fluctuate greatly, and although there had been *Mantella* nearby in years past, it wasn't clear that they were there anymore. My hopes rested on Angeluc's answer.

"The *Mantella* . . ." He paused, seeming to search for words. "There are *Mantella* in Montagne d'Ambre," he reassured me, "but not many, and not close."

"How far?" I asked. "Not close" might mean a fifteen-minute walk, or it might mean two days of hiking.

"About eight hours," he admitted.

I was stricken. This wouldn't do at all. Pitching a tent eight hours from the nearest building, which itself was a long way from food or other resources that I didn't bring in myself, wasn't a possibility.

"Eight hours," I said aloud to myself, then I asked Angeluc, "toward the edge of the park, toward town, or toward the middle?" I thought, maybe, that if the *Mantella* populations were near the village just outside the park, I could still make this work, even if I couldn't take advantage of the glorious new research facilities.

"Toward the middle," Angeluc replied quietly.

Angeluc is an amazing man in many ways, always surprising. One of the qualities I treasure most in him, when he is my guide, is that he tells the truth even when he knows I won't like it. This seems to be a rare trait in the developing world, where people often want to please in the moment and often give misleading or downright false answers if it will bring a smile to another's face. Angeluc knew, probably from many years of working with Ron and Chris, that the *vazaha* didn't appreciate wrong answers in the long run.

"Well," I said, turning up my hands in defeat, "I guess I won't be working here for the next few years."

"Too bad," Bret said, looking around. "Nice digs."

"Yeah, they sure are." I turned to Angeluc. "Let's go to Ankarana."

Ankarana is a phenomenal, mystical place, largely unspoiled by human intervention until recently. About seventy miles south of Diégo, Ankarana is on a plateau, a calcium-rich massif 150 feet above sea level. The plateau is traversed by underground rivers, which have dug deep into the earth, forming vast caverns 150 feet high in places, and more than seventy miles of underground caves and passageways. On top of the plateau, atop these vast caves, the limestone surface is a highly eroded karst formation called tsingy. Little grows on the tsingy, these vast rock seas, and the razor-sharp stones can easily cut through leather boots.

In several areas the caves have collapsed. In their place, forests have sprung up, isolated by the remaining caves and tsingy formations. The only access to most of these forests is through the caves, so they are isolated pockets of life in a surreal, otherworldly landscape. Where the caves are intact, the rivers flow underground, but they lie exposed in these forest pockets, and animals flock to the water in an otherwise bone-dry landscape.

Ankarana has recently been targeted by people more interested in industrial-grade emeralds than in natural beauty, and it is quickly being destroyed. These are not even stones to grace the hands of the vain beautiful, but slivers of stone to attach to grinding wheels, stone that could surely be harvested from a less glorious place than Ankarana. But labor is cheap, and the existing caves make mining relatively easy, so a few men are making a profit on the destruction of a place unique on the planet. In 1996, it was still desolate, forbidding, and largely pristine.

We only had a week to scout Ankarana for *Mantella*, so we hired a *quatre-quatre*, a 4×4 pickup, in Diégo to take us to the back side of the reserve. From there, we would hike out, catching a *taxi-brousse* back to Diégo when we emerged from the mix of caves, forest, and savanna of Ankarana. The expanses of dry land we went through in the *quatre-quatre* were scattered with villages. Lovely bright fields of green sprang suddenly out of the rolling yellow hills, rice paddies in a scorched climate. The Malagasy adore their rice, and they will plant it even in the most inhospitable places. The earth was red, as everywhere in Madagascar, and soon we and our things were covered in a fine silt. When the road was impassable, due to past flooding, the driver made his own road. We went through a village comprised entirely of small thatched houses on stilts, suggesting that there was heavy flooding on a regular basis. A little girl hid behind the stilts of one house, then ran behind the truck, waving at us as we bounced out of sight.

"*Sali, vazaha!*" they shouted, using the shortened form of *salama* employed by children across Madagascar.

After a long, dusty trip, we arrived at a spot in the shadow of an impressive massif, where nearby an underground cave opened up enough to allow people on the surface to retrieve freshwater from the depths. For reasons that were never clear to me, this spot was called the "*campement des américains.*" We set up our tents, then cooked some rice and beans over a wood fire for dinner.

"Do you think we'll see *Mantella* tomorrow, Angeluc?" I asked him as we sat around the fire after dinner. He laughed and looked at his feet.

"*Ongomba.*" He nodded his head. "*Peut-être, ongomba,* maybe." The way he strung these together, the French, Malagasy, and English words all meaning the same thing, there was a melody, a lilt that was almost calming. If Angeluc says so, it must be okay. He meant "Probably not, but who can predict these things?" But his tone was reassuring. *Peut-être, ongomba,* maybe.

Ankarana was dry as sand this time of year, and I suspected we wouldn't find any *Mantella*; that they would all be buried two feet under, their lives on hold until the rains resumed. Even if we did find *Mantella* in Ankarana, I was doubtful that this would be my study site. The almost complete lack of surface water scared me, as did the fact that the nearest village, which had no electricity or radio, was a four-day hike away.

We went out for a night walk, a *tsangatsangana,* as a walk or hike of moderate distance is called in Malagasy. Angeluc, true to form, unearthed huge numbers of reptiles. He found countless leaf-tailed geckos, *Uroplatus,* which cling to trees, the fringes of skin around their bodies utterly camouflaging them. He found sleeping chameleons, and some wary but docile snakes. We came to a small watering hole at the entrance to a cave, where during the day we had gotten water, and where we would try to wash the next day. It was the only surface water for miles, so all of the animal kingdom was in attendance. I was relying on Angeluc to tell me the names of the species of herps I would see, but when I spotted small yellow frogs sitting on a rock, I was sure they were *Mantella*. The thing about being brightly colored, though, is that unless all of your predators are walking around wearing headlamps, it doesn't make any sense to be active at night, when your coloration is wasted in the darkness. I could see that they were yellow, but then, I did have a light strapped to my head.

"Are those *Mantella*?" I asked Angeluc, incredulous.

"Yes. *Mantella viridis*," he asserted.

"Are they often out at night?"

"Sometimes." He shrugged, as if to say, So the frogs don't always follow the rules. What am I going to do about it? I frowned. If these frogs turned out to be nocturnal, my field work was going to be even more difficult than I had thought. One of the few saving graces of working on brightly colored poisonous frogs in Madagascar is that the field work is done during the day. Another is that there are no dangerous snakes to worry about. If you're a human.

The sound of screaming pierced the forest. A dreadful, desperate cry, persistent and repeated. The three of us looked at one another, then tried to follow the sound. We all went in different directions at first, but quickly equilibrated, and soon found the source. A larger frog, not poisonous like *Mantella*, was being engulfed by a boa. The snake had a firm grip on the frog's back end, but the front end was still quite alive, and loud. We watched for forty-five minutes as the frog slowly gave up the fight, the calls died, and the snake finally swallowed its prey.

I wandered back to the rock where I'd seen the *Mantella*. A snake with an aggressive reputation and a tendency to eat frogs, *Madagascarophis colubrinus*, was lounging nearby. In fact, there were four of these nasty-tempered serpents. The *Mantella* appeared to be unconcerned. They were in groups, from three to fifteen individuals, hopping about on the surface. I caught a few frogs and dropped them in front of one of the snakes, trying to induce a predation attempt. But the snakes didn't go for the frogs. I was curious if these snakes, which ate other, nontoxic frogs, would try to eat these toxic ones, but I would have to devise a better experiment to test the hypothesis that they avoided frogs that were bad for them. All I demonstrated by dropping frogs in front of snakes was that frogs hop away when dropped.

———

The next day, Angeluc led us to a place he called the "*jardin botanique*," which, though wild, was comforting after so much dry land. After three hours of walking across land without trails, we arrived at a set of pools, where a stream rushed between large rocks even in this dry season. There were, however, no frogs.

"Watch this," Angeluc instructed as he splashed water up onto the rocks. *Mantella viridis*, the same species we had seen the night before, instantly emerged from between the rocks. There seemed to be hundreds of them, suddenly, where before there had been none. They dashed out of view again when we tried to catch them.

"Where are we, Angeluc?" I liked the spot, the availability of freshwater, and the fact that even in the dry season there were frogs of the sort I was looking for. But if I worked here, how would I get food? How would I get help if I needed it? Who would know if I just disappeared?

"*Le jardin botanique*," he told me again.

"Yes, but . . ." The question was difficult to phrase. "How do you get here?" He looked a little morose.

"Very difficult without a vehicle. The nearest village is many, many miles, and even there you can't buy rice." Rice means food. If you couldn't buy rice, that meant you couldn't buy anything. I sighed. As lovely as the spot was, I was coming to realize that the northern tip of Madagascar would probably not be where I would conduct my research when I returned the following year.

We spent the next day hiking through caves to isolated patches of forest formed when the tsingy collapsed and let the light in. The caves were cool and wet, the entrances filled with geckos. Overhead were fruit bats—*Rosettus*—talking to one another, twittering, jostling for space. The floor was sticky with bat guano, and cockroaches swarmed over it. A short way in, in a narrow, inky pool, a four-foot-long black eel-like fish swam back and forth, making U-turns as it hit one end and then turned, elegantly, upon itself. Angeluc called it a "long fish," and we had no better name for it than that. As all light but that from our headlamps disappeared, we walked on, softly crunching through bat guano on the cave floor. Occasionally, we found a bat skeleton in the giant silty guano piles that lined the edges of the cave. As we continued in, the only life detectable became the occasional gleam of a spider's eye, a jewel sparkling in the dense blackness of deep cave.

Emerging into an island of forest from the pitch-black, we saw troops of lemurs playing and foraging in the trees, isolated by the tsingy from others like them. There were geckos and chameleons, living there undiscovered. We were enchanted. But there was no way I was going to work in a patch of forest accessible only by hiking through a long expanse of cave, in which wrong turns were likely, and the network of connecting caverns had never been mapped.

So the next day we moved on, trudging across an expanse of savanna with no surface water, few fruit trees, and incessant sun and biting flies. Angeluc called the fruit "*makaotra*." It was gourdlike, and when he broke the round shell open, disk-shaped seeds swam in a viscous liquid, attached by tenuous fibers to the seeds. Angeluc raised the shell of the fruit to his mouth and drank the liquid, then sucked on the seeds to detach the remaining pulp. Bret and I followed suit with other *makaotra*. They were both sweet and slightly tart, almost gummy, but the liquid was a welcome relief. We couldn't tell how close we were to the forest we were aiming for on the other side of the savanna, and until we got there, the only water we had was what we carried, and what we could steal from the *makaotra*. When we passed the last of the *makaotra* trees, our eyes playing tricks on us in the cruel heat, all we could do was aim for the distant trees, a line on the horizon, trying not to focus on our parched lips and our skin browning in the fierce orange sun as we scuffled through red dust and dry riverbeds. In January, Angeluc told us, those same desolate riverbeds that we hiked through would be impassable, due to inconceivable amounts of water. In January, when I might return. It was hard to believe that this barren landscape could be transformed so quickly, and so regularly, into a menace of a different type, where flash floods threatened crops, livestock, and children.

Finally, we arrived at the forest, then, shortly thereafter, the river camp, Amposetelo. Just downhill from two flat areas where we pitched our tents, a stream snaked through the small valley. Tamarind trees were in fruit high overhead, and a troop of crowned lemurs sprang from tree to tree, chattering and clicking. Often a few lemurs would come down to the stream, one apparently acting as sentry while the others carefully edged down a rock to drink from the cool water. Usually, they bent over and lapped the water with their tongues, like cats. Sometimes, they cupped their hands and drank from them, like any thirsty human without a cup. Any movement sent them bounding back into the trees. *Galidia elegans*, speedy, slender little russet mongooses with black-and-red-striped tails, raced about in pairs, chasing each other, eating insects. As night fell, frogs began calling from the banks of the stream, and more aggressive snakes lay in wait, occasionally lunging at a frog made obvious by his song. In this part of Ankarana, the *Mantella* knew the rules and didn't come out at night.

"Tomorrow," Angeluc promised, "I will take you to where the *Mantella* are."

"They will be out now, at this time of year?" I asked. I thought our experience at the *jardin botanique* was probably an exception.

"*Ongomba,*" Angeluc replied. "*Peut-être, ongomba,* maybe. But we will try."

That night, thinking of *Mantella,* and scratching furiously at fly bites, I dreamed of water, though now we were so close to clean fresh water, we could hear it gliding by from our tents.

The next morning, rehydrated but sunburned from our trek the day before, glad for a day's reprieve from our heavy packs, we set out to find *Mantella.* We failed. While doing so, we hiked through forest rich with striped mongooses, miniature chameleons, and curious lemurs.

After we had given up on finding *Mantella* for the day, Angeluc took us across a vast expanse of tsingy, sharp gray shards of stone eroded by millennia of weather. We arrived at the edge and peered down two hundred feet into what had once been a cave. Now a forest had grown there and an emerald green lake had formed. Crowned lemurs bounded from tree to tree far below us. Birds soared high over the lake, looking for prey, but we were high, too, and could look them in the eye as they circled. Angeluc led us around the perimeter of the tsingy and down to the lake, one of the few that can be accessed from the top of the tsingy, not just through the caves. The lake still fierce green, the birds and lemurs now high overhead, we saw brief flashes of fish as they surfaced. At the entrance to the cave, on top of which we had been standing an hour before, a river emerged from the depths, feeding the shimmering lake. Inside the cave, all was cool and dripping. When the lake fell into shadow, we retraced our steps back to camp.

The next day, we hiked out; crossing over more dry riverbeds, and past a few lakes that were drying up. Briny from the evaporation, they were home to both crocodiles and the ancestors of local people. These were sacred lakes, Angeluc told us, and we could not drink from them, lest we upset the ancestors. If we needed water, we could dig a hole many yards away and let it fill with water seeping in from the water table. This water was old, salty, and thick. You could taste its voyage through the earth on your tongue. But it had the promise of life.

Frogs were scarce during the day in Ankarana, but the forest was filled with them at night, their calls resonating far. But the *Boophis* and *Manti-*

dactylus frogs we found were not what I was looking for, and when the time came to leave Ankarana and catch a ride on an overstuffed old pickup truck back to Diégo, I wondered how feasible my plan to study poisonous frogs somewhere in Madagascar actually was. When we left Angeluc, I felt a pang of misgiving—as if I should be hiring him to accompany us all over Madagascar, for he was knowledgeable, clever, and fun. But I didn't have the money to do it, so this was good-bye.

"Will you be back here next year, Erika?" he asked me.

"*Peut-être, ongomba,* maybe," I said a little sadly.

"Oh." He nodded. He knew what it meant. "I hope you find the *Mantella* you're looking for."

5

Because It Is Natural

From Diégo, we flew on a tiny prop plane to Maroantsetra, a town at the northern tip of the Bay of Antongil, on the west edge of the Masoala peninsula. The Masoala has the largest remaining tracts of lowland rain forest in Madagascar, and two sites in this northeastern region held the greatest promise for long-term research. There was Nosy Mangabe, a small island just three miles off the coast, and a camp called Andranobe, much farther away, on the Masoala itself. Andranobe had been launched by Claire Kremen when she was doing her dissertation work on butterflies. Now she and the Wildlife Conservation Society (WCS) were working to make the whole region a national park. Though I hadn't met her, we had talked at some length before I went to Madagascar, and she had recommended Andranobe as being a forest rich in frogs. I was coming to realize, though, that while most of Madagascar is rich in frogs, the particular ones I was looking for were a bit harder to find.

After we landed on the dirt airstrip at Maroantsetra, which sported a single wind sock, and unpiled from the plane to wait in the sad lone building, our bags sat by the tiny plane for fifteen, twenty, twenty-five minutes. The plane was going on to Sambava, so there were about fifteen Malagasy wandering about, waiting to board, but our bags just sat there. I approached the man who looked like an authority; he was standing behind the scale used to weigh luggage and make sure it came in under the twenty-kilogram limit. A sign on it read, in French, NOT ACCURATE BELOW 25 KG.

The man behind the scale said they would bring us our bags, and he told me to wait. I was frustrated, hot, and impatient, so Bret decided to take the matter into his own hands. We were the only *vazaha* around, and were surrounded by a group of children who had come from the village to see the plane land. Bret extracted himself from the curious little ones and strode purposefully out to the tarmac, such as it was, deftly picked up our two heavy frame packs, and began marching back with them. All activity in the airport stopped. All eyes were on the odd *vazaha* who was carrying his own bags from the plane. Even the children stopped their whistling and chattering to watch this slightly scary *vazaha* carrying bags, one hanging precariously off each shoulder.

In this building, there were four places where doors ought to have been, but only one door. At the other openings, there was just air. Similarly, there were no windows, just holes in the wall. The ceiling hung in tatters, wet and dark, fallen through in several places. As Bret approached the one remaining door in the building, he turned slightly to get through, but not enough. One of the backpacks grazed the door, which fell, crashing, to the concrete floor. Its hinges were rusted away, as if it had been waiting for a lumbering *vazaha* to take it out. All was silent. Bret looked at the door on the ground, at me, at the breathless children, and at the passengers waiting to board. Carefully, with exaggerated movements, he put our bags down, picked up the door, and rested it up against the building. He appraised his handiwork, as did everyone else in the airport. We left as subtly as we could manage, which is to say, with much noise, and an entourage of little children.

Maroantsetra thinks it is a beach town, and it has all the appropriate trappings, except one: It lacks a beach. On the Bay of Antongil, its climate is hot, and its reputation as the wettest spot in Madagascar is warranted. The main drag was once paved, and there are still remnants of asphalt. There are no roads that service Maroantsetra throughout the year. The one road into the region—a coastal route up from the large port town of Tamatave to the south—has on it fifteen or so ferries, running across waterways out to the Indian Ocean. During the wet season, the chance that all ferries are up and running has been estimated to be less than 5 percent. In the dry season, when all parameters are optimal for a road trip from Tamatave to

Maroantsetra, the trip can be completed perhaps 50 percent of the time. Maroantsetra is thus isolated from the rest of Madagascar, at least by road.

When we got to town, we headed to a place called the Motel Coco Beach, a curious name for a hotel in a town with neither vehicles nor a beach. We found a dozen dingy thatched-roof bungalows, which, we were told, usually had electricity and running water. The Coco Beach was relatively clean, very quiet, about a twenty-minute walk from the center of town, and cost about ten dollars per night per room. There was a restaurant in a larger thatched-roof building near the bungalows run by Monique, a friendly Malagasy woman who, I later learned, intensely disliked vegetables.

Throughout Madagascar, guides are required for tourists and first-time researchers, but we did not yet know how to find one in Maroantsetra. Soon after getting settled in our bungalow, though, a man came up from the river nearby, asking us what we were looking for. Not knowing what he meant, I tried simplicity.

"*Grenouilles,*" I offered, using the French word for frogs. At first, I thought he didn't understand me—my tongue has a particularly difficult time with that word. "*Sàhona,*" I added after a moment, the Malagasy word for frog. He grew animated.

"I know where to find the tomato frog, here in town. I can be your guide!"

The tomato frog is a large bright red frog found only in the northeast of Madagascar. I was interested to see it but wasn't going to study it. I was realizing that the vast diversity of frogs in Madagascar was actually impeding my ability to find the frogs I was looking for, because everyone had seen one frog or another. So as not to encourage the man, who didn't seem to know much about nature except that a bright red frog sometimes attracted *vazaha*, we excused ourselves and walked into town.

Maroantsetra was flat, dull, and hot. I feared getting trapped, as we had been in Tana. Bret and I wandered down to the office where permits were stamped and access to the forest was granted. There, we hoped to get a guide, arrange for a boat, and figure out how to get provisions. As if he had been waiting for us to appear, a short, smirking man named Emile was immediately in the doorway, extending his hand and asking if we needed a guide. We would be spending two and a half weeks with whomever we hired, so it was important that we get it right, but we hadn't a clue how to interview a naturalist guide. I asked Emile if he knew the frogs called *Mantella*. He did.

"Can you find them at Andranobe?" I pursued. He paused for just a moment, then assured me that you could.

"Do you know where?"

"Yes," he said.

He was feeding us answers that would get him hired, but what choice did we have? Bret, who studies bats, though not the bats of Madagascar, asked Emile about the bats on the Masoala. Emile perked up and began talking about various bats he had seen. It seemed he thought Bret would be making the hiring decision, so he was working on impressing him more than me. I needed someone who could show me where the frogs were. As if reading my mind, Emile spoke to me again.

"On Nosy Mangabe, there are many *Mantella*. Easy to find. Andreone found them."

I raised my eyebrows at him. He had invoked the name of an Italian herpetologist I knew, Franco Andreone. What's more, Franco had told me himself that there were many *Mantella* here. I thought this auspicious.

"Where on Nosy Mangabe?" This island reserve was the second site I intended to visit in the region.

"All over." He spread his hands out as if to suggest they carpeted the place. "Everywhere you go."

This, I didn't believe. But we wanted to get into the field, and so far Emile was the only guide we had met who seemed legitimate, so we hired him. Two days later, we were on a small boat to Andranobe, with Emile and several baskets of rice.

Andranobe is a stunning spot, the outflow of a watershed encompassing an expanse of primary rain forest, steep-sloped and lush. There are a few tent platforms and small cabins. One belongs to the Peregrine Fund, which hires Malagasy researchers to search for the serpent eagle, a species of bird only seen once, many years ago, in this very spot. The Wildlife Conservation Society, which administers the lands with the Malagasy government, has a cabin as well, and here we were allowed to store our bags, and our rice. One permanent resident, Solo, acts as camp guardian and cook. When he visits his family in the village of Ambanizana, five miles away, he goes by coastal footpath or pirogue—a small dugout canoe, the likes of which are common throughout coastal Madagascar, the same sort we had taken to find crocodiles in Manakara. Other villagers walk the same footpath, some-times with cattle in tow. Solo's wife, Pierette, farms vanilla in his absence.

When we arrived at Andranobe in 1996, Solo was there, as well as two Peregrine Fund workers, who remained nameless to us, as we did to them.

For three days, Bret, Emile, and I headed out into the forest on one of few paths, looking for *Mantella laevigata*, the species of *Mantella* I was most interested in. For three days, we came up empty. We did find another *Mantella*—*Mantella betsileo*—but this cryptic frog was by far the least interesting to me of the many *Mantella* species, and I wasn't satisfied with it. Emile didn't know where to find *laevigata*, and now that we were here together and he couldn't be fired, he admitted that he hadn't seen any here at Andranobe.

The rain forest of Madagascar is filled with weird and extraordinary things. As biologists, Bret and I react to seeing such things as a large blue bird or a flower that opens only at night and smells of buttered popcorn by asking questions: Why? What is the purpose of this odd trait? Who benefits, and how? When we asked Emile the same questions, though, his answer was always the same.

"Why are the ruffed lemurs on the Masoala red, when everywhere else they are black and white?"

"Because it is natural."

"Why does this gecko have black chevrons on its throat?"

"Because it is natural."

The bechevroned gecko, one *Phelsuma guttata*, was a beautiful specimen, a vivid green with shocking red spots, and of course the chevrons on its throat. The thrill of finding amazing animals and having a sense of what they are is great. But here was Emile, always at my side, with his pat, uninvestigated answers.

He began to grate on me. Bret and I schemed to escape into the forest without him. Some mornings, early, before the others were awake, I would sneak into the forest alone, leaving Bret to deal with the increasingly morose Emile, who recognized that he wasn't particularly necessary, or wanted. Lacking the *laevigata* I was really after, I began watching *Mantella betsileo* at a wide, shallow, slow-moving stream where a population of them routinely came out in the mornings. The males called from rocks, and sometimes they fought with one another at what seemed to be the borders of territories. Once, I saw an interaction that could have been interpreted as females vying for male attention, very rare in any species that isn't monogamous. I wasn't sure—not confident that I had sexed the players correctly. But I was intrigued.

It was the wrong season to see frogs, so I was lucky to observe any frog behavior at all. Most mornings, I sat watching perfectly still frogs on rocks for hours at a time. But in this comfortable forest with ample water, so unlike Ankarana, I was easily lulled, and even mornings spent watching completely immobile frogs were tolerable.

In the afternoons, Bret and I kept looking for *laevigata*. One day, we asked the Peregrine Fund men if they had seen little yellow-and-blue frogs. After equivocating a bit, they pointed south out of camp and told us to go about a mile. Emile asked if he could go into the forest with us, which softened my heart a little, and the three of us began searching together again. We spent an afternoon wandering around the general vicinity the Peregrine Fund men had directed us to, but we found no *Mantella*. We did find more geckos and tree frogs and even a boa, but no *Mantella*. Emile was sluggish, and he seemed tired a lot of the time, which slowed us down. Over our bowls of rice that evening, we asked him if he was okay.

He nodded yes. Most of our conversations were in French, as my French was better than his English. But Bret didn't speak any French, so the communication was slow and halting, as various translations occurred.

"You are healthy?" I repeated. Emile turned his sad eyes on me. He looked at the table.

"I have malaria," he mumbled. Bret and I exchanged looks.

"How do you know?" I asked.

"I've had malaria for a long time. It comes and goes. Usually, I'm fine. But now, I'm not."

There are four different strains of malaria, and the two most common have very distinct epidemiologies. Falciparum malaria is associated with cyclic fevers every day and a half or two, it sometimes "turns cerebral," and is the form of the disease most likely to kill a person. It is also common in northeastern Madagascar. The advantage of falciparum malaria, if it can be said to have any, is that if you purge it, it's gone, and it won't come back unless you get reinfected by another mosquito. The more common form of malaria is vivax, which is also associated with fevers approximately every two days, along with aches and pain, but it is a lower-grade infection than falciparum. Vivax doesn't tend to kill people, but it does retreat into the liver at whim and stay there, dormant, for long periods of time, reemerging sporadically and making its host sick again. Emile was describing a long-term battle with vivax malaria.

"Did you know you were sick before you came out here with us?" He nodded again. This was a man so desperate to earn a bit of money for his family that he had hired himself out as a guide for almost three weeks while ailing and listless from chronic malaria. But though his body was slow, urging him to sleep, his mind was active, and he had been forming intense questions about us, the *vazaha* in his care. He steered the conversation away from his malaria.

"Why are you looking for frogs?" he asked me.

When I had explained the basic questions before, he hadn't seemed very interested. "Well," I replied, breathing in, ready for another round, "I want to understand what they do, and why they do it. There are no other frogs like this in the whole world." He looked unconvinced. "Why do you think I'm here?" I asked him. Clearly, he had been thinking about this.

"I think you're here to get rich," he announced confidently.

Bret and I laughed spontaneously at this, which perturbed Emile a bit.

"No, no," I said, thinking that would be enough to assure him. "There's no money in this."

"But Madagascar has many unique things," Emile argued. "It must be possible to make money. . . ."

"Yes, but . . ." I began.

He continued, urgent now. "Why would you come here except to make money? To be a researcher, it is a good job, no?"

I couldn't explain it. His world seemed so insular and tiny to him, and he had heard enough about what happened outside its borders to wonder why anyone would willingly come inside. The only driving force he believed strong enough was that of money. Emile had previously told us that he did not come from Maroantsetra, but from Tamatave, the larger port town down the coast. There he had been exposed to literature and philosophy in school, and these were his passions. He didn't care much for the forest, and he had never been taught biology, but guiding was a job. He and his family lived in a tiny one-room house with a thatched roof. They had never had enough money to buy a "real" roof, one made of corrugated zinc. He had, he felt, a life of the mind, but he couldn't escape the pressing everyday realities of life in rural Madagascar. He didn't have enough money to have a dog, he explained, because a dog eats a kapok (a tin can measure) of rice every day—the equivalent of about two dollars a month. He couldn't afford to smoke cigarettes. In this world of constant want, how could anything besides money motivate anyone? he wondered.

"You like to read philosophy, Emile, and learn that way. I like to learn by going into the forest and looking directly at animals, to figure out what they do."

He shook his head, and the smirk on his face betrayed a lack of confidence in my words.

"But the learning is in the books," he said; "there's nothing to be learned here. The forest is useful, but books are for learning."

"You said yourself that Madagascar has many unique things, extraordinary animals and plants found nowhere else on the planet. So many things here are endemic, found nowhere else. . . ."

"Endemic?" he repeated, eager to learn a word new to him.

"Yes, endemic," Bret interjected, realizing that Emile was beginning to understand his well-enunciated and careful English. "The animals are so different here; it is worth studying them to see how they are different, and to think about why."

"They just are," said Emile, but Bret interrupted him.

"No, that's not a good-enough explanation. This work that Erika is doing, and that I do in other places, is about figuring out why." Emile wasn't convinced. His religious convictions prevented him from fully agreeing with our worldview, as he believed that God had put humans on the planet for reasons we hadn't yet discovered, but the animals and plants were here for us to use as we pleased.

When Bret and I had been in Madagascar three years earlier, we had a brilliant guide named Maurice in the eastern forests. One day, out of the blue, he began talking about religion. We assumed that he, like most Malagasy, identified as Christian, while still retaining belief in the animism of native Malagasy religion. Maurice surprised us.

"When people ask me what religion I am," he said clearly and loudly, as if he had been practicing for this, "I tell them I am not a Christian." He paused. "Sometimes they are shocked. Then I tell them I am not a Christian; I am a Naturalist." He looked at us expectantly. We were delighted. Here was a man who had come to atheism on his own. Immersed in a culture of ancestor worship, and exposed to a recently introduced Western God, he had explored the forest day after day, week after week, year after year and had come to the conclusion that nature explained what he saw.

Emile, by contrast, was a religious man, and he specifically believed that the fruits of the earth were put here for us to use. But he cherished his job. So publicly, at least, he didn't approve of lemur hunting in protected areas, or of the routine eating of bats. He was no Naturalist, but he was a smart man, and his eyes were always open.

The next day, Emile stayed in camp while we took a new direction into the forest, going where we hadn't been before. We crossed a few rivers and climbed over and under tree falls, figuring that if we got lost, we could just go downhill, toward the coast. We never left our watershed.

Bret and I had separated. I was looking in the leaf litter for frogs, without any luck, when I heard him yell to me. As quickly as I could manage, making my way through the vines and other obstacles a rain forest presents, I got to him. In his hand, he held a beautiful neon green-and-black frog, a frog that had to be a *Mantella*, though why I knew that, I can't explain. A flippant but confident field biologist mutters "gestalt" by way of explanation in such a situation.

"Do you know this species?" he asked me. I didn't. As far as I knew, it was new to science.

"Where did you find it?" I asked.

"Here, on the ground, underneath the tree fall. There are more." He gestured to the leaf litter. I was mesmerized. This *Mantella* wasn't in the one decent field guide that described the herps of Madagascar. Still, the field guide wasn't completely up-to-date, and there are always species yet unnamed that researchers somewhere in the world are writing descriptions of for publication.

As I was ruminating on the significance of Bret's find, he wandered off to find more, scrounging in the litter for them. He yelled again. I went to him, only to find him holding a *laevigata* in his hand, a juvenile.

"*Laevigata*," he said, almost a question, but not quite. He knew that he had found the elusive *laevigata*. Only one, but there had to be more. That, along with the new species (the green-and-black frogs), the *Mantella betsileo*, which was drab put populous, and the atmosphere of lush tranquility at Andranobe, made my decision for me.

"I'm coming back here next year," I announced. "Here, and Nosy Mangabe. These will be my research sites."

We collected a few of the green-and-black frogs, which hopped in Ziploc bags, and took them back to camp. None of the men there had seen this frog before. Later, we discovered that our "new species" had, in fact, been collected by herpetologists already but had not yet been formally described as a species. So we weren't first, but the thrill of discovery at that moment wasn't diminished for it.

While we were sitting in camp admiring our new frogs, some fisher people wandered through. Emile went to talk with them, then approached us with the wide grin that meant he wanted something and was going to try to convince us that we wanted it, too. At his signal, the fisher people presented several large flat fish that had been smoked over a wood fire. They were shriveled, their skin coming off in large flakes, and when Emile lifted one to display its quality, a large cockroach scuttled out from inside the pile. It didn't make me want to eat. But Emile wasn't used to a diet without animal protein, and we had refused to buy any of the gray, fly-laden beef in the market when we were shopping for provisions, so we bought all of the dried fish, then let Solo do what he would with it. For the next three days, our meals consisted of rice and a murky broth made of reconstituted fish to pour on top of it, the fins, tail, and head swimming in it. I wasn't going to starve to death in the time we had left, so at some point I stopped eating the broth with dried fish chunks, its flavor too smoky, dusty, dried. Emile, however, was very satisfied.

Bret and I spent the last hour of daylight one night sitting on the rocks by the water, mudskippers at our feet, the sun glinting onto the water through clouds hovering on the horizon. Usually, the Andranobe pirogue rested on sand and rocks nearby, hatchet marks from its carving visible on its side. This evening, though, Solo had taken it to Ambanizana, asking us before he left if we wanted anything. When we looked blankly at him—we thought Ambanizana was a tiny town without any commerce—he told us his family sold pineapples and bananas, *toka gasy* (rotgut rum), vanilla, and chickens. He implied that he could do wonderful things with a chicken. Yes, we enthused, yes please, some of everything.

When Solo returned, we did indeed have a delicious chicken (and rice) dinner, and luscious tropical bananas, tiny sweet-tart ones, the likes of which you can't get in the States. Solo also slit a few vanilla beans, put them in the *toka gasy*, and let it sit for two days before letting us taste it. Instant vanilla extract. We asked Solo if we could buy more vanilla—a lot more, to take home with us. Nothing could have pleased him more, this relatively poor but honest, engaging, friendly man who had been told his product was desirable. We bought a kilogram of vanilla from him, more than 250 beans. He wanted twenty-five dollars, which was a fantastic price—less than ten cents a bean for luscious, hand-pollinated, organically grown vanilla straight from the people who grew it. This seemed to him an exorbitant amount of money, but for us, it was a tiny price for a product that runs almost two dollars per bean in the States. He asked shyly if we might buy him a rain jacket like the one I had, a bright red anorak. He wanted to pay me, in money or vanilla, and asked that I bring it back when I returned. The jacket had cost me eighty dollars, and I knew Solo couldn't afford such a price.

He made the equivalent of something between one and two hundred dollars a year. I told him I would try to get him a jacket but that it would be a gift, not something for him to buy. He broke into a huge smile, ran off, and then returned with another half a kilogram of vanilla for us as a gift.

We left Andranobe, promising to return the following year. Solo waved to us as the small motorboat turned and headed for Nosy Mangabe. When we got to the small island reserve, excited to arrive in a new place, Emile turned to me and asked if I wanted to be back home in Michigan.

"Sometimes," I admitted, "but not usually."

He shook his head in contradiction. "No, I believe you are thinking about home, that you always want to be there."

I couldn't convince him of his error, because he was always imagining our home, and wanted to be there himself. Since he was eager to learn English better, I taught him a new phrase. "The grass is always greener on the other side of the fence, Emile. It means you want what other people have." He thought about it, and seemed to believe that much at least. In fact, Emile couldn't have imagined what I missed. The long days of summer in the northern temperate zone. Freedom to move of my own volition, without waiting for a boat or a *taxi-brousse*. The ability to walk down a street without attracting the attention of everyone around, without being yelled to and pointed at and touched. Emile thought I missed the things we had told him most Americans have, things many Malagasy have never even experienced: electricity, television, phones, cars. But he was wrong. I didn't crave a telephone. The freedom from such conveniences was wonderful. I did, though, often want to be in my world, where the people around me had essentially my set of experiences, where the assumptions were established, and things went smoothly.

"What do rich Americans have?" Emile asked us.

Off the top of our heads, we said, "Lots of cars, large estates, perhaps a boat, jewelry, and a lot of free time." He didn't understand the concept of free time. The stuff, though, was of interest.

"How many cars do you have?" he asked.

"We have one."

He eyed us suspiciously.

"Boats?"

We laughed. "No boats. We're not rich." He scowled. We were clearly lying. Obviously, we *were* rich. We had just spent twenty-five dollars on vanilla. We each had two pairs of shoes. He had one pair of flip-flops, which were falling apart. And in rural Madagascar, he is not poor. Emile is middle-class, which must make us rich. A person who hasn't experienced the different economies of the First and Third Worlds cannot be expected to understand that you budget differently in your different locales but that you do not become as impoverished as the local people just because you're trying to save money. In the five weeks I had been in Madagascar, I had spent six hundred dollars, including domestic airfare, hotels, food, hiring a car, and paying Angeluc and Emile. Six hundred dollars was an inconceivable amount of money to Emile. He would never in his life see that much money at one time. I felt frugal. In his eyes, I was fabulously wealthy.

Nosy Mangabe is known primarily as a sanctuary for the aye-aye. Aye-ayes are the weirdest of the native primates, with their long middle fingers and big bat ears, and we were eager, our first night on the island, to look for these shy beasts. A Swedish tourist couple were on the island, too, with their guide, Felix. That night, we saw a single aye-aye, high up in a tree, picking fruit and hanging upside down, looking wide-eyed into our lights and camera flashes. The animal was engaging and slightly repulsive, but Felix, he was a gem. After more than two weeks of being distrusted by the forest-ambivalent Emile, we appreciated the joy Felix displayed about everything—about the aye-aye, the night sky, the leaf-tailed geckos, and the *tsangatsangana* we were taking through the forest. His enthusiasm was contagious.

The next day, Emile, Bret, and I went to the higher of the two summits on the island to find *Mantella laevigata*. We found plenty. While Bret and I rummaged in the leaf litter looking for frogs, Emile sat reading his English-Malagasy dictionary, much more interested in teaching himself English than in the forest. He was picking it up unusually quickly, with his remarkable language skills and critical mind. When a troop of black-and-white-ruffed lemurs passed overhead, Bret and I stopped hunting for frogs to enjoy the spectacle, but Emile didn't even look up. To a Malagasy, having lemurs pass by may be like having squirrels cross the telephone wires overhead in the States. At some point, it's just not new anymore.

I was finding the *Mantella laevigata* I'd been looking for. On the summit, there was a population. On the way down from the summit, another. The next day, I walked down the coastal path and found several stands of bamboo. Calls were emanating from them. I had hit the jackpot. I found frogs calling, chasing, aggressing against one another. Where the bamboo had broken or been cut and rainwater had collected, I found small wells with tadpoles in them. In some of these, there were many tadpoles, with an adult frog of a different species with them. In some, though, just one or two tadpoles lived, and I felt that these were the tadpoles of *Mantella laevigata*, the species for which I wanted to decipher reproductive behavior. So I parked myself by one of these wells with a presumptive *laevigata* tadpole in it and sat down. Around me, frogs cruised by, calling, hopping along the ground, going up trees and bamboo. A hundred feet away, waves lapped on the shore. After three hours, the tadpole had done nothing in particular, nobody had visited it except for me, and most of the frog activity in the bamboo stand had stopped. Late afternoon brought thinner, warmer light, and soon no frogs were in evidence. Nothing continued to happen with breakneck speed. But I was content.

On our final morning on Nosy Mangabe, waiting for a boat to come pick us up, I realized I was already addicted to *Mantella laevigata*. I sat at the closest bamboo stand to camp, with instructions to Bret to run and get me when the boat showed up. I felt that every minute I was away from these frogs, I might be missing some crucial aspect of their story. I saw astonishing things just as the boat arrived. First, a male and a female mating inside one of the bamboo wells. Then, in a well right next door, a single frog egg being eaten by a tadpole. Why was the egg there? Simply because it is natural? I didn't think so. Could it have been deposited by the tadpole's mom, in an act of maternal care? These were exactly the sort of fantastic life-history observations I had been hoping for, although not expecting at this time of year, when the rains were relatively rare and the weather cool. I had to be pulled away from the frogs so the boat wouldn't leave without me, but knew that I would be back, when it was hotter and wetter and the frogs were even more likely to be doing wondrous things.

We left Maroantsetra in a *brousse*, an old pickup truck with a canvas-covered bed that was stuffed to the gills with people and luggage on the way to the dusty little airport. Emile insisted on going with us to see us off. I couldn't see the driver, as the cab was already filled to the ceiling when we crammed ourselves in the back. We circled through the center of town several times, perhaps looking for more passengers, though it is the rare Maroantsetran who has a ticket to fly away. On the ride, Emile tried to chat with us nonchalantly, still picking our brains about our weird *vazaha* ways. One thing that still bothered him, it seemed, was that we didn't pray before meals. Emile did, and he was concerned every time we failed to join in.

Finally, we got to the airport. We extracted ourselves from the back of the truck, then carried our bags into the room without doors. I looked around for the driver of the *brousse* to pay him, and found a man standing behind Emile, looking expectant. He looked at me and smiled, and I tried to hand him a ten-thousand FMG note. He backed off, surprised, and laughed.

"This is our pastor, Erika," Emile informed me, his eyes narrowing a bit as he assessed me in light of my most recent error. It seems I had tried to buy my way into heaven with a bribe of two dollars and fifty cents.

6

Escapes from Tana

Back in Tana, city of contrasts. Gated houses with freshly painted blue shutters sit, protected, next to three-walled shacks, next to rice paddies. Old men rummage through burning piles of trash, keeping ahead of the smolder, picking out pieces of rags, half a bottle with no bottom. Smartly dressed women in fitted suits gingerly walk through this city of sudden holes that drop thirty feet to sewage below. Children in T-shirts down to their ankles, eight or ten holes in the backs and sides, always of the same dingy hue, wander barefoot through remnants of chicken butchering. Some wait in line at the neighborhood water pump, where families come to retrieve water with which to cook and wash, brightly colored buckets at their sides. The taupe of their shirts, deep brown skin showing through, against russet clay earth, all dims next to the vibrant artificiality of their buckets—red, blue, yellow.

We struggled to escape Tana's grasp as soon as possible. Next we were headed to Ranomafana, the park with the most logistic support in all of Madagascar. We were staying at a house in Tana reserved for researchers working at Ranomafana. Every day, we visited ICTE (the Institute for the Conservation of Tropical Environments), also called Projet Ranomafana, the organization funded by American universities and government subsidy to help administer the park. Benjamin Andriamihaja, the chief of operations there, is a highly organized, efficient, honest, and warm man. He is also perennially stressed, as he has to take care of all the mistakes made by those less organized, and less honest.

Because we were going to Ranomafana, Projet Ranomafana was going to allow us the use of one of their vehicles and drivers to get to the park, which is about a twelve-hour drive over horrible roads. *Vazaha* don't drive themselves in Madagascar, as a rule, and certainly not long distances in vehicles owned by other people. Unfortunately, none of the Projet Ranomafana vehicles was in working order. A couple of Toyota *quatre-quatres* were the least compromised, and they had different things wrong with them. So it was logical that ICTE attempt to hybridize the two. One had no tires or brakes. The second had an inoperable piston ring which caused the car to be filled with smoke when the engine ran—itself a rare occurrence. Unfortunately, they weren't the same models of Toyota. After two days, the effort was abandoned.

Meanwhile, Bret and I loitered in the small courtyard, told every hour or so that we would be leaving for Ranomafana shortly. We amused ourselves in the mornings by getting pastries from one of the city's fine bakeries. The French first imagined baguettes, croissants, and *pain au chocolat*, and they sold their recipes to the Malagasy for the small price of imperialism. We occupied ourselves midday by going to the Indonesian restaurant up the street, an unexpected find. Its only drawback was the proprietor, who took a liking to us and insisted every time we came in that we visit his private museum. This alleged museum was mysterious, and a bit scary. We had only a murky understanding of the museum's contents or purpose. The proprietor made allusions to Malagasy-American collaboration and richly decorated rooms, but we never learned more.

After days of this, Benjamin suggested that we rent an entire *taxi-brousse* for the journey and said that ICTE would split the cost with us, as they needed to send down some luggage for EarthWatch volunteers currently in the park. Alas, the drivers went on strike—against whom was unclear—and blocked all the roads out of the city. We went back to the Indonesian restaurant for lunch and received another invitation to the private museum. The drivers abandoned their strike, and the search for a rentable vehicle was back on. Finally, one was found, and we were off on a long, grueling nighttime road trip to Ranomafana.

———

Ranomafana is in the long, lone remaining strip of eastern forest still standing in Madagascar. Higher in elevation than the lowland rain forests of the Masoala, with a base elevation of 2,600 feet and rising from there, Ranomafana's two basic seasons aren't wet and dry, but cool and cooler. We were there in the cooler season. The forest is dense and steep, and many small rivers snake through the region. Rainfall is in excess of eight feet a year, most of which falls as drizzle during the cooler season. We were in for a cold, damp time of it. The lemurs, not themselves immune to the constant spitting rain, hunkered down and made a habit of looking miserable in trees overhead.

Base camp at Ranomafana, in keeping with its reputation as a logistic powerhouse, has a kitchen building, a one-room library/laboratory, and several cleared areas where tents can be pitched. When we arrived, all tent areas were taken by the EarthWatch volunteers, who had been welcomed with open arms by Pat Wright, the American primatologist who founded the park. The place was a zoo, with *vazaha* do-gooders crawling all over it, and no research being done. We remembered, from our previous trip, that there was a remote camp at a higher elevation, Vaturanana, and decided to hike to that as soon as possible. Pat Wright wished we would stay—more researchers interacting with EarthWatch volunteers meant a better experience for them—and to entice me, she insinuated that there was a high density of *Mantella* near base camp. Bret had made it clear that he hoped to find the endemic sucker-footed bats that hung out, suction-cupped to the insides of young rolled-up leaves, and she suggested the presence of many of these bats, as well. After a cursory look around the area near base camp, with the ambient noise level high due to so many people, and most animals hiding as a result, we decided it wasn't worth staying more than one night. We set up our tent and then played along, interacting with the innocent but research-obstructing EarthWatchers and with one distinctly non-naïve young woman who called herself Jessica.

Perhaps she had heard Pat Wright talking about us and our research interests, or perhaps she was being ingenuous. Regardless, when Jessica introduced herself to us as a future biologist who wanted to work on herps, or bats—she hadn't decided which—we were completely charmed.

"Are you one of the EarthWatchers?" Bret asked.

"No no." She waved her hand dismissively. "I'm volunteering here, watching propes for Pat Wright's project." *Prope* is researcher slang for *Propithecus*, a remarkable genus of primate unique to Madagascar. Technically not lemurs, but close, they are sifakas; they sport long, lithe limbs and pointy, quizzical faces. They bound through the trees in a unique form of locomotion called "vertical grasping and leaping."

"They're wonderful," she added, "but I'd rather watch herps. Nobody seems to know anything about the frogs or lizards. There's female dominance in lemur society, and gripping social interactions, but lemurs aren't the only things *behaving* in this forest." She seemed downright passionate.

As a student of behavior myself, I have long felt it critical that the organism of choice spark deep interest in the researcher doing the work. Scientist or no, we all have to follow our passions. As with good literature, I find the stories of what animals do timeless and deeply engaging. The natural histories that weren't good have disappeared, continually replaced by classics, so every bit of animal behavior is rich with history and possibility. Unraveling the patterns that define animal lives and explaining them are puzzles I enjoy. The same was apparently true for Jessica.

I asked her where she was going when she was done volunteering at Ranomafana.

"I'm starting at Oxford in a year," she said, a bit abashed, as if this were a strike against her. I assumed she was starting a graduate program there, taking a year off between college and grad school. But no. She was only seventeen at the time, had just graduated from the French lycée in Tana, and was taking a year off between high school and college. The daughter of a UN diplomat, she is British, but had never, at that point, lived in Britain. She grew up in Kenya, Swaziland, Burkina Faso, and Madagascar, and she is fluent in French. Her keen mind for evolutionary biology had her looking for field adventures until she started school in September of the following year—she wouldn't be volunteering at Ranomafana for the entire time.

The next day we hiked to Vaturanana—Vatu, for short. There were four researchers there already, which was for the best, as if there had been nobody, we wouldn't have known when to stop hiking. Vatu is a research site, in so much as there is a space flat enough to have a food tent, fire, and table. A river runs nearby, but unlike in Ankarana, water isn't limited in Ranomafana. Flat spaces are. Two of the researchers were working on lemurs, the other two on the elusive fossa, the largest member of the carnivore family in Madagascar. There aren't any cats, dogs, or bears native to Madagascar—no leopards, grizzlies, jackals, or hyenas. The native predators are all mongooses and their ilk, and the fossa is one of these. Unlike the cute little red-and-black critters we had seen playing in Ankarana, the fossa was reputed to be the size of a German shepherd, sand-colored, and fierce. *Cryptoprocta ferox*. Even the Latin name sounded menacing.

Luke, the graduate student studying the fossa, was pissed off. A juvenile fossa he had put a radio collar on had gone missing. Carnivores are rare in any ecosystem—it takes a lot of space to house enough rodents and other prey to feed a carnivore—so the loss of one marked individual was a big problem for a carnivore project. Luke suspected that villagers living in the park had killed it, as he had originally trapped it by baiting it with live chickens, and it had developed a taste for them. Now it was probably stealing villagers' chickens, which wouldn't make the villagers happy.

The Ranomafana forest was strangely quiet. The constant buzz of frog and insect calls of other forests was missing. Many tropical frogs aestivate, or go underground, during the cold season or during dry periods, emerging once the conditions are again to their liking. In my few days at Vatu, I found no *Mantella* at all, though I was assured that they were there in the "right" season. Odder still, I found very few of the other frogs that were prevalent elsewhere—none of the pale green tree frogs, and few of the drab brown numbers so common on the Masoala. There were some lovely geckos, living in prickly palmlike plants called pandanus. But even in a swampy section, where I sat for a day, silent and still, waiting for animals to emerge from the gray and drizzle, the forest was eerily quiet.

At night, the six of us sat around eating rice with vegetables and soy sauce—big bottles were available in town, and every week a local man was hired to carry supplies up to Vatu, an all-day trip. Sitting with the other researchers, we heard the park gossip.

There was ongoing logging, and a generator, *the* generator, had been stolen by one of the park employees. To put this in perspective, Pat Wright, who has arguably done more than any other *vazaha* can hope to with regard to conservation efforts in Madagascar, hired essentially the entire town of Ranomafana to help in various capacities with the new park—porters, drivers, and the elite positions, naturalist guides. She brought in money and resources. Still, one of the top people in that local organization was profiting from logging in the park.

But this was old news to the researchers at Vatu. The sudden death of the brother of one of the guides was breaking news. When Bret and I hiked back down to base camp in pursuit of promised bats, we found that another man had died in town, and a third was deathly ill. A nasty gastrointestinal infection appeared to be eating holes in their intestines and causing them to vomit up black sludge. When we suggested that it sounded rather ominously like Ebola, which isn't known in Madagascar, we were silenced. One of the bodies was transported back from town in an ICTE car. Plans were made for the EarthWatch volunteers to attend the funeral. No mention was made of the potential for the spread of infectious agents this way.

We were finding no frogs or bats, and the possibility of an outbreak of something truly nasty scared us, so we decided to leave. Ranomafana offered up the car that had transported the dead man, but we declined. Thanks to Luke, who was Pat Wright's student and had decided to leave as well, we got a ride in an uninfected car. Three-quarters of the way to Tana, in the dead of night, the *vazaha* had to pee, and we asked the driver if he could pull over to the side of the road. The Malagasy don't often reject the suggestions of the *vazaha*, so he pulled over. The men stayed near the car, while I walked a short distance away to a ditch where I could squat in relative privacy.

"Hurry up! Get back here!" I heard Bret yell. I was annoyed. What was the hurry? We were making good time, especially for Madagascar. I got back to the car and we sped off.

"What the hell is going on?" I asked. Bret explained.

"The driver told us there have been shootings here recently. People killed on the side of the road."

"In Madagascar?" I was incredulous.

"That's what he says."

I was never so pleased to get back to Tana.

With one week left in Madagascar, we headed to the final region I had been considering as a research site, even though I had already decided on the Masoala and Nosy Mangabe. Less than one hundred miles from Tana by either train or surprisingly good road, the reserve called Analamazaotra by the Malagasy, or Périnet by the French, is probably the most visited, and certainly the most crowded, of Madagascar's nature reserves. A huge area around the reserve, an area known as Mantady, had been slated for national park status for years, but nothing had yet come of it, perhaps because there was mining interest in the area, as well. The town of Andasibe is the closest human settlement to all of these areas, and it was there that we went.

This town, unlike many of the places we were revisiting from three years prior, had truly changed, and it seemed possible to point to a single cause.

Previously, there had been two hotels in town. One was the old Buffet de la Gare, a grand old French colonial hotel with polished floors, run-down about the edges but with an air of grace; at the train station on the edge of town, it was now being run largely by local people. The other was the Orchidées, a Malagasy version of an old western bar and whorehouse, complete with swinging doors and wooden balconies that ran around the building. The floors were splintery, the rooms spare and none too clean. This Malagasy-owned establishment sat right in the middle of town. Most tourists stayed in the Buffet de la Gare, somewhat removed from the daily activity of the townspeople but still contributing to the local economy. We had stayed in the Orchidées before and intended to do so again.

This year, there was a new hotel in town, a grand *vazaha*-owned and -operated affair with individual bungalows, and no glitches in the electricity or service. Most importantly, this tourist hotel offered the implicit promise of a buffer from the local culture. There would be no chickens or small children running past you as you sipped your drink here. No wooden-wheeled wagons rumbling past at six in the morning on the way to market. No sad eyes or hands extended, no shouts of *"Vazaha, vazaha!"*

In the wake of the new hotel, the Buffet de la Gare had fallen on to even harder times, and the Orchidées was close to ruin. Few people but tourists had reason to need a hotel in a town like Andasibe, and the new hotel had attracted most of them. In town, the locals were less friendly than before, less eager to interact with the backpack-wearing *vazaha* as we walked into town. Walking through the doors of the Orchidées, we found a dank, dark room that took a few minutes to adjust our eyes to. Two Malagasy men sitting at a table began talking to us in boisterous, largely unintelligible French. A pretty young woman sat with them, staring down at her plate, while the two men tried to engage Bret in increasingly loud conversation. We stood looking dumbly at them for a while, until finally I understood their meaning.

"They're trying to sell her to you," I said to Bret. The woman still hadn't looked up from her empty plate. We escaped from the would-be pimps, got a key, and went upstairs to a room far darker and scarier than the one we had known three years earlier. What had once been a town of dirt roads and open-air shops selling the usual assortment of toothpaste, twine, biscuits, and rice, where laughing children pushed rings of metal with sticks, now seemed poorer, more desperate, and, understandably, more filled with resentment at its fate.

Later that night, Bret went out for a night walk into the forest in search of wildlife, a little *tsangatsangana*, with the only other resident of the hotel. I stayed in the room alone, nursing a head cold, uneager to go out into the cold drizzle that had stayed with us since Ranomafana. In that small space, with only three empty rooms and an open-air communal bathroom sharing the second floor of the Orchidées, I began to hear footsteps on the balcony outside and taps on the wooden shutters I had bolted shut. Men began to sing outside the shutters, slightly off-key. I heard no women. Anyone who had been paying attention in this small town would know that a white woman with a lot of gear was alone in a room at the Orchidées, in an unlit part of town, where *vazaha* didn't go. The strains of song rose and fell, and occasionally there was a crash, which started dogs barking. If they had really wanted in, they could have broken the shutters by standing on the balcony outside and forcing them in. But they didn't, and a few hours later, when Bret returned, I wasn't ready to talk about the noises, preferring to wait until morning, when I could confront the place that had scared me, even if not the ghosts who had roamed and sung and tapped the night before.

The next morning, Maurice the Naturalist took us into the forest. Maurice didn't remember us from three years earlier—a naturalist guide near Périnet sees a lot of *vazaha* come through—but we remembered him and his proclamation of belief in Nature, as there had only been a few Malagasy guides in our lives. The rates for guides were hourly here, and extremely high because of the rich tourists who came to see the forest for an hour, then retreated to the new hotel for drinks. Maurice had assured me I wouldn't find any *Mantella* this time of year—winter here meant average temperatures of less than sixty degrees, and a lot of fog and drizzle. So we hired him for two days, one day to show us a region most people not hunting lemurs or cutting wood didn't see, the second to hike us in to a remote spot where we could camp, and hopefully find our way out again on our own.

The first day, we rose in the chilled pink dawn and walked through rock quarries and tiny shacks with smoke drifting from them. By the time we went past the last shack, we had been walking long enough that its inhabitant was already out working. In this landscape of massive rock formations, the Malagasy government had hired poor men to break rock for roads. Some men quarried large pieces and collected them in piles. Other men broke these pieces into gravel with hand-sharpened, human-powered metal tools. This man was enormous for a Malagasy, probably six feet tall, muscles rippling with each stroke at his pile of rocks. He gave us a huge smile as we walked by, then asked a question in Malagasy.

"He wants to know if the *vazaha* have had their rice yet today," Maurice translated for us. We shook our heads no, assuming the beautiful rock-breaking man spoke no French.

"I have already had one bowl," the man told us in French, surprising us—a day laborer bilingual in the language of the colonials, he could hardly have routine use for his French. "We Malagasy," he continued, "have many bowls of rice a day to keep us strong." He flexed his biceps by way of demonstration. I was almost ready to sign on for the all-rice diet. He looked at us with some pity. "How do the *vazaha* stay strong?" We had no answer for him. To tell him we did so by eating vegetables and carrying heavy packs around seemed a weak response at best. Breaking rocks into gravel by hand and eating several bowls of rice a day was clearly a quicker route to impressive strength.

Maurice thought we should press on, so with promises to eat more rice, we left the man to his rocks. That day and the next, the three of us engaged in mild competition to find the most, the best, and the most agreeable lemurs. Indri, the largest of the nonhuman primates on Madagascar, were plentiful in this forest, and though they were skittish, bounding away from noises on the ground, with patience we were able to find a few couples. Indri are monogamous, pair-bonded, and vocal, their twice-daily duets reminiscent of the songs of humpback whales. There were also more sifakas—Jessica's propes—a species of almost pure white. When we found them in large groups, they made alarm calls before leaping away through the trees. The related *Avahi* often sat in the crooks of trees and stared, unblinking. Maurice asked us if we wanted to see more *Avahi*, then took us to a spot in the forest, nondescript to our eyes, and told us to wait.

"Just after dusk they will be here," he said, peering up at the fading light. Sure enough, at 6:40 by our watches, several *Avahi* bounded through. The next night, we went back, and at the same moment, we again saw these graceful primates leaping into our field of vision, from tree to tree, then gone.

Bret and I stayed a few days in the forest alone, camped at the top of a glorious waterfall. We were looking for animals of all sorts; we found no *Mantella*, but plenty of lemurs and geckos. The forest was dense, and we neither saw nor heard any other people during this time. When time grew short, we packed up our tent and hiked out several hours to a dirt mining road that led back to town.

A Frenchman in a truck laden with Malagasy workers stopped to pick us up not long after we had reached the road. His Malagasy was fluent, his English nonexistent, and though his name was McDonald, he insisted that he was a real Frenchman. He had lived in Madagascar since 1964 and was currently heading a road crew to improve the existing mining road. He was picking up workers to take them home for the day, though it was early in the afternoon. As we stopped to pick up a man digging white quartz by the side of the road, our man McDonald said to himself, "It's two o'clock. He's worked hard; he is done for the day." He volunteered then that each member of the road crew earned 130,000 FMG per month—a little over thirty dollars.

"Is that sufficient for a family to live on?" I asked.

He smiled ruefully. "If a man is single, it is enough, but for a family, no."

It struck me that Maurice, with his marketable skills as a naturalist guide, made one and a half times the monthly wage of these road workers in just two days. But his work, and therefore his pay, wasn't consistent, so some months he might make nothing. When Maurice left us, he returned to his wife and four-day-old son with full pockets, money enough to feed them, at least for a while.

Our plane left Tana on a Sunday night. On Monday morning, President Zafy was due to be impeached. Parliament had voted him out of office, but he had already declined to leave once, arguing that the army was on his side. One might speculate that the only reason for Madagascar to have a military is to back their favorite governmental factions. The existence of a prime minister, in addition to a president, and a shadowy king figure who might not even be real, makes the balance of power opaque to outsiders. I asked Benjamin, who had been a government official before taking the job with ICTE, who wields the power in Madagascar.

"You know how it is." He shrugged his shoulders.

I didn't know how it was. That's why I had asked. I asked two other Malagasy at ICTE, as well as a woman selling pastries, and they all gave me the same shrug, the same noncommittal "You know how it is."

The night we left, there were rumors that military helicopters were flying in erratic circles over the city, as if taunting Parliament to try, just try. Before then, I hadn't suspected that Madagascar owned any military helicopters.

"You're leaving at the right time," Benjamin told us. "Probably nothing will happen, but just in case, better to be gone by tomorrow."

As soon as our plane left the ground on what was to be a multiday, seven-leg journey home, the experiences in Madagascar began to fade, hard to recall in vibrant, living detail. Did I remember correctly that no diagnosis had come of the strange GI-related deaths at Ranomafana, and no autopsies were scheduled, as that would be disrespectful to the dead? In the air, on hold between two worlds that couldn't understand each other, this seemed implausible. I took Vermox, a dewormer available over the counter in Madagascar, not because I really thought it would treat whatever had struck people down in Ranomafana, but because it was the only thing in my arsenal that seemed vaguely relevant. And I thought about returning to Madagascar.

"I don't want to work there completely alone," I told Bret while we sat on the ground in Djibouti, tucked in between Ethiopia and Somalia.

"I don't think you should," he agreed. "It wouldn't be safe."

I hadn't even been thinking of my physical safety. I was concerned about my sanity. I was going to need someone to talk to besides frogs over the course of several months. Then it came to me.

"You know who would be perfect as a field assistant? Jessica, from Ranomafana! She wants to do behavioral work on something other than lemurs . . . and she's already in-country . . . and she speaks French. It couldn't be better." I was immediately focused: If only I could compel Jessica to come be my field assistant, all would be well.

I fell into a reverie, trying to recall some of the wonder and craziness of being a *vazaha* in Madagascar, now that it was remote, although only hours in the past. As Madagascar receded as daily reality, it came back in slow, dreamy waves that suffered from a lack of plausibility. The tsingy of Ankarana, and learning from Angeluc to suck the insides of gourd fruits for their precious water. Being ferried to shore in a pirogue by Solo, ripe forest glistening ahead of us. The ghosts from the balcony of the Orchidées, and the curious native primates nearby.

But the reason for all of this experience, the science, came back, too. Discovering *Mantella laevigata* in bamboo wells, fighting and mating, had been glorious. There is such grand biodiversity in the tropics. All seems disorder at first glance, but it can be parsed, identified, and understood. In the tropics, many of the rules made by temperate-based ecologists fall apart, and field biology explodes in a chaos of unknown vectors, uncontrollable variation within and between seasons, watersheds, populations. In the tropics, discovery can still happen routinely—it is almost difficult to avoid, if only you keep your eyes open.

Waiting on the tarmac of the St. Louis airport, our last stop before home, the little boy next to me asked his mother persistently but pleasantly, "Are we up in the sky now? Are we up yet?" He had been told he could have his tuna once we'd taken off. Tuna, he knew, was what he wanted. Being airborne was only incidental. Finally, we departed, and four-year-old Scott had his tuna at last. Then he looked out the window in disbelief and wonder at the scene below. On the final leg of this particular adventure, I shared the company of a curious little child who was just beginning his. Tuna was his goal, but flight, with its surprises and discomforts, might prove to be just as enduring.

PART 2

7

Reentry

Five months later, I returned to Madagascar, unnerved and excited by what awaited me. Jessica had been exuberant about the opportunity to be my field assistant, and she was waiting for me in Tana.

For this trip, in addition to pharmaceuticals, gifts, field clothes, and a tent, I had to pack research equipment. Assuming that nothing would be available to buy, I second-guessed what I might need; since I didn't yet know what the animals did, I couldn't predict what experiments I would design. So I took scales, a dissecting kit, calipers, rubber bands, a hacksaw, stopwatches, sound-recording equipment, tiny beads and needles, paracord, Tupperware, turkey basters, and epoxy. This list is not exhaustive. Were there turkeys in the field? No. But most of the specialized objects of our First World existence have uses far beyond their names.

I also put together a small solar electricity system to power my laptop computer. The energy output of such a system is dependent on weather conditions, and it is impossible to predict how often the sun will actually shine in the rain forest, so none of my calculations were certain. Most of the components for such a system are straightforward, but the battery that I would use to store energy coming in from the sun, before it would be discharged to my computer, proved more difficult. Broadly speaking, there are two kinds of batteries in the world—those that benefit from being discharged and those that do not. Car batteries fall into the latter category—when fully drained, they tend to need replacing. By contrast, rechargeable NiCad batteries—which come in AA, C, and D—need to be discharged regularly to function at top form. They develop a memory if you top them off frequently, and stop holding as much charge in the long run. Given the job I was trying to do, I needed a battery that could be discharged regularly, as my demand for electricity, though small, was going to be fairly constant, while my energy source, the sun, would not be. Deep-cycle, twelve-volt, absorption glass matte (AGM) batteries are designed to be discharged regularly, and are fully sealed so the acid in them cannot escape. Superficially, they look like car batteries, but they are functionally very different. They were also, at the time, the only kind of twelve-volt battery that was legal and safe to transport on a plane.

So I embarked with a fifty-pound AGM battery, connected to countless wires of various gauges and ominous-looking switches, and a digital multimeter that flashed incomprehensible numbers when turned to the wrong setting. I feared my bag would get torn apart by overzealous bomb-seeking dogs as soon as it was out of my sight.

Landing in Tana thirty-five hours after I left home, I was bedraggled and unhappy. But I was whisked through the normal protocol by virtue of being accompanied by Jessica and her father, Peter Metcalf, who was then the resident representative for the UN's Development Program (UNDP) in Madagascar. My stress would have been at an all-time low in Tana, but for one snag. The small plastic crate containing my AGM battery, inverter, and most of the hardware for the solar electricity system didn't come off the plane. After some discussion with the airport employees, the lid of the crate appeared, and the workers were astonished that this wasn't satisfactory. I had hand-carried the solar panel from the States and could piece together the rest of the system with the redundant hardware I had packed, except for the storage battery and inverter. Without these things, I had no system. Some lucky Malagasy airport worker was now the proud owner of a brand-new AGM battery. Even with Peter's intervention on my behalf over the next several days, Air Madagascar (usually aptly shortened to Air Mad) refused to take any responsibility. American FAA guidelines dictate that Air Mad, as the final carrier, were responsible for the loss, but not even the UN could convince them to do the right thing.

The Metcalfs, Ros and Peter, took good care of me. As I was slipping into incoherence and panic, they were contacting a friend of theirs who was in New York but would be returning to Madagascar shortly, and she agreed to bring me another inverter. Inverters turn the 12-volt DC energy stored in a battery into the 110-volt AC energy used by computers and other tools. Thankfully, they are light—just a few pounds.

The battery was another issue. I had no chance of getting an AGM battery, with their high power ratings and impenetrable cases, in Madagascar. The Metcalfs' driver took Jessica and me to a row of shacks in town that sold twelve-volt batteries. I picked one out, blindly. There was no indication of amp hours; I had no idea how much battery I was getting. I assumed it was a car battery, and thus designed not to be discharged. So for the use I intended, I was sure to destroy it. Hopefully, it would last four months.

On the box my new battery came in there were Chinese characters and a single English word in large red letters on the side. EXCELLENT. I had to buy the lead acid separately. I toted the toxic liquid, along with my new Excellent battery, away, bitter at the Fates for smashing my plans to have a smoothly running solar electricity system in the field.

While in Tana, I also had to go through the usual rigmarole of obtaining research permits. The various offices are scattered widely throughout the sprawling capital city, and it can take half a day to get from one to another. The employees at the various government bureaus that administer the lands and waters of Madagascar see no reason to hurry unless there is evidence of a deadline. The *vazaha*'s diminishing sanity is not viewed as an immutable deadline. A plane ticket is.

At the Département des Eaux et Forêts (DEF), we were told to come back the following day with four copies of my research proposal in French. The next day, Jessica and I were back, and they told us they needed six copies. Come back tomorrow. The next day there was nobody there to help us. The day after . . . well, by then I had bought us plane tickets. I told them we had a flight to Maroantsetra in three days, and they gave me my protopermits. From there, it was another several days of wrangling with a different government office before I was finally handed the actual permits, which were made of flimsy brown newsprint and covered in official red stamps.

Ros and Peter showed me all possible hospitality. I stayed in their house, made use of their car and driver, and had several doors opened for me that otherwise would not have been. Out the window of the room in which I slept, I looked across a lake, on the shores of which clothes were drying in the summer sun. Children bathed and ran around naked, and errant rice

plants grew out of their paddies, into uncared-for waters. Past the shimmering lake were mountains that turned pink at sunrise and sunset. In this
house, books lined the walls, the conversation was stimulating, and the people were deep, warm, and comforting. This was a Tana far more peaceful
than any I had ever imagined.

Jessica and I flew to Maroantsetra, gateway to the Masoala, where the airport was still without a door. Bret's legacy lived on. In town, little had
changed but the season. The people were still walking barefoot, or in plastic
sandals, through the sandy streets. The dirt roads were now spotted with
dark puddles, which took over when the rains persisted. Despite the lack of
road connections to the rest of Madagascar, Maroantsetra is a port, and
boats often come in from Tamatave to the south. The Masoala is the primary supplier of spices for Madagascar's export business, so the marine
traffic usually consists of spice boats, come to pick up a cargo of cloves,
nutmeg, cinnamon, or vanilla. There were a few pickup trucks in town—a
few more than there had been only months earlier, it seemed—though one
wondered how they got here, and if they stayed only because there was no
way out. The single road running through town, a strip of two or three
miles, turned to dust and rocks as the hustle and bustle of the rice market
of Maroantsetra receded. Bicycles had become increasingly popular, and two
of the Indian-owned shops had gleaming new Huffys for sale on their patios.
A few young Malagasy men had little motorbikes, as did the couple of
vazaha in town, which their slinky young Malagasy girlfriends sometimes
rode.

The best bet for a night's lodgings in Maroantsetra was still the Coco
Beach, where Bret and I had stayed the year before. Coco Beach's grasp on
electricity was still somewhat tenuous. I specifically requested a room with
electricity, but when I plugged my computer into the single outlet, I got
no response. My voltmeter told me there was no current coming out of the
wall. I went to the main building to ask if it could be fixed, or if we might
get a different hut, one with juice. Monique yelled for a small barefoot man
to go back with me to investigate the problem. He brought a fork.

When we got to our hut, the man went straight for the socket, looking at
it inquisitively. I explained the problem, then produced my voltmeter as evidence. I put the two leads into the socket and it read zero volts. The small
man wasn't convinced by my electronic answer. He took off his shirt and
wrapped it around his left hand. Placing that hand firmly on the wooden bed

frame, he then grabbed the fork with his right hand and jammed it into the socket. I was shocked, though I knew he wouldn't be, as the socket was dead.

The man came to the same conclusion I had, and motioned for me to follow him. I took my voltmeter with me, and we went to the bungalow next door. He found the socket and began to arrange himself in a similar manner. I tried to stop him, suggesting that I could again test it with my voltmeter. He would have none of it, however, as he had been called on to do a job and was going to finish it. So, this time in horror, I watched as he wrapped his left hand in his shirt, grasped the wooden bed frame with his mummified hand, then, grabbing the fork firmly in his right hand, jammed it into the socket. A small spark, and the man flew backward onto the bed. Two hundred and twenty volts could easily have killed him. He got up, retrieved the fork, which had flown to a far corner of the room, welcomed me to my new room, and left.

Our next task was to visit Projet Masoala, the regional office of both the Wildlife Conservation Society and CARE. Between them, these two non-governmental organizations are largely in control of administering the protected areas of northeastern Madagascar. There are several such NGO conservation groups in Madagascar, and they have divvied up the island, each taking some region so as not to step on each other's toes, and plans. I had gone by the WCS office in Tana, where they had approved my research permits and assured me that the employees at the office in Maroantsetra knew I was coming.

Projet Masoala is headquartered on the eastern side of the Masoala, in the comparatively rich vanilla-exporting town of Antalaha. The *vazaha* who runs WCS Madagascar, Matthew Hatchwell, lives in Antalaha, at the eastern edge of the new national park. The Maroantsetra office, at the western edge, is but a poor cousin.

It was two o'clock in the afternoon, during the daily *sieste*, when everything and everyone shuts down. We looked inside, found nobody, and climbed the stairs to the second floor, where a balcony looked out over the center of town. Dogs wandered by. Two-year-old children ran past, exuberant and bowlegged, followed at a distance by their older siblings, seven- or eight-year-old caretakers. The air did not move.

By a quarter to three, things began to pick up. Vendors in the market emerged from underneath their wooden tables, where they had been napping. Even the chickens seemed more energized. Soon we heard rustling downstairs, and went down to look. At the desk, a dark wooden affair with a grimy rotary phone on it, sat a woman with a hostile glare. She eyed us with suspicion. I wasn't sure exactly what I needed from her, but knew I was supposed to check in, find out what the boat schedule was, and ask when we could go to our first site.

"Hi," I stumbled, "I'm Erika, this is Jessica. We are here to study frogs. On the Masoala. The WCS office in Tana has approved all of my paper-work." I stopped. The woman just looked at me.

"Well," I continued, "we would like to go, with our provisions, to An-dranobe as soon as possible. When will the boat be available?" I asked.

"Not today," she said.

"Okay. Fine. But when . . . ?"

"The boat is busy. For how many days do you want to go?" This was a question for a tourist.

"We will be here for four months."

She exhaled sharply, a sort of hiss. I had surprised her with this bit of news. I tried another tack.

"I have been told that as a researcher, I can use the boat for the price of gas . . . ?"

"No. The boat is very expensive."

"But . . ." I stammered, and looked helplessly at Jessica, hoping for some fluent French to bail us out.

"We were told by the office in Tana that for the price of gas we could use the boat to get to our sites. If you would like, you may call them." Jessica gestured to the phone.

"The phone is not working," said the woman without batting an eye. "The phone only works occasionally."

She was probably telling the truth. Phones rarely worked in Tana. They would be even less likely to here. I remembered that upon arriving in the Maroantsetra airport, I had seen a sign for the Coco Beach. On it was a phone number—incongruous enough, given that there were no phones with which to dial the number. But odder still was the number itself: 57. A two-digit phone number.

"Perhaps you can radio Tana," Jessica continued. With her experience in Ranomafana the year before, she knew that radios were the usual mode of communication. The woman looked at her with some interest.

"No, the radio only connects to other places on the Masoala. Sometime the phone will work. Until then, you pay the tourist price."

I didn't have the funds to pay tourist rates, and ultimately she conceded. We scheduled a boat for three days hence.

"Now, why are you here?" she asked me.

"To study frogs," I told her again. "I was here last year, too. Didn't WCS tell you I was coming?"

"No." She seemed irritated, but not, for the first time since our conversation began, at me. I had a glimpse of the frustrations of being a small-town administrator, the sort to whom nobody tells anything, even information of direct relevance to her job. I decided then and there to win her over, though I had no idea how I would do it.

"Would you like to see our permits?" I asked eagerly, thinking that all of those red stamps might impress her.

"No." She waved her hand dismissively. "Later, before you leave town." It seemed she wanted us to leave her alone.

"Well," I said brightly, "can you tell me one more thing before we leave?" She looked skeptical. "What, please, is your name?" A slight smile. Recognition of humanity behind the desk.

"Clarice," she said.

"It is a pleasure, Clarice. Thank you for all your help. We'll come back tomorrow." And we left.

By the time we left Projet Masoala, word had gotten around that two *vazaha* had arrived in town. As usual, this had the effect of attracting old friends, as well as the merely curious. Patrice, one of the guardians whose job it is to protect the Projet Masoala building against theft, began talking to us in his unique blend of Malagasy, French, and English. When Emile and Felix, the guides I knew from the year before, arrived and Patrice spoke to them, he used the same garbled language with them. For once, I wasn't the only one having trouble with the native tongue. Emile was looking better now—probably his chronic malaria was latent—and as always, Felix, was cheerful. After opening pleasantries, I asked Felix about Clarice. He indicated that the two most important things she did were to make the *programme*—the boat schedule—which meant I would have to rely on her to get to my research sites and back to town to replenish provisions, and man the radio. There was a radio on Nosy Mangabe, and one in the village of Ambanizana, five miles from the site at Andranobe. The phone in the office, Felix agreed, rarely worked. It was connected to the phone at the post office, the central phone in town. It, too, rarely worked.

A slight man, paler than most Malagasy, approached. Emile introduced him as Yves, the boat captain. His eyes skittered across our faces, landing briefly on Jessica's. Then, without a word, he left. By way of explanation, or apology, Emile told me that Yves's father, whom he had never met, was French. Emile, book-educated man that he was, knew that differences existed between the *vazaha*. Though he didn't know what it meant to be French, or American, he understood that we were divergent, somehow.

Before Emile and Felix left us, disappearing into town to pursue their normal lives, I asked them how much rice Jessica and I would eat. We needed to shop for provisions. They assessed us, couldn't quite get a fix on how the *vazaha* differed from the Malagasy in this regard, and finally concluded that since the Malagasy eat three kapoks of rice a day, we should plan on doing the same thing. A kapok is a medium-size tin can used by vendors to measure out uncooked rice. Three kapoks cook up into more than ten cups of cooked rice. Ten cups of rice per person every single day for four months. Rice was to be our primary, and often only, source of nutrients, but we couldn't possibly have eaten that much. We didn't know that, though, and began the long process of buying rice, beans, cooking oil, candles, and scant other provisions in the market, and hauling them away.

The shops in Maroantsetra—true shacks, with walls and ceilings, as opposed to the open stalls in which rice and other staples are sold—fall into three categories: food and sundry shops lining the market; drinking establishments; and general stores. The food shops lining the market offer brightly colored plastic cups and bowls, candles, mosquito-repellent coils, biscuits, salt, and cooking oil. The oil is spooned out of a large dirty vat swarming with flies and put into the container you bring; if you don't have a container, you don't buy oil. Stores selling liquor offer beer, *toka gasy*, and Coke. There are few bars in Maroantsetra, and even these seem like family establishments, not places for men to go when they want to escape.

The general stores, unlike the rickety food stalls at the market, sell rare specialties that come in on boats—mustard, chocolate, vinegar, and Lazan'i Betsileo wine, the one and only Malagasy vintage. Each shop has some item that is not available elsewhere in town. One of the general stores has chicken wire. Another sells screwdrivers. A third offers brooms with hand-chiseled wooden handles for fifteen hundred FMG—thirty-five cents. I tried to buy one of these, but there were no more. I had to put in an order for one to be made.

"How many do you want?" they asked me.

"Just one," I said, before I knew how inexpensive this act of labor was to be.

Everything centers around the *zoma*, the marketplace. The stalls and commerce are there every day, but on market day, when people come in from the countryside, the marketplace teems with life, then truly becoming the *zoma* of Malagasy legend, rich with activity and commerce. A sand road broadens, and narrow cement platforms, poured into place in the ground, identify the marketplace. The covered part of the market consists of a large cement floor. Under the corrugated zinc roof are tables with slabs of meat on them, swarming with flies, and small piles of onion and garlic, waiting to be purchased by discerning but parsimonious buyers. Women sell baguettes and baskets, pineapples and *brede*, a local weed boiled into a broth and then eaten.

As potential customers walk by we are plied with their prices, though sometimes what we want to hear is an explanation of what they were selling.

"Five hundred per kapok," offered a rice vendor.

"One thousand each," I heard as I walked by neat triangles of golden brown.

"What is it?" I asked. I was intrigued.

"One thousand," the seller repeated, "one thousand." He was eager now, pursuing a sale as best he knows how, iterating the price until it became a mantra, until the consumer could do nothing but buy it, for fear the price would suddenly change. If I guessed at what the product was, he would agree even if I was wrong, for he was eager to please. These crisp golden triangles smelled like honey, but maybe they were soap—the vendor nodded in agreement at both possibilities.

Buying rice is the central activity of provisioning yourself in Madagascar. It would be an absurd understatement to suggest that rice is the staple of the Malagasy diet. The Malagasy are intensely proud of how much rice they eat. Every meal that a Malagasy eats consists primarily of a plate piled high with slightly sticky rice. The market in Maroantsetra is dominated by the rice vendors at rickety tables, neatly lined up, with umbrellas overhead.

There are so many rice vendors, it is difficult to make a choice. The slight variations in price mask vast differences in quality, if you believe the experts, which is to say, every Malagasy who has eaten the many subtly variant forms of white rice. Questions from the *vazaha* are gross, tactless, uneducated. "Is there any brown rice?" "How can you tell the difference among the rices?" "Does it really matter?" Brown rice, with the husk still on, increasingly the rice of choice among gourmands in the First World, is low-class, not pure, somehow sullied. If you have to ask about the differences among rices, you are perhaps not fit for the job of choosing your own rice. And finally, of course it matters, for rice is central; if one does not care about rice, what is there left to concern oneself with?

8

Maybe Tomorrow

Town life doesn't prepare one for forest life. After two hours of a lovely boat ride across the Bay of Antongil, Jessica and I arrived at the mouth of the river that Andranobe ("big water") is named for. The last hundred feet of the trip to Andranobe is accomplished in an unstable pirogue piloted by Solo. He paddled out to the boat, where we sat bobbing in the heavy surf, and his face broke into a wide grin when he recognized me. Finally, some-one who knew I was coming and was glad to see me. Before sinking into that comfort, though, we had to get ourselves and all of our stuff into the small dugout pirogue and to shore. Malagasy pirogues are particularly prone to tip, and even the calmest voyages are precarious. It took seven trips, each one likely to tip and deposit our gear at the bottom of impossible waters. Great white sharks had been spotted in the rough, unswimmable sea. Trans-porting heavy equipment in that pirogue, through high surf, was one of the most arduous parts of the entire journey.

Once safely on land with our gear, I admired Andranobe anew. The Masoala peninsula, on which Andranobe sits, contains the largest tracts of lowland rain forest still standing in Madagascar. The world's remaining rain forests tend to be in inconvenient places—extremely steep, or remote, or both—and the Masoala peninsula is no exception. This is no accident. It is precisely their inconvenience that has protected them from being cut by people needing to plant crops or wanting to harvest wood. These inconvenient places are not immune, though, just lower down on the list. The whole region, including the Masoala and the island of Nosy Mangabe, had recently been designated a national park, named for the peninsula on which it sits.

Andranobe hadn't changed much in five months. There were still a few roofless tent platforms, five small cabins measuring perhaps eight by ten feet each, a pit toilet, some laundry lines, and an old fence, which had sprouted, becoming a living fence. There were two different Malagasy Peregrine Fund employees living there now, mist-netting for birds. Wood smoke drifted out of the kitchen cabin. Within hours of our arrival, Solo had transformed the porch of his cabin into a tiny area in which we would eat.

Solo had been talking about my return for months. When I had gotten back to the States after my previous trip, I wrote the company that made my jacket, Helly Hansen, and described the situation—Andranobe, Solo, his desire for a jacket like the one I had—and included with it some photographs that Bret had taken of the place. They sent me a free jacket to give Solo, in exchange for the negative of one of Bret's photos. So this year, I arrived in Andranobe, rain jacket in hand, and Solo was rewarded for his patience. Though he was silent, his eyes grew bright as he received the gift with obvious gratitude.

Bright heat has a sound in the rain forest. The cicadas call unceasingly, like a complaint about the stifling, still air. Their sound, when you stand directly underneath them, is as oppressive as the temperature. Instant relief from both is found in the river—cool, clean, kinetic, it dissolves the fatigue that comes not from extended effort but from merely existing in the drowsy heat of the rain forest. At Andranobe, the cicadas, inescapable ten miles inland, are often drowned out by the waves crashing on the rocky shore and the river tumbling out of the hills to join the bay.

At the far end of the river pool lives a kingfisher, arrogant and regal. Bobbing his head, squinting, he looks indignant, though at what, one can hardly imagine. Wild ginger flowers nearby, amid palms and grasses on the bank of the river. Melastomes, the ubiquitous understory plants of the wet tropics, bloom as well, small lavender stones amid a sea of lush pale green. Red-ruffed lemurs cackle in the distance, as if at a private joke. Back at camp, men sit on a stoop eating rice. The two Peregrine Fund men seem to barely perceive us, and I feel anonymous in their presence. They probably would not recognize me on the street of an American city, where all the white faces blend together. One of them has a radio, which he plays at such times, usually light and pleasant Malagasy music, sometimes mideighties American pop—Culture Club, or Michael Jackson. It is always background, though, to the waves pounding on the shore, meeting the river.

In the hottest part of the day, when there is no rain, the forest shuts down. Blue mountains sway in the pure haze across the bay. Nosy Mangabe is the closest, and it does almost look blue—*manga*—in the heat. Farther is the mainland of Madagascar, one peak looking like a volcanic cone, others receding behind, increasingly obscure. I sit, waiting for rain, sheltered from the bright, harsh, adored sun by the roof of the research cabin. It sometimes feels like a life on hold.

At night, the cicadas are quiet, but other insects and rare frogs join in a chorus, and the wind picks up and blows the few man-made structures— zinc roofs on the five small cabins, the tarp over our tents—in an eerie melody. Sitting at my computer with a candle at my side, I can see the outline of the keyboard, the almost-full moon rising over an emergent tree at the river. Lightning flashes over the bay. And I wonder, Will my tent really keep me dry, a little nylon shell on the edge of the world?

After the moon has come out, the forest reveals itself only as a silhouette. Its sounds, like parts of a symphony, ring on and off abruptly, as if a conductor is instructing whole hosts of insects to suddenly, after the tuba, begin. The ceaseless background is waves, regular but not exact, receding and returning to nobody's baton.

The remoteness of Andranobe is exciting and dangerous all at once. I wanted to stay for two months before moving on to Nosy Mangabe, but I couldn't find my study animals. Every day, Jessica and I went in to the forest at dawn, seeking the bright yellow-and-blue frogs that should have been prevalent now that it was the wet season—the right season for frogs. Every day we were disappointed. We observed *Mantella betsileo* instead, their close relatives, and watched them establish territories after rains reorganized their tiny landscapes. We tied fashionable beaded bands around the waists of *Mantella betsileo* and cut off their toes, looking for just the right combination of marking techniques to proceed with the work efficiently. (Unlike waistbands, toe clipping is standard practice for marking amphibians.)

I intended to ask so many questions of these unknown frogs. How do they spend their time? Are they territorial, mostly arboreal, social, polyg-amous? How do females choose their mates? What environmental variable is limiting for the population? Do mother frogs return and give their young parental care? Most of these questions required that I recognize individuals on sight, without catching them every time and traumatizing them again. There are well-established, much-practiced, if still flawed, methods for marking mammals and birds without doing them damage. Revlon hair dye works as well on rodents as it does on human hair. Radio collars are put on many mammals to track them. Small plastic leg bands are used on birds to distinguish them. But frogs are less often studied with an eye toward long-term social interactions. Their wet skin won't accept hair dye. Collars require a neck. And these frogs are too small to put leg bands on them without risking splinting the joints they need to move. So I spent a lot of time working out various ways to mark the frogs, first among them this combination of toe clipping and beaded waistbands.

Tying waistbands around frogs was fairly engaging, but these drab frogs weren't what I had traveled halfway around the world to study, so we made plans to push on, knowing it would be days, if not weeks, before we could actually accomplish the move. As I grew despondent because of the lack of appropriate animals, I spent more time at the swimming hole. There I watched the resident kingfisher dunk himself repeatedly in the water, his crest flattening with every dive, then perking up of its own volition when he emerged. He delved into his breast with his beak, to reveal bright red feathers. He fluttered and preened and glowered and bobbed and came out looking fastidiously well groomed, a bird with the very best tailor, and good taste to boot. I was watching animals, just not the right ones. This little bird seemed to be the only thing awake and moving during the middle, hottest hours of our days at Andranobe, when the rest of the forest went down for a nap.

When a storm came in like tanks invading a quiet town, it gave as warn-ing only a quiet tinge to the air, a vaguely ominous graying as high clouds moved in. Winds started howling, blowing clothes off the lines, and within moments the rain was beating down so torrentially on the zinc roofs, it bounced off, sounding like a thousand drummers out of sync. The Peregrine Fund men ran to their cabin, scooped up their shoes, which they had left out to dry, and stood on the porch, looking morose, as if this were the end. I believed them for a moment, peering out from under our roof at the sky, so close at hand and yet endless. Concerned about the security of the tarp we had erected over our tents, I trod over to the platforms in my bare feet, actually enjoying the freedom of the rain. Rain, like snow, gives perfect cover. When under an umbrella, you're not expected to make eye contact with anyone, or greet the world. The rain closets you, puts you in a shell of protection, gives an excuse for privacy.

Come night, thunderclouds covered the moon. The night was deep, darker than usual. During a lull in the rain, the men's voices floated from the kitchen cabin, slowly, then swift, melodic. Solo had gone to Ambanizana for the evening. During a brutal downpour, he left in his pirogue, waving at us in his new rain jacket as he paddled against the surf. Until now, he had had no protection but his skin against the fierce rains, which are so prevalent in the Masoala. He would use the radio in Ambanizana to tell Clarice at Projet Masoala of our change in plans, as there was no way to contact the outside world at Andranobe.

When Solo returned from Ambanizana, bearing sweet pineapples for us, the *vazaha* in his care, he asked if I would bring him good shoes the next time I came from the States. I was disturbed by the request. It seemed that what I brought would never be enough, that no good deed would be sufficient. Transporting more than 250 pounds of equipment to Madagascar was already an ordeal, and with every new item, it became more of one. This year, I had brought a new rain jacket for Solo, and also some clothes for his two daughters and wife. I allowed myself to feel generous for these actions, but I also felt put-upon when he asked for more.

After thinking more about Solo's request, however, I changed my mind. I did feel that I was now, forever, in a bind with this kind man, but I realized he had no choice. What else could a perceptive man do in his place? Solo is a reasonably well-educated man, with a good job for someone from Ambanizana, that of guardian and cook for Andranobe, an often-uninhabited research site. He paddles his pirogue along the coast between Ambanizana and Andranobe, and lives in many ways like most rural Malagasy. The critical difference, however, is that he sees, every now and again, *vazaha* researchers arrive with their stuff. And what stuff we have! Not just cameras and computers, scales and waterproof notebooks—the likes of which he may have imagined but has no real use for—but durable plastic water bottles, hiking boots that last, Swiss army knives, fine-quality cord. Solo sees that, though not necessary, these things would make life easier, and more pleasant. So he asks, "Do you think I could pay you—in cash or vanilla—to bring me back a rain jacket like yours?" Most people probably rebuff him; Bret and I responded with enthusiasm, seeing in this man a gentle person who had identified something of real worth for himself.

My first reaction, when he asked me for more things, was to say no. But what of *his* position? He had received, surprise of surprises, a beautiful new jacket, and as a gift no less! He is kind to the *vazaha*, gives her gifts of vanilla, supplies his own special sakai (hot peppers and onions steeped in vinegar), which he knows she enjoys, fetches pineapples. And he lies awake at night, thinking, She is kind, and brought my family and me clothes; perhaps she would find me a pair of shoes, and I would happily pay her for them in return. She has already indicated a willingness to bring me things. Surely I should ask. There is no harm in asking.

He asked only because I was there and had demonstrated willingness to communicate with him. He had no other options. He did not *need* shoes, any more than I *need* the computer I write on. He had lived this long without shoes. He just wanted them very much and knew that they would make his life more comfortable. I took the information from him, the type and size of shoe he craved. I have never been in that position, utterly isolated from material things and dependent on kind souls to bring me that which I desire. Solo had seen how much stuff I had, and must have known in his heart that there was no inherent reason that I should have it, and he should not.

Sunday in the rain forest. Here, the days of the week lose all meaning. We spent the morning climbing up hills and scampering down streambeds. On this day, we had a particular goal, a place on some map, though no map we had ever seen. I asked the men hired by the Peregrine Fund if they had seen the tiny yellow-and-blue frogs this season, and first they said no. Then, after thinking about it, they agreed that yes, they had seen them, but they couldn't remember where. Finally they were in agreement. Now they were certain.

"Go one thousand meters up trail C, then descend off-trail to the left, until you get to the small waterfall. There you will find the frogs," they assured us.

Trail C seemed nearly vertical. Two-thirds of a mile took a good hour and a half. Once we turned off-trail and started going down, things only got harder. Falling down through the rain forest with no semblance of a trail is always an adventure. Vines threaten to cut you off at your throat and ankles, spiderwebs are constantly showing up after you've walked into them, and, though there are no noxious ants or vipers here to worry about, the most innocuous-looking vines often have razor-sharp spines on them.

We fell for a ways, paused to listen for water, heard nothing, continued, until finally I saw a trickle, though it hardly qualified as a waterfall, even one described as small. We made our way there and, hearing song that sounded like *Mantella laevigata*, we scrounged around for a while. One bane of field zoologists is tracking an animal by its call, waiting patiently each time it falls silent, inching forward oh so slowly when it calls again, and finally coming face-to-face with a cliff or a tree, out of which the call is clearly emanating, but on which the animal is utterly invisible. At some point, the intrepid field biologist may throw all care for the well-being of the animal to the wind and start to dig furiously through the leaf litter or soil that conspires to hide the animal. Nine times out of ten, though, this strategy fails utterly, and the researcher is left with no animal, no call, and a heap of leaves and dirt where once there had been a microhabitat. This is exactly what we did on this particular morning, and we found no frogs.

Once we had failed, spectacularly, to find our animals, we were left with the question of how to get back. We could scramble back up the slope to trail C, and retrace our steps, or we could take what would surely be the more ridiculous route—follow the water. Having never left the large watershed for which the river Andranobe is the outlet, we assumed the trickle of water that we were standing in would ultimately take us home. The problem with this logic, of course, is that water can fit through some alarmingly small spaces and drop off precipitous edges. Opting for adventure, we began to make our way down. After weaving our way down, up, around, down again, and down some more, finally, we had to rest. No, of course we weren't *there* yet; nor, at this point, did we have any idea where *here* might be. We were merely exhausted, covered in moss and dirt and spiderwebs, sweating through the seats of our pants. During one descent down a mossy rock face with water spilling over it, using all four limbs and my butt as an anchor, small rocks gave way beneath my feet and I slid several feet to the bottom, landing with a squeak and a curse.

Two and a half hours after leaving the "waterfall," we came out at the pit toilet. It was still only ten in the morning, but we'd been out climbing and sliding since five. In another hour, all frog activity would stop anyway, for the midday *sieste*. We made the short trek to the pool where we had marked *Mantella betsileo*, hoping to observe them for a while. By the time we got there, all frogs were already lulled into inaction, perhaps by the heat of the early sun or by the drone of the cicadas. Jessica and I sat watching frogs do nothing for an hour. Sometimes they lunged for an ant or mite. Occasionally, we drank some water. Observer and observed engaged in equally fascinating tasks. Then we picked up our stools and went home—home, that is, until we packed up our tents and moved again.

We spent three days in suspended animation, waiting to move to Nosy Mangabe. Solo had received word that the boat would come on Tuesday. So on Tuesday, we got up with the sun and took our tents down. I packed my solar electricity system, and our rice—the extent of our provisions. If the boat came, we would have to be ready to load our gear into the pirogue and paddle out to the boat immediately, before it smashed onto the rocks in the heavy surf. Looking across the bay, I imagined that every shimmer on the water was the boat. By midafternoon, I had lost hope, and I began slowly to reinstall the great blue tarp that had been battened down over our tents, which kept us miraculously dry in the torrential rains that happen almost every night at Andranobe.

There is no radio at Andranobe, no connection to the outside world at all. When you have arranged for a boat in advance, which is the only way possible to arrange for a boat from Andranobe, and the boat does not show, you are left without an explanation. Along with the boat not showing up, the people responsible for deciding that it would not show up have also not shown up.

As the sun rose in the sky toward noon on the second day, and I continued looking expectantly toward the horizon, my hopes fading, I glanced over at the now-barren tent platform, wondering when I would have the heart to undertake putting up the big blue tarp again. Wistfully, I asked Solo if he thought there would be a boat that day. A compassionate and empathetic soul, he looked searchingly to the horizon himself, as if hoping to find an answer in the vast expanse of empty water. Finally, he shook his head slowly, and in a mixture of French, English, and Malagasy, he told me that no, there would be no boat. I looked distressed and put-upon, and he looked distraught on my behalf. Jessica and I then indulged in the meal of carbohydrates he'd made for us that noon. Ramen noodles and potatoes over rice is Solo's crowning success.

The next morning, Thursday, the charade began again. I reflected that the previous day, and the day before that, could have been spent in the forest but instead was spent waiting in camp for a boat, taking down and then putting back up the various shelters that kept us dry. Solo felt responsible for the boat's failure to show up, but of course he had as little control over this as I did. While I sat idly in camp, everything packed, I asked him again if he thought the boat would come.

"Maybe," he acknowledged, and his response was unaccompanied by its usual sister word, *tomorrow. Peut-être demain. Ongomba rapitso.* Maybe tomorrow. May*be*, always with the second syllable accented, as is normal with the Malagasy and French equivalents. In English, this has the effect of making the speaker sound as if he is stressing the element of existence in this word, rather than the tenuous nature of both existence and schedules, which is suggested by the first syllable.

"*Ongomba*," I repeated wearily and, as always when I made an attempt at Malagasy, Solo brightened. Despite the interminable waiting, Solo lightened my mood, as well. The boat would not arrive that day. I wanted to go *now*, but my impatience was utterly out of place. In Madagascar, time is slow, and schedules get made out of deference to a First World pace but are forgotten in the next breath.

Ultimately, the boat did come, as almost everything does in Madagascar, if you give it enough time. We were deposited on Nosy Mangabe, which was to be our home for the next three months.

In Malagasy, Nosy Mangabe means "big blue island," though it is neither particularly big nor blue. Blue is the color of wondrous things, and so is attributed to well-loved things and places. It is, perhaps, analogous to the word *golden* in the English language. Nosy Mangabe is beautiful to those who live near it, in the northern reaches of the Bay of Antongil. Compared to Madagascar, it is small, at 510 hectares (about two square miles), but one cannot see from one end to the other, nor to its coasts from much of the interior. Nosy Mangabe is a high island, most of its area comprised of two summits, which descend steeply to the sea, although in some areas the slopes are more gentle.

Nosy Mangabe, originally protected as a sanctuary for the aye-aye, is now administered as part of the new national park. In theory, only people with valid permits are now allowed onshore. It is reputed that centuries ago, there was a Dutch sanatorium on its shores, though its precise function is shrouded in mystery. Before Nosy Mangabe was protected, it contained sacred land for the local people, including a small cemetery in a cave, and was a base for fisher people, who used it as a refuge during storms and a place to preserve the day's catch over a smoke pit. It is but three miles from the town of Maroantsetra, and locals say it used to be even closer. A Dutch pirate map from the 1700s represents Nosy Mangabe connected by a thin isthmus to the "mainland" of Madagascar. Perhaps it was over this strip of land that the Malagasy carried their dead and buried them in the cemetery, returning every few years to speak to their ancestors, and rewrap their bones in fresh shrouds to honor them. Long-untouched body boxes, in which the freshly dead were wrapped and placed, and the much smaller bone boxes, containing only the bones and remains of shrouds, remain in the hillside cemetery, deep in the forest.

The three miles between it and Madagascar are so shallow that larger spice boats that come to pick up cargo sometimes cannot moor in Maroantsetra. Northeastern Madagascar produces much of the world's vanilla and cloves, and a fair amount of cinnamon and nutmeg as well, so the movement of spice boats is of considerable economic importance. These boats moor in the small bay on Nosy Mangabe's western edge, and sea-weary men tumble onto land.

There is evidence of recent human presence in the disturbance of the forest, particularly near camp and along the one-thousand-meter stretch of flat coastal land that looks west toward the small bay, and toward the east coast of Madagascar. The only structures on Nosy Mangabe are in the main camp and eight hundred meters south, down coastal trail G, where the fishermen's camp sits. In the main camp, there are three tent platforms with thatched roofs, built in the expectation that ecotourists would discover the island. There is one small cabin, in which two local men, hired as conservation agents by Projet Masoala, sleep and eat. A few meters away, a tiny cabin houses a wood fire and two aluminum pots. Across the path is a cement bunker, which is called a "lab," although it is only a room, perhaps twelve by thirty-six feet, with four wooden windows and a small stoop.

There is a stunning waterfall not one hundred feet from camp, which makes a lovely shower. A piece of PVC pipe has been run off the top of the waterfall, diverting some water to a wooden closet, which makes for a less exciting shower but a more accessible one. The PVC pipe then runs to the other end of camp to supply two newly installed flush toilets. When we were there, these didn't work very well or often, so the nearby pit toilet was still a necessity. The water in the streams was clean and good, and we drank it without filtering it or treating it with iodine. There is also a small wooden dock, where boats larger than the little Projet Masoala motorboat can tie up.

The conservation agents are the only two human residents of Nosy Mangabe. These local men are paid by international environmental organizations to protect the land. In this particularly poor region of an impoverished country, people and cows are increasing in number, and there is not enough food for all. Rice, which is land- and water-intensive, quickly leeches all nutrients from the already-poor rain forest soil, but this is the agricultural crop that the Malagasy know how to plant. Ecotourism could potentially save the local economy, so training local people such that they gain from protecting the forest is one of the few reliably effective conservation tactics.

The conservation agents on Nosy Mangabe, who live closest to the forest, should have insight into its value to them. Their job involves patrolling the island to keep unpermitted visitors off and to prevent hunting and wood cutting; doing trail upkeep; and greeting the rare tourist and the odd researcher when they arrive, showing them the ropes. The ropes include, in full: You may set up your tent on one of the tent platforms; the bay is often safe to swim in if you don't go out too far (where there are great white sharks, which have demonstrated a taste for human flesh); and researchers may store their equipment in the lab, protected from the inevitable rain. The trail system is extremely limited, but two trails along the coast are passable, though tree falls punctuate even these.

The two conservation agents at the time, Lebon and Fortune, shared at least one goal: to step foot into the forest as little as possible. They suffered, as so many Malagasy do, from stultifying forest fear, even though Madagascar has some of the safest tropical forest on the planet. There are no poisonous snakes, no large predators to prey on the unsuspecting. But the fear persists. Otherwise, they were wildly different in temperament. In terms of both intellect and charisma, Lebon was the leader. He was amiable and ready to please when we arrived, once I produced the proper permits. I had hoped to pay the conservation agents to cook for us, but Lebon brushed the suggestion aside. Of course they would cook for us, so long as their fare—rice every day, and a lot of it—was acceptable. They seemed eager for our company, as otherwise they were alone out there.

During our first afternoon on the island, Lebon helped me punch holes in the roof of the lab so that I could bolt down my solar panel. We were off to a glorious start, a relationship founded on little shared language (both of us spoke some bad French) but an enthusiasm for life. Only one thing about him concerned us on that first day. As Jessica and I were setting up our tents and moving our rice and equipment into the lab, he followed each of us until he got us alone, then asked if we were married. He proclaimed that he wasn't. Later, we learned that he had three children by the woman he had been living with for fifteen years, but they were still saving for a grand formal wedding party, as is the custom.

The other conservation agent, Fortune, proved expert at giving dumb looks. A bit thick about the middle, and correspondingly slow-moving, he didn't say much, and when he did, it was generally about the quality of the rice. Lebon appeared to be the clear winner in the personality game.

9

Cute, Furry, Desperate, and Alone

People the world over find comfort in cute and furry animals. Throughout the developing world, people take animals from the forest as pets. Then when the animal grows too large, or too difficult, it is returned, sometimes to a different forest entirely. People think they are doing the animal a favor. In truth, that animal, all other individuals of its own species that it may encounter, and often any humans whom it meets are worse off for its existence after being an ill-treated pet.

The word *pet* may be misleading for those in the developed world, who conjure up images of a well-groomed dog, lovingly taken for walks, played with, and given food designed for the well-being of the animal. Pets in the developing world are a different phenomenon, and exotic pets, such as primates from the forest, are yet one more step removed. Some of the omnipresent dogs in developing-world villages are pets, insomuch as someone would notice if they died. Similarly, the rarer cats are tolerated in people's doorways, more occasionally inside a shack, as they keep the rodent population down. They are pets in the same way cats on a farm are pets— acknowledged but not enjoyed.

Exotic pets are unique, as the owners of these animals have recognized in their surroundings some element of the local biota that fascinates. You do not find marmosets as pets in Africa, nor lemurs in Central America, nor scarlet macaws in Madagascar. Exotic pets in these locales are taken directly from local habitats. Many middle-class families in Tana have had a lemur as a pet. It is chic and suggests a sophisticated recognition of the animal's unparalleled persona. Many of these people later discard their animals. It is no great loss for the families, for these animals were never loved, or treated as one of the family. Primate pets are often kept in cages, sometimes outside on a dead tree, tied with a short lead, unable to climb, obtain fruit, or escape from their own excrement.

A spider monkey I once met in the Osa Peninsula of Costa Rica, a frugivore, was being fed bread and milk by his master. The man objected to my giving the monkey bananas and mangoes from the local market, food the animal ate with a voracious appetite, having knocked over the unwanted plate of bread and milk in his eagerness for the fruit. The man explained to me that fruit is bad for monkeys and that he was doing it a service by generously giving it expensive milk. In truth, milk can't be digested by most adult mammals, as when we mature, we often stop producing the enzyme that breaks down milk sugar. The milk that monkey was being fed probably caused him painful stomach cramps, in addition to lacking the fruit pulp his anatomy demanded.

In Tana, the most obvious place to abandon lemurs is at Tsimbazaza, the underfunded zoo in the middle of a poverty-choked city. Already swamped with more animals than it can handle, Tsimbazaza receives these pets, born wild, taken into captivity and treated badly, now loved and wanted by no one. When Tsimbazaza can truly take no more, people do what must seem like the right thing to do, the kind and generous thing to do: They put their pets back into the forest. There is, however, especially among the urban middle class of the developing world, an utter lack of recognition that one wilderness differs from another. Thus, an animal that came originally from the spiny desert of the south might be replaced in high-elevation cloud forest or in the lowland rain forest of the east coast.

People who do not know the United States, and do not recognize its vastness, assume we all know one another. "Ah, an American. I have an uncle who moved to America, to Norfolk, Virginia. He is a mechanic, balding—do you know him?" All Americans look alike to those unfamiliar with discerning our features, and a country of this size is too large to believe. We make the same error, of course, when we assign to people a nationality—Chinese, for instance—which speaks hardly at all to the experience they have had in the specific region of China from which they come. Even Madagascar, a comparatively small country, has more than twenty distinct tribal affiliations, and the plateau people, the Merina, are offended at any suggestion that they look similar to coastal people or those from the south. Within our own worlds, we recognize subtle differences between communities, based on neighborhoods that may be but a few blocks long, but still we have the impulse to assign character traits to whole continents of other people.

Similarly, most people assume that one lemur is like another and can live anywhere that lemurs exist. Recognition of an animal's need for certain trees, or a particular kind of terrain, is, understandably, beyond most people. When a lemur of a lowland rain forest species is placed in a forest on the cold plateau, it will not fare well, and it will never find any others of its kind. Its existence will be solitary and short. Even when care is taken to provide an animal its native habitat, no individual—human or other—without experience in that habitat can be expected to assimilate and survive. Imagine a Los Angeles native being yanked from his comfortable urban existence, washed up on the southern shores of the Mediterranean, and told to thrive.

At dusk on our first day on Nosy Mangabe, as I returned barefoot from showering at the waterfall, Lebon called to me from the steps of the conservation agents' cabin. He was picking through rice, culling the stones from it.

"Close the lab," he suggested. "At this time of night, the lemurs sometimes try to steal things." As he said this, a female brown lemur, *Lemur fulvus*, the most widespread of the nonhuman primates on Madagascar, scampered by on the ground. She made what I took to be a playful swipe in the general direction of my leg. I laughed, made noises at the animal to discourage her from getting any friendlier, and continued on toward the lab. There is a troop of brown lemurs resident in the camp area at Nosy Mangabe, and I took this animal to be one of them.

The next evening, as I again returned from the waterfall at dusk, the same lemur ran by my feet, grabbing at them but missing. The lemur also made a swipe at Jessica as she left the lab, and she responded as I had, shouting at the animal, merely to dissuade her from making a habit of such behavior. We never saw the lemur approach Lebon or Fortune this way, and they said nothing further to us about her. We were not even certain that it was a single lemur who was so playful, but perhaps several females in the resident troop who were a bit aggressive.

On the third day, I rose 5:00 A.M., dressed for the field on my tent platform, and took my toothbrush and paste to the place where the small stream pools. I sat on a rock and bent down, splashing water onto my face. Dawn is a meditative time on Nosy Mangabe, still cool and subdued. The nighttime frog song is dissipating, the squabbles of diurnal lemurs and insects have not yet begun, and the understory is tinged a deep blue. My mind floated easily in this place so far from home as I casually planned the day's work.

Searing pain suddenly enveloped my left arm. The female lemur raced by me, not two feet from my face, and leapt up to my right, where she perched in bamboo eight feet away. I stood abruptly, uncomprehending. She made another movement in my direction, and as I picked up a rock to throw at the beast who had bitten me, I felt the blood flowing down my arm. Twisting to look at my wound, I was horrified to find a deep gash, which looked more like a knife wound than an animal bite. My triceps muscle was exposed, bubbling out of the wound and bleeding profusely. Before I could internalize this, the lemur was on the ground, coming at me again across the rocks. I kicked at her and yelled, and she retreated. Hurriedly, confused, I splashed my arm with cold, clean water and picked up my things. Walking slowly back to the lab, I couldn't think, didn't grasp how this fit into any bigger picture, refused to comprehend how bad it might be. I called to Jessica, told her I'd been bitten by a lemur, and showed her my arm. She was horrified by the wound. My fears were validated. I had indeed been ripped open by a wild animal, unprovoked. The wound would surely demand stitches, and the behavior an explanation.

I was dazed. The wound was open to the air, attracting the biting flies that pervade the forest during daylight hours. I slathered my arm in iodine and Neosporin, but this didn't provide much of a barrier to the outside world.

"Can you stitch me?" I asked Jessica. She was pallid. She had never had stitches herself, had never even seen them. Despite this, I believed, naïvely, that she could sew me up without much trauma to either of us. Before proceeding, we got Lebon's attention. He was just waking up, preparing to rake the camp, the one job that was done every day. He was suitably appalled by the situation.

"Do you know how to do stitches?" I asked him.

"Ah, stitches are very difficult, I think." This was his polite way of saying he couldn't do it. I had failed to include sutures in my medical kit, but I did have a set of sewing needles, including a thick, curved mattress needle.

I sat down on a wobbly bamboo bench, held my arm over my head so Jessica could access the bite, asked Lebon to hold my wound closed as best he could, and told Jessica to puncture my arm with the mattress needle. After about two minutes of this, the needle was halfway embedded in my arm, no stitch was yet apparent, and all three of us were shaking. I suggested, much to the relief of Jessica and Lebon, that we abandon the plan.

"I'll need to see a doctor," I told Lebon. He would have to radio Maroantsetra to arrange for a boat to come pick me up. He looked alarmed.

"No need for that. Earlier, someone was bitten on the foot by the same lemur, but it was not bad, so you will also be better soon."

I was feeling unsure of my judgment, but I did think I needed to get to a doctor. I waited for him to expand on his position.

"Perhaps," he continued, "you should just sit here, wait for a few days, and see what happens."

He and Fortune were already demonstrating expertise at sitting around and waiting to see what happened, but I was not of a mind to follow suit. I did, after all, have a gaping hole in my arm, possibly inflicted by a sick animal. By this time, my thoughts had turned to rabies, then to other infections, like gangrene, and all the possible nasty things that can happen as a result of a deep animal bite in a persistently hot, wet place.

"No, I must see a doctor. Now." My mind was growing more confused, but I could repeat myself with some success.

"But it's only six in the morning, and I cannot use the radio until eight, because nobody is on the other end until then," Lebon argued. Even then, there was a chance that the communication wouldn't be possible, as the radio was frequently low on batteries or shorting out.

"Okay, I'll come back in two hours." I started myself on a course of antibiotics and retreated to the dock to lie down and consider my fate. My arm throbbed, and my thoughts raced, then flitted, from one incoherence to the next. Why would a wild animal attack a person unless it was rabid? How did Lebon know that this was the same lemur that had previously bitten someone else? Could I go home now?

After two hours of this, I stood up, light-headed, already imagining every ache as the beginning of the end. I staggered the thirty feet back to camp and asked Lebon to radio Maroantsetra.

"Why?" He looked genuinely confused. I repeated my plan to go see a doctor.

"But," he warned, "the park boat is not in town, so you will have to hire a private boat, which will be expensive."

The Projet Masoala motorboat was on the other side of the peninsula. There were only two other boats for hire in the area, and they were, as he said, quite expensive. For Madagascar. Even if they had been expensive by American standards, it hardly seemed relevant. I wasn't going to risk my arm, perhaps my life, to save a few dollars. Finally, I persuaded him that I was going to town, with his help or without it. He radioed and arranged for a private boat to come out and get me immediately. He was outraged at the price they would charge me for the three-mile trip—the equivalent of twenty-five dollars in Malagasy francs—and tried again to dissuade me. He knew I was being robbed. But he had no idea how little that mattered. The economies we live in are too different for Lebon to comprehend. I spent on a single boat ride what he and his family might spend on life in a month.

Jessica and I got to town as it was turning into a steamy, swooning day. Nosy Mangabe is always cooler than town. The forest, long gone from Maroantsetra, helps insulate against heat on Nosy Mangabe, water surrounds the small island, and the waterfall is always there, beckoning. Maroantsetra, by comparison, is hot and dusty, cramped with people.

In town, Clarice's compassionate nature came through, and she took us to a man I came to refer to as "the good doctor." The good doctor's French was easily understood, even by me, but it was a relief to have Jessica there to help translate just in case. He worked in a small, cool building with bamboo walls and a thatched roof, and his manner was professional but amused. I watched carefully as he poured alcohol over all the instruments he would use, then set them on fire to sterilize them. I carry my own sterile syringes in the field, but not a complete doctor's kit, and there is always the fear of disease. AIDS is not formally recognized as a problem by the Malagasy government, but it is surely there.

Once the good doctor had anesthetized my arm and had me lying helpless on his examining table, he began extolling the virtues of lemurs.

"Lemurs, you know, are smart and funny, quite clever, and beautiful, too." I gaped at him, then asked Jessica for a translation just in case I had gotten it wrong. I hadn't. He continued: "They don't usually do this sort of thing. You mustn't hate lemurs because of this."

"I love animals; that's why I'm here in Madagascar." I paused. This was true, but incomplete. "But I'd like to have this particular lemur for lunch."

He laughed. "Oh, no, we can't eat lemurs. Some people do, of course, but it's not right. . . ."

"I don't want to make a *habit* of it, you understand, just this particular one." I wasn't making myself clear. Having a lemur for lunch may have been the wrong way to convey that thought. I asked Jessica to step in and help me. The doctor seemed relieved by her explanation.

"Oh, yes, that particular lemur. What were you doing to provoke her? Did you try to pet her?" The good doctor was beginning to get to me. Did I try to pet her? A wild animal? Did I look mad? Was the rabies manifesting already?

"No, I was only sitting at the stream, brushing my teeth."

"Ah, they love toothpaste. She probably wanted your toothpaste."

I cast a glance at Jessica, who is expert at looking simultaneously bemused with and removed from a situation. She was doing it now.

"Lemurs like toothpaste?" I repeated.

"Yes." The doctor nodded again, his needle in my arm. "Really, they like anything that's sweet. They eat fruit, you know."

I was beginning to understand. This good doctor did know something of lemurs, but he couldn't put my story together in a way that made sense to him. It was possible that the lemur liked toothpaste, but I doubted it, as mint has a very particular aroma, and besides, she didn't make a grab for my toothpaste, just me.

"Voilà, we are done."

I twisted to look at my arm, surprised how quickly he had put in several large stitches. "Come back in three days. I'll check for infection again then. And don't have the lemur for lunch." He chuckled. We had come to an understanding. As long as I wasn't living out on Nosy Mangabe with a yen to eat all lemurs, he could accept my ire at one of them.

As Jessica and I walked back through town, we ran into Felix, perhaps the best of the local naturalist guides, along the way. Felix is the happiest person I have ever met, with the possible exception of his young son Alpha, who shares his father's exuberance at all that comes his way. Felix is a young, smart, almost trilingual, forest-loving Malagasy, and he has no chance of ever living a life outside of Maroantsetra. He is just Felix, with no last name, and when I ask him about it, his eyes grow distant, and he says his mother just called him Felix, that's all. He is enchanting, with deep, soulful eyes, a wide smile, and a laugh like wind chimes. The story of the lemur attack on one of the two *vazaha* women living on Nosy Mangabe was already circulating through town, and he had come to find us and hear the story firsthand. I recounted it. He looked as serious as I'd ever seen him, then announced, "The lemur must have wanted your toothpaste."

My mouth hung open. "You think so?"

"Why else would a lemur do something like that?" I had to admit he had a point. "You weren't trying to pet her, were you?"

I almost yelled at Felix, even though he was the last person deserving of my anger. *No*, I didn't pet the lemur. *No*, I didn't bring this on myself. *No*, I'm not the one acting unpredictable here. I wanted to scream, it's the lemur! I'm the victim, not her! Instead, I said, "No, I didn't try to pet her. She's rather mad, you know." Maybe if I started saying that, it would catch on and circulate through town. The lemur's toothpaste alibi would disappear into her madness.

The truth eventually did come out, emerging slowly from many sources. A woman in town had been keeping this lemur as a pet for a few years. The lemur was never socialized, never even allowed to climb trees. She didn't know any of her own kind. Over time, she did seem to grow mad, and began lunging at the neighborhood children, who had tormented her with sticks and taunts. The lemur's human owner wouldn't tolerate such behavior, so she looked for someplace to discard the animal. The woman was a member of Lebon's extended family, and when she approached him, he was all too eager to help. This, he was sure, was a clear example of what conservation agents should be doing—saving poor lemurs, and putting them back in the forest. He had done this the day before I arrived on Nosy Mangabe.

Though I now recognized that the lemur was probably just crazy from having been chained up alone for years, she was still a threat. When we returned to the island that night, we went with instructions from Projet Masoala for the conservation agents: Trap the lemur and bring it to town. For the next two days, nothing happened. I was jumpy, scared at forest noises, whereas I'd always been comfortable before. And the lemur continued making advances on Jessica and me. Raised among people, perhaps she mistook us for females of her own kind, encroaching on territory where before there had been only males.

Finally, we gave Lebon and Fortune an ultimatum: Trap that lemur, or we'll find a way to do so, and it may not be pretty. The next day, a lobster trap showed up in a tree by the lab. I've never caught lobster myself, but I have a feeling that they are . . . well, different from lemurs. I laughed at the trap, wondering how long it would be before I went into town again to find—what? Twine? Lumber? How would I trap a lemur? I had no idea. But it seemed clear that I would have to.

When Jessica and I returned to camp that evening, the lemur was sitting in the lobster trap, eating fruit Lebon had given her. She and Lebon had a relationship, it was clear, but nobody else could get close. I congratulated him on having caught a lemur with a lobster trap. He thought nothing of it.

After the lemur had been caught and caged, Lebon radioed for a boat to come get us. It was time for me to go in for my follow-up with the good doctor anyway. On the short, choppy ride across the bay to Maroantsetra, the lemur looked stricken in her lobster trap. She threaded her hand through the wire mesh, extending it toward Lebon, and he took her hand in his. They sat hand in hand for the ride to town.

Later that day, Lebon asked me if I knew why the lemur had to be taken away. My mind boggled, but rather than sharing the rather obvious answer, I said, "No, Lebon, tell me—why did this animal have to be removed?"

"Because," he answered, speaking with authority, "if she stayed here, she would get sick and die. As a conservation agent, it is my job to keep all lemurs healthy."

This concept of conservation—simply to keep all that is charismatic alive—had never before occurred to me. Frankly, it scared me. The conservation agent charged with protecting a fragile nature reserve had failed to recognize the difference between protecting whole ecosystems and protecting individual animals. Of course, many Americans make exactly the same mistake. One reason the cause of environmentalism is at risk in the States is because people erroneously think it pits spotted owls against the workingman. But spotted owls, charismatic as they may be, are only a proxy for the entire threatened ecosystem we hope to save.

Lebon's vision of the lemur's future was also sadly ironic. In Madagascar, information travels slowly and with much mutation, like a massive game of telephone. Early rumors that the animal was headed to a retirement home for old and disturbed lemurs in southern Madagascar were probably false, possibly started to soothe Lebon. It is far more likely, as later reports suggested, that the animal was put down. Tsimbazaza, the zoo in Tana, already had far more unsocialized lemurs than it could handle. And this animal would never successfully reenter lemur society. Killing it was the most humane thing to do.

I have repeatedly entered the lands and cultures of the developing world and started making value judgments. Don't tear down trees for crops that are pure luxury. Don't hunt bats if you have other things to eat. Don't take wild animals out of the forest and keep them as pets. Don't tell me about conservation and saving mad lemurs, for I know better. Where do I get off?

Left to their own devices, preindustrial people don't tend to destroy the land they live on. The fisher people of Nosy Mangabe disobey the letter of the law regarding coming onto the island, but in their case, that law shouldn't be enforced anyway. They smoke fish with dead wood they have collected and they spend the night camped on the beach, but they use this land well, as their ancestors did for hundreds of years. They respect the land and use it sustainably. Most important, this island was taken from the local people and made into a reserve some years ago; some of these people were using this land as a base for their fishing, their livelihood, before it was ever designated a reserve. The land belongs to them. It does not belong to the Malagasy sailors who come off spice boats for freshwater and lemur meat, nor to the Western conservation NGOs who administer it with the best intentions, and certainly not to me, a white researcher who has come to look at frogs.

But the Western NGOs come in and declare, with the tacit approval of the Malagasy government, that this land is theirs to protect. Wisely, they hire local people like Lebon and Fortune to act as guardians. The guardians get the fancy title of conservation agent, so their friends and family in town don't so easily see them for what they really are—policemen keeping local people off their ancestral lands. The problem is, these particular conservation agents don't understand conservation. They, like so many in the Western world, make the mistake of believing that only those things that are big and cute and engaging should be protected, and they fail to protect all that doesn't so easily grip their imagination. Lebon's mistake in understanding is not so different from the one we make when giant pandas or lions or whales are paraded in front of us to evoke a visceral reaction of guardianship and compassion, and we respond with our pocketbooks. How much of our grassroots money-from-the-gut goes to protect eels, after all?

The customs of the local people usually make a lot of sense in context, even when the *vazaha* who effectively parachutes in from outer space can't make sense of them. Problems tend to arise at the junction between native and Western culture, and Westerners shouldn't point to these, nod sagely, and say, What would they do without us? I desperately want vanishing Malagasy ecosystems to be protected before they are entirely lost, and I don't know how best to help the cause. I do know, though, that going halfway is not the answer. Putting local people on the payroll and telling them that they are conservation agents, without ensuring that they know what that means, is irresponsible. If these men don't understand why we might want to protect a whole forest rather than a single lemur—and why should they, at first—it is our job, if we are already intervening, to ensure that they learn.

As my wound healed, so, too, did that part of my brain that had, in an instant, searing flash, turned on me and warned me repeatedly that lemurs were dangerous. On nights when the moon was full and the water apple trees in camp were fruiting, the resident troop of brown lemurs spent all night awake in a long fruitfest, dropping the cores and bad fruit down onto the roof of my tent platform. Sometimes a lemur would scamper by on the ground, going after a piece of good fruit, and if I was in my tent trying to sleep, I would wake and tense in that moment, fearing, irrationally, that it would come for me, too.

By the time I was again able to sweat during fieldwork without wincing from the salt in my wound, and shower in the waterfall without constantly trying to keep one arm out of the spray, I enjoyed the lemurs fully again. The comic ruffed lemurs make such a production of a human going by, it's almost impossible not to hoot back at them, egging them on with cackles as they peer out of the trees at the strange being on the ground. The brown lemurs did show a noticeable interest in the lab whenever we returned from town with bananas, and their spirit was contagious. Lemurs were again wonderful coinhabitants of my small world, rather than unpredictable and treacherous foes. And it turns out that rabies isn't known in lemurs, so I probably was never at risk of turning up rabid. All the same, I'd rather not put my arm to the lemur test again.

10

Weather Is Everything

A hurricane had been spinning toward us across the Indian Ocean when we went into town with the errant lemur. But without connection to the outside world, even in Maroantsetra, we didn't know until later what to call the week of almost solid rain and punishing winds.

We were stuck in Maroantsetra for three days while the rain poured down and spindly palm trees twisted in the fierce winds. The short trip across the shallow bay to Nosy Mangabe was impossible. We stood on the second-story balcony of the Projet Masoala building and looked out on the swampy marketplace, where even the rice vendors had abandoned their posts. Early on the fourth morning, there was a break in the wind, and the captain took us back to the island, grudgingly, for he was scared that the weather would turn ugly again before he could get back to town.

Would we have gone back to the island had we known we were about to get smacked with a hurricane? Maroantsetra had services, and the theoretical possibility for escape, but it was dense with other people who needed services and food. On the island, isolated though it was, we had enough food for three weeks, and our water supply wasn't at risk of contamination, given that only a couple of people lived there.

houses washed away, corpses floating by in the streets, and, in the middle of everything, two helicopters and the new president landing in town. Lebon regaled us with stories of the helicopters, how they landed, what they looked like. When I asked him about the president, he didn't have anything to say. He hadn't noticed the president.

DAY 10

Now that the hurricane was past, the reliably unpredictable weather had returned. We had a lazy, gorgeous afternoon, wind and blue clouds washing in and out of the hills across the bay. The Masoala, they say, is the rainiest spot in Madagascar. It is a place of many clouds, of interminable rain, of unending damp. Even though the rain had isolated us for days, we could expect a respite, a golden day of sun and scattered clouds, a day with enough heat to finally dry the socks that were beginning to befoul everything they came in contact with, a day to walk around barefoot, to have a swim in the sea and a shower under the waterfall. A day to let everything dry. All things had to be attended to, or else they would rot, and mold, and fog over, and be ruined. After a night of piercing rain, the sun shone so fiercely that by midday all was dry—perfect frog-watching weather.

The world never went blankly gray on Nosy Mangabe. The sea had intrigue even when gray, whitecaps receding to a blue mountain horizon, a gray sky with flecks of white, blue, green. On this particular morning, a rainbow over the distant gray sky plunged onto layers of hills. Electric sounds from cicadas, tiny birds, and frogs pierced my ears like flashes of hot color. And the depth of the sky held in it such dimension that even when entirely gray, it was a palette of grays, hundreds, sometimes yielding to a perfect white or black.

DAY 11

The only way to enjoy the forest is to accept dirt and sweat, to immerse oneself in getting filthy. I came in from two hours of focal observations—in which the observer watches a single animal for a set period of time—just as it began to rain. I was on the fence. Should I remain in camp, changing into dry clothes and staying still so as not to dirty them with sweat, moving one step closer to having nothing dry and clean at all? Or should I hike to stand three, forty minutes away along a hilly trail, knowing that as the rains began pouring down I would be dripping wet within minutes of embarking?

Stand three beckoned, and the rain freed me from trying to feel clean.

THREE WEEKS

DAY 1

Finally back on Nosy Mangabe, I was eager to resume my work. In the pounding, ceaseless rains, Jessica and I went out to search for frogs, demarcating areas of particularly high density, mostly bamboo stands, where they congregate. We numbered bamboo stands as we found them, and each of us chose one we would go to every morning and sit in, watching, waiting for revelations from the frogs. My stand, number four, was a small affair with a lot of activity. It was on the coast, a frontier between the rain forest and a thick-grained sand beach. A mango tree hung over the water. The canopy was open, the rain immediate. Inland, when the rains grow fast and sharp, there is a delay—you can hear it begin, pounding the leaves above, but the water doesn't reach the forest floor for a minute or two, and then it is subdued, softened. After the sky has emptied, water percolates through the understory for half an hour, as the drip tips on leaves empty the foliage of water.

In between squalls, the waves coming up almost into our stands, Jessica and I alternated between watching unmarked frogs and chasing them with green mesh aquarium dip nets. We captured them and took down their length and mass data before adorning them with snazzy little beaded waistbands. We also clipped their toes, so even if they lost their belts, we could identify them.

When it rains hard, even frogs dive for cover. A Costa Rican frog biologist once told me that a single raindrop can kill a small frog. This is an exaggeration—small frogs survive being nailed by a rapid succession of raindrops all the time. Still, it doesn't look comfortable.

When the rains lashed the ground, I searched for frogs, but after a while I gave up, retreating to the fishermen's camp just three hundred feet away to wait out the downpour.

DAY 3

It had been raining for days. My frogs were ample, but they were doing nothing I could understand. Half of each day was spent marking individuals, a thankless task. When I was not marking them for identification, I was out again in the pouring rain, watching them. We were trying to get a feel for what they do, not coding any behaviors yet. Neither Jessica nor I was gaining much sense of them, but patterns take time to reveal themselves. Who knows how much of what we now saw was due to the ceaseless rains, the howling winds, the high, ominous seas. The usually inconsequential streams running down from the summit were powerful and hungry now, breaking everything in their path.

These frogs usually called from or near natural wells—tree holes and broken bamboo filled with a cup or two of rainwater. Maybe only males called, as is true in the vast majority of frogs, but since nobody had investigated this species before, I had to figure that out myself. I found one bamboo well with eight frogs inside, all amplexing one another—the near universal position for frog mating, male on female. This amplexus was extraordinary, though, eight frogs lined up, one on top of another, in one long string of frog sex.

Other organisms in this forest moved in more easily interpretable ways. I had seen frogs from a different evolutionary lineage perform paternal care of their froglets. I had watched a chameleon laboriously dig a hole into which she then deposited a clutch of eggs. Ubiquitous zonosaurs—speedy ground lizards—engaged in breakneck courtship and sex. But what could I do with these observations? They were anecdotes, not science. I enjoy theory, and the forest, but I hadn't yet put the two together so that they sang.

DAY 4

Hailing rain again, the sound of giant liquid pellets penetrating the ground. The drops were reviled, the soft earth full. The streams were engorged, running pregnant, foaming. A boat moored in the bay slipped its anchor and slammed into the dock in the night, crushing a piling. The sea fought back with intolerably high tides, waves slamming the newly broken dock, making cliffs of the coarse sand beach.

A brief radio transmission from Maroantsetra informed us that this was a hurricane, one of the worst they'd seen in years. In the river in town, corpses were flowing down from the hills. Pirogues were necessary to get through the streets of town, and only the few buildings with two stories were still accessible. Rumor had it that the French had loaned the Malagasy government helicopters so that newly elected President Ratziraka could come and investigate the disaster that was northeastern Madagascar.

DAY 5

The beaded waistbands we had been putting on the frogs for identification were failing. Most had fallen off, and those that hadn't needed to be removed, for they were constricting the animals. My new marking plan was

to stitch unique combinations of beads into their backs, but for this, I needed smaller needles than I had in camp. There were tailors in town, so we radioed Projet Masoala and asked Lebon to bring needles with him when he returned on the boat the next day. But the rains continued, and we did not have faith that the boat schedule would be adhered to.

The sea was agitated, high and gray. The tides had disappeared into the storm, and the dock was pounded day and night by whitecaps. My tent platform was fifteen feet from the dock, which itself was almost submerged. The water was but one vertical foot below my tent. Soon we might have to move to higher ground, perhaps to the cemetery cave, among the body and bone boxes of the ancestors.

DAY 7

Still no boat, no Lebon, no needles, and no explanation. The rain was still constant, though not as rageful as a few days before. The radio wasn't working, so here we were, Jessica, Fortune, and I, on this small island, expecting a boat with provisions and necessary equipment, incapable of knowing when it might show up.

In the meantime, we had identified six coastal bamboo stands that were home to hundreds of *Mantella laevigata*. Males defended the bamboo wells; extended courtships led to them; mating and egg deposition occurred in them. I tagged ninety-nine wells, largely in the six bamboo stands, and was taking data every three days on each of them. I had two consistent goals: to understand everything about this system and to keep downtime at bay. When there was no work to do, the hours stretched endlessly, with nothing to do but watch the sea rise.

DAY 8

Finally, a break in the rains. The boat came, and with it, the needles we had radioed for. The needles worked wonderfully in marking the frogs, piercing their skin with relative ease, but this was the only aspect of this frog-marking campaign that was going well. Less than 10 percent of the frogs we were finding now were recaptures—what had happened to all we'd marked with waistbands? Were there many more animals than we had imagined? Were the animals previously caught more wary of us, thus harder to catch? And, even worse, had many of the animals died from our first marking campaign, only to be quickly replaced by eager competitors from the sidelines, the forest?

Lebon came back from town with more stories of utter destruction:

I was quickly soaked, and by the time I arrived, I had no inhibitions about crawling around on all fours looking for frogs, reaching under logs, or sitting on the wet litter, striving to become part of the background. As the rains eased, I was in perfect position to watch the frogs emerge after the downpour. Sure enough, they began to appear, calling, fighting, courting, patterns unfolding in front of a soggy but satisfied biologist.

DAY 12

The day was hot, bright, dry. I sat out in my stand, trying to watch frogs, but when there is no nighttime rain, they spend the day hiding under the litter. So I sat idle, waiting for my animals to reappear, watching anything that showed up. Unlike the wet-skinned frogs, most animals like the hot, dry days. A brown lemur troop came overhead, the males yelling at me. Later, they came back through, stopping to feed at the mango tree that overhangs the beach. A resident chameleon was also out sunning herself, and she accommodated me by turning a bright green when I touched her, then a deep, scary brown. She opened her big jaws and assumed an aggressive pose. As she reached out with a strange mitten hand, she lost her balance and fell, catching herself with her tail. Hanging from her tail while scrambling to reattach herself to the plant she was on, she was an artist's palette. The frogs remained hidden.

There is a fisher family who use this island, respecting it and treading gently. It is a second home for them, and they treat it as such. The matriarch is often out in the family pirogue, casting nets, along with the little boy. On this day, the adult son had a guest, a pleasant young woman. With new people come new ducks. I do not know if these ducks are valued for the eggs they lay, if they will someday be eaten, or if they are just hangers-on, but the fisher family always seem to have one or two ducks with them.

Sitting in stand 4, trying to observe frogs that were nowhere in evidence, I found myself gazing out to sea. Suddenly, the young woman, bare-breasted, ran past, laughing, looking back over her shoulder. Five seconds later, the young man ran past in pursuit, also naked to the waist, also laughing, also looking back over his shoulder. Five seconds later, a duck ran past, chasing the hominids. Was he laughing? I didn't have the presence of mind to ask.

DAY 13

While we marked frogs, we made use of the old fishermen's camp close to both of our stands. It consists of a palm-frond roof over a dirt floor, and a wooden platform sporting a similar roof. Whenever it's raining, it's more pleasant to weigh, measure, and mark frogs under a thatched roof than in the forest. It's also easier to retrieve them when they escape. So we go out armed with Ziplocs, catch two or three frogs each, and come back to the fishermen's camp to mark them all before returning them exactly where we found them.

When I arrived at the fishermen's camp, a crowd of fisher people, emerging silent from the forest, surrounded me.

"*Sàhona,*" one man with laughing eyes said to me, looking at my bags of frogs.

"Yes," I agreed, to the Malagasy word for frog, "*sàhona.*"

"Are there many frogs in France?" he asked me in French. He could not conceive of another possibility—you are either from Madagascar or from France.

"I don't know in France, but in the United States, yes, there are many frogs. But none are like this."

He understood my poor French, and repeated, "Oh, United States . . ." trailing off at the end.

A woman approached, saw the frogs in the bags, and exclaimed, "They're beautiful!" I smiled at this, which evoked a smile from her as well as she backed into the crowd. I was becoming uncomfortable holding frogs hostage in bags while surrounded by fisher people who had appeared out of nowhere. Jessica wasn't yet back from her frog-catching attempts.

The man with laughing eyes piped up again. "Do you eat these frogs?"

"No, not these. They are toxic." He wasn't sure what to do with this information, and he wandered off, dispersing the crowd. In South America, some of the appropriately named poison-dart frogs are used by native peoples to poison the tips of their hunting darts. In Madagascar, the poison frogs are mostly ignored.

DAY 14

A day with no rain, all crystal blue, soft and gentle. The sun makes watching and marking frogs more enjoyable, except that the frogs don't come out for dazzling sun. They retreat, hide in cool, damp places that my hand won't reach and my eyes can't probe.

In the town of Maroantsetra, the sun rises over the river's mouth, where the fishermen take their pirogues out to sea.

A fisherman pauses near the reeds, in the shallows where the river and the Bay of Antongil mix. (PHOTO BY BRET WEINSTEIN)

Primary rain forest, replete with pools and streams, in the middle of Nosy Mangabe. (PHOTO BY BRET WEINSTEIN)

Mantella laevigata engages in lengthy, complex courtships. Here the male, on top, is emitting a soft courtship call while resting his head on the female's head—a behavior I refer to as "chinning."

One of two species of boa endemic to Madagascar, this *Boa madagascariensis* individual lived near bamboo stand 6, where I could reliably find it every day for almost two months.

Leaf-tailed geckos (genus *Uroplatus*) are also endemic to Madagascar. This species, *Uroplatus fimbriatus,* were relatively common in the forests of the Masoala region, though hard to find, as they are remarkably cryptic when they flatten themselves against the trunks of trees. (PHOTO BY BRET WEINSTEIN)

Sifakas (genus *Propethicus,* often called *propes* by researchers, such as this one) are closely related to the indri. They are intensely curious and social animals. (Photo by Bret Weinstein)

Hop on Pop: *Plethodontohyla notostica,* one of the frogs that competes with *Mantella* for well space in which to breed, displays extended paternal care. Fathers stay with their brood as the eggs develop and until the tadpoles metamorphose and leave the well. This father is somewhat indulgent, allowing a metamorph to sit on his head. (Photo by Bret Weinstein)

From the dock on Nosy Mangabe, the view is south toward the small summit and west across the bay to the mainland of Madagascar. (Photo by Bret Weinstein)

High up in the forest in a cave on Nosy Mangabe, the ancient Malagasy cemetery remains, body boxes and bone boxes no longer regularly cared for. (Photo by Bret Weinstein)

Shortly after arriving on Nosy Mangabe as a new conservation agent, Vincent and his brother Joe built gym equipment from bamboo in camp.

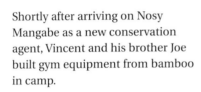

One of the daily rituals on Nosy Mangabe involved preparing food. Rafidy and Bret are tending charcoal fires in the "kitchen" outside the lab.

Solo, a vanilla farmer and friend, holds his daughter as he looks out the window of his cabin at Andranobe. (Photo by Bret Weinstein)

Lebon takes an ax to the tree that fell in camp, which almost killed Bret and crushed our tent platform in the same instant.

Retournement ("turning of the bones") ceremony. The gathered
villagers wait for the sacrifice of the zebu.

In the special reserve of Ankarana, limestone formations called tsingy form the roofs of vast cave complexes. Where the tsingy collapses, islands of forest grow. Here I am looking out of one of the caves into a pocket of forest. (PHOTO BY BRET WEINSTEIN)

Just outside Ranomafana national park, children play with what they can find. Here several little boys have found enough components to put together a game of marbles. (PHOTO BY BRET WEINSTEIN)

I more narrowly defined our study area, as trying to mark this seemingly infinite population had been making us both lethargic and dull. We had been focusing on stands four and five, excluding the large stand six, where so much had happened, but there were too many frogs, always losing their beads. Bad frogs.

I floated, languishing in a field of open questions, having discarded so few of the possible answers. These frogs could be hermaphroditic, for all I yet knew, though I didn't believe so. I was beginning to suspect that only males call, which would be normal in frogs. Just keep watching, I told myself, watching, until things start to click into place. That is how I needed to proceed.

On this morning at five the sky was pale, high clouds tinged with pink from a sunrise, which I was on the wrong side of the island to see. Over Madagascar, the fluffy storm clouds, which at night would turn electric with peach lightning, were watercolor rose, pure white only at their thickest. A glorious morning, and the frogs in stand four were doing their thing, letting me watch a territorial dispute, a border successfully defended. Then, as the sun rose and turned its rays on my little stand of bamboo, my mango-filled patch of forest, the frogs closed up shop and went to bed, stopped sharing their lives with me. I sat diligently, waiting.

DAY 15

It was hot and gorgeous again, making the frogs lethargic, unwilling to let us in on the soap operas of their lives. Even large wells were drying up— the stump from a tree fall long ago, full of water and *Mantella* eggs the previous week, was now almost dry. Fisher people had stored mangoes in it. I removed them and placed them in a neat pile nearby, hoping that even without language my message would be clear.

By 10:00 A.M., we had given up on the reticent, silent creatures, which left a day to fill. I couldn't begin my experiments yet, lacking either enough baseline data to design them or recorded calls to set them up appropriately. So what to do with a day like this? I washed everything I could think of in the waterfall—the fly from my tent, sticky with animal droppings from the raffia roof; my day pack, just beginning to rot; and, of course, my field socks—*mes chaussettes des recherches*—pungent and stiff. Things dried quickly in this clear sun, and I tried to find more to wash, knowing that soon enough the rains would resume, and everything would become sodden again, quick to mold.

DAY 16

Another hot day. I was up before dawn, and rewarded with a pinkish sunrise while I began watching frogs in stand four. Though the sun came up from in back of us, over the island, the mountains across the bay and the clouds over them lit up with the sunrise. Again, there were mangoes in the dry tree stump, and again I removed them, not taking them, but moving them away from the frogs' microhabitat.

Jessica and I saw a zonosaur, the speedy ground lizard, eat a *Mantella*. Jessica pointed it out, and we watched as the lizard chewed on the limp frog, then dropped it, licking its lips furiously. The lizard rubbed its snout and head on the ground, picked up the corpse of the frog again, and thrashed it about in its mouth like a dog. After several iterations of this—thrashing, dropping, head rubbing, corpse retrieving—the lizard ate the frog, headfirst. I was intensely curious to know how it would fare after its poisonous lunch. We had no lizard-catching equipment with us—just our little dip nets for catching small frogs. So we took off our shirts and ran around the forest, throwing them at the lizard in an attempt to catch it, but it eluded us.

At five o'clock, the sun was beginning to acquire its late-afternoon sheen, an edge off the bright heat of midday, a predictor of another blue evening. It had caught the bay at many angles, glinting fierce white. While swimming, I thought I saw the head of a sea turtle come up for air, though it is possible I only saw a briefly surfacing piece of driftwood.

The sun sank, casting its late-afternoon light on everything I saw, lending it an air of fantasy. As the sun fell behind peach-white clouds, it left the island in dark green shadow. As the spinning Earth fell away beneath it, the sky grew bluer, inky, deep. When the sun blazed, the vegetation glowed yellow-green, sallow, the leaves looking haggard but well fed under the weight of so much light. In the cooler light, the greens turned soft; there was no immediacy to them, nothing pressing. These greens could wait until tomorrow, when they would once again be useful.

I knew I would dream of this place when I left it. I was often caught, in a consciousness that I can't quite define, in which I was swimming in the warm bay, or gently sliding into sleep with the sea breeze ruffling my tent, or watching frogs while in the distance a rainbow appeared, or hiking through forest, listening to lemurs and frogs; then I would enter an awareness of time and realize I would be there much longer, yet had already been there for so long.

DAY 17

Early morning, an oh-so-brief rain shower, just enough to bring the frogs out of hiding for a few hours of observation. A possible courtship here, a definite fight there. A lot of calling back and forth, and I began to recognize individuals by where they were. When I got close enough to see their marks, confirming their identities, I found that the males were acting territorial, but the females were not. By ten o'clock, though, the rain was long gone, and the searing blue sky had again taken hold. The frogs settled in to the leaf litter and stopped moving. By afternoon, we were baking again on our little island.

The sun set over the bay, flashing yellow darts into my eyes and rendering the plants on the beach a luminous pale green. Everything looked bewitched by this sun, the blue of the water deeper, the green of leaves more alive, the brown of my arms golden against wrinkled white linen.

I escaped from a dinner of hot rice and *ranon' ampàngo*, the burned rice water that had become a staple in our diet, into the cool air, a slight breeze coming off the bay. I went down to the dock to watch schools of little fish jump out of the water, running from some unseen predator. Jessica and I watched needlefish, five of them. One nonconformist swam away from the others, the other four holding close to one another in the water beneath the dock.

At night, the moon's phase decided my mood. At home, I rarely know if it is waxing or waning, or keep track of it for more than a few nights. On Nosy Mangabe, it set me, reminded me of the unstoppable nature of time passing, brought with it change to look forward to, a schedule to know and take heart in. Lebon told me that the boat would be canceled that Friday, which meant that its next scheduled appearance would be over two weeks away. It was hard to have the things I looked forward to so far away, especially when they were small things, the little goalposts that signaled the passing of time. I should be living now, I told myself, thinking about and enjoying each day. My life was good and pleasant in many ways, staggering in the bewitched nature of existence, a foggy stroll through days that came early and ended early.

DAY 18

The clouds had rolled in with promise the evening before, seeming to foreshadow a great storm, or at least a touch of rain. No water fell from the sky, though, and the next morning, the frogs went into hiding again.

Although I watched one social interaction between two frogs before 6:00 A.M., by 6:45 all was quiet. By 7:30, Jessica had come to me, hoping I was ready to give in, for though days are long when there is no fieldwork to do, they are even longer when you are trying to force fieldwork that isn't there, sitting and staring at nothing for hours on end. By eight, I had forfeited, the whole charade pointless on this dry, hot morning, following on the heels of others just like it. I climbed to the summit of the island, knowing that there were ten hours of daylight left, too much time to fill in and around camp. I was looking for new populations of my frogs, and doing a casual survey of the herps on the island. Several delicate thumbnail-size chameleons were out, surprisingly visible on the leaf litter. These *Brookesia*, like their larger relatives, hovered over each careful step before taking it. Drab brown frogs, leaping at odd angles, seemed bulky and erratic in comparison.

DAY 19

Another gorgeous day, bright and hot, causing the frogs to sink deeper into inaction, the wells their tadpoles were in drying a little more. The large stump well was totally dry now. There were no more mangoes in the stump, though I could still see the shadowy forms of fisher people wandering about the forest, filling their skirts and shirts with mangoes. The young fisherman, once chased by a duck, approached me shyly as I sat watching frogs sit. We shared no language. He came to me with a hand outstretched, offering two tangerine-coral mangoes. I hesitated, but he insisted. Thanking him in poor Malagasy, I smiled, and he laughed, exposing a mouth of pure white teeth. Silently, in his bare feet, he turned and disappeared back into the forest.

I reveled in a sun-kissed beach and sky. The mangoes were a luxury, sweet flesh clinging to their large flat central stone. There was so little happening with the frogs, I had to wonder why I was there, entrenched in a life of fieldwork when there was no fieldwork to be done.

In the afternoon, I went back out to find frogs in the stifling heat. It was important to quantify the obvious: no rain, no frogs. After two hours without a single sighting, I returned to camp, then organized my field observations, tallying time spent in focal observation and counting fights and courtships that we had seen. I was quickly exhausting all of the little tasks I was saving for the times when I could not proceed with actual fieldwork, and there was no sign yet of rain on the horizon. The winds picked up that evening, but Lebon predicted the next day would be much the same.

DAY 21

Rain at long last. It was wet all day, the frogs improbably active when it wasn't pouring rain, so excited by the wet that they engaged in group sex and rowdy fights, calling exuberantly to no one and everyone. Would that there could have been a happy medium, wherein frogs were active, but not behaving with such agitated abandon that it was difficult to see pattern in their movements. I recorded page after page of notes, after several days when my field notes read like an elementary school primer: See frog sit. See frog twitch. See frog disappear.

Not so during the rains, though. The intrigue was thick—I could say with some certainty, even so early in this study, that the males defend wells, and that they attract females by calling, but also attract other males to fight with. Courtships are long and involved. Males lead the females around, resting their chins on top of the females' heads while chirping softly. Other males leap in and interrupt, and a wrestling match ensues, while the female sits on the sidelines, watching. If the fight goes on too long, she leaves.

This day, I saw two females show up at the same time, attracted by a calling male. He couldn't decide, and ran back and forth between them, courting each of them in turn. Ultimately, he lost both females. In one wet morning of observations, I saw more social interactions than I had during all of the previous week.

The next time I went into town to get food, the bodies of cows were still floating by on the river, victims of the hurricane. At the stands that usually sold colored sugar water in plastic bags, there were cheap photos of the French helicopters for sale. Lebon wasn't alone in his focus on them. There were no pictures of the president. It was the helicopters that piqued the townspeople's interest, understandably improbable to people who had never seen such machines.

Months later, when I returned to the Western world, I found out that the hurricane had actually made the news in the United States. My friends, who knew approximately where I was, had tried to find out how close the storm was, and reports were that it had missed northeastern Madagascar entirely. They were relieved not to have had to worry about my well-being. So much for weather reports.

11

The Good
and the Fortunate

Living in a tent for months on end has its advantages. The phone doesn't ring at 3:00 A.M., electricity bills are low, and I never find myself wandering from room to room, wondering what I've been looking for. Mud wasps do build their homes on mine, though, their crusty mazes growing until I knock them off, and they must begin anew. Mold grows into the very being of my simple home, leaving behind a persistent smell, and creeping black spots. Lizards take advantage of the sleeves holding my tent poles, moving into these new haunts that are so tight the animals have to back out when they leave. One night I woke to find a soft, slightly moving mass beneath me. When I prodded it carefully, the form revealed itself as a large snake, curled up warm, underneath my tent, perhaps waiting to strike at a hapless lizard emerging from the fragile walls. But these are minor inconveniences. I have free waterfront real estate, and when day breaks, I don't need an alarm clock. The forest and I wake together.

This forest, though, is different. It is not simply that all Madagascar forests are unique. Indeed, some families of organisms are well represented both here and in the neotropics, such as the understory melastome plants, with their slightly fuzzy, latticed leaves and small blue fruits. Of course the lemurs and chameleons and leaf-tailed geckos of the Madagascar forest are wildly different from the monkeys and parrots and toucans that one is likely to see with some regularity in a neotropical forest. But there is more. This place doesn't seem saturated.

When a tree falls in a neotropical rain forest—and they do, often—it creates a light gap into which light-loving, pioneer species move, using, in part, the nutrients left by the tree now fallen. There is evidence of a tree fall for many years after the fact. The canopy is no longer closed. The plants that thrive under these conditions include spongy-wooded species such as many palms, balsas, and *Cecropia*—light-adoring species that will disappear when the canopy above closes and the light dims. The many vines that the tree brought down with it grow up from where they fell, producing a shrubby area, ripe with smaller, tangled vines. There is, however, often no evidence of the actual tree that fell within months of its falling. It is utterly absorbed, first by fungus and termites, ultimately by all the things that grow to take its place. There are no spare nutrients in a neotropical rain forest, so a windfall of organic matter is immediately seized upon. When a tree falls on Nosy Mangabe, though, it lingers where it fell, not immediately sinking into itself, eaten from within by microbes and fungus. For many years, its carcass remains an impediment to those wishing to pass.

On Nosy Mangabe, in particular, many groups are simply missing. There are no members of the Carnivora. The niche that would be filled with big cats or hyenas in Africa, or mongooses in the rest of Madagascar, is apparently unfilled. There are relatively few birds. Only four species of lemur are present, two of which were introduced by humans, or, more likely, reintroduced, after being hunted out many years ago. The only group that seems to be well represented is the frogs.

Even the ants are scarce. In a neotropical rain forest, when you drop a piece of food, it swarms with ants within minutes and is completely gone soon thereafter. On Nosy Mangabe, when you drop a piece of food, it may stay there for weeks. Bananas hung on a string are a sure attractor for lemurs, but they don't generate streams of ants. In a Costa Rican forest where I worked, I had a poison-dart frog in a plastic container for the afternoon, intending to use it in a behavioral experiment the next morning. I thought, in my naïveté, that the frog should be fed, so I put a very small piece of banana in the container with the frog, to attract ants, which the frog could then eat. Half an hour later, the little girl who lived there ran up to me, panicked. I had attracted ants, sure enough, and they had devoured my frog. In the neotropics, ants are unstoppable. On Nosy Mangabe, they seem to beg for encouragement.

Spiders, on the other hand, are prevalent. In my experience, people who like snakes are often repulsed by spiders, and vice versa. To my mind, the smooth muscle of a snake body is an invitation to touch, whereas spiders have far too many legs to contend with. I hate walking into spiderwebs. Every day, each trail I walk on has fine threads woven into elaborate patterns strung across it, and every day, I get covered in them. This gossamer string, faintly sticky and imperceptibly strong, covers me, nets my hair, drips from my arms, masks my face. Occasionally, I see them before I walk into them, and tear them down with my arm. Usually, I walk unaware through the thick, juicy center of the spider's lair. When it stops raining, the spiders all put up webs. When it ceases to blow, or becomes very sunny, the spiders put up webs. And I come along and destroy them.

Many of the forest spiders and wasps are in a continual struggle, the wasps aiming to parasitize the spiders, the spiders hoping not to be used for someone else's goals. Parasitoid wasps are relatively common throughout much of the world, and Madagascar is no different. Some wasps paralyze large spiders, then drag them back to a hole in the ground, where the female wasp lays her eggs in the still-breathing but immobile spider. That spider, slowly eaten from the inside by developing wasps, will feed the next generation of parasitoids. Smaller mud wasps pack huge numbers of tiny spiders into their little mud homes, where they, too, serve to feed the young wasps.

The trails are rife with spiders. Higher up, lemur troops hoot and whistle, scream and cackle. The ruffed lemurs are intensely curious, grasping branches firmly with their hands while peering down at the odd bipedal primate on the forest floor below. A mile and a half from camp, along hilly trail F, I had set up a new experiment. A troop of ruffed lemurs often hangs out in this area, making terrifying noises and peering with their improbable dog faces from the trees. They started screaming while I took data on a precipitous slope, matted wet leaf litter beneath my feet, and I fell. The tumble was minor, but annoying, and surely scared into silence the frogs I was hoping to find. The lemurs continued on, though, cackling and bounding through the trees, while I lay in a wet heap at the bottom of a trail in the darkening forest.

Back in camp, protected from some of the hazards of the forest, there are still few barriers between nature and people. All over the world, people invent stories to explain what they see around them, but these may serve mostly to betray human fear, rather than to convey real understanding.

Jessica and I stood at the gateway to Lebon's and Fortune's world and looked in, confused and wary.

We were sitting in the lab, transcribing field notes, when Lebon came to us, holding his right hand limply in his left.

"I am in much pain," he said. He was staggering slightly as well, though this was purely for emphasis.

"What from?" Jessica asked.

"A fish bit me," he said, producing his limp right hand as evidence.

"A barracuda?" I asked, knowing there were barracudas here, and thinking this was the only fish that would have hurt a man, except for the great whites, which would surely have done more damage. I had not yet looked at his hand.

"No." He looked morose.

"What kind of fish?"

"A little fish," he said, then added, "I didn't sleep all night." Jessica and I caught each other's eyes, amused, and confused.

"Misy maharary?" I asked Lebon, using my paltry knowledge of Malagasy to say, "Is there pain?" He looked at me startled, surprised to hear Malagasy emanating from my mouth.

"Misy maharary," he affirmed, cringing. Yeah, there's pain all right. I had learned the Malagasy word for pain, *maharary*, from Bret during our first trip to Madagascar. Bret had ripped his leg open on barnacle-laden mangroves. We got him to the nearest medical facility, but nurse-nuns wouldn't let me go in with him, and he spoke no French at all. They were trying to anesthetize the area so they could give him stitches, but they couldn't read his *vazaha* facial expressions, so they didn't know if the anesthesia had taken effect yet. Finally, they managed to communicate the only two phrases he needed to know: *Maharary* (pain)? *Tsy maharary* (no pain)? When next I saw him, he was several stitches, and one Malagasy word, better off. I needed such a simple binary system now, with Lebon.

"Do you want something for the pain—"

"Yes."

"—or for the infection?"

"Yes," he agreed.

I tried again. "Do you want something for the pain, or for the infection?"

"Yes."

I looked gloomily at Jessica, hoping she could discern what it was that he wanted. She asked the same question, and she, too, received simply an affirmative answer.

"He wants some of everything," she said to me, not surprised.

Rural and small-town people in much of the developing world seem to be in awe of the Westerners who arrive with a vast supply of pharmaceuticals. We appear to have panaceas for every disease, every physical ailment, and there is little understanding that these same cure-alls often have side effects, and that a full course must be taken for them to be of any use at all.

Finally, I went over to Lebon and looked at his hand. There was a tiny cut, hardly visible.

"Is this a deep cut?" I asked him, testing.

"No," he admitted.

I went to my first-aid kit and got topical antibiotic, a Band-Aid, and some ibuprofen. He held out his hand, and I put some Neosporin on the slight cut, covering it with the bandage. I handed him the pill.

"This will keep the pain away for at least eight hours."

"Eight hours?" he repeated, looking at it.

"Yes, eight hours." I wanted him to go away and let us get on with our work.

"I swallow it?" he asked.

"Yes." I was exasperated with him, but the question made sense. He had little access to pills—who knows what you might do with them.

"With water?"

"Yes, with water, swallow it with water."

He limped off. We never heard anything more about the aggressive little fish. Probably, though, it was not a bite he had suffered, but contact. We later learned that stonefish were common off the shores of Nosy Mangabe. Contact with the extremely toxic spines of these bottom-dwellers can be deadly, and is reputed to be fiercely painful. Lebon didn't have the words in French to explain this to us, so he said simply, if incorrectly, that he had been bitten. He was always trying to prove his manliness to us, and this unexpected display of weakness made no sense unless he was truly in distress.

Later that week, I was going into town to get provisions. I had arranged for a boat to take me there, and Lebon decided to take advantage of this opportunity to go to town, as well.

"Why are you going into town?" I was curious.

"My wife and child are very sick."

"Your wife?" I couldn't help myself. "But you said you didn't have a wife."

"Uh," he stammered, "my future wife, and her kid."

The next day, when I was returning to the island with provisions, he met me as I waited for the boat.

"Um, Erika, I will not be going back today. . . . My wife is still very sick—uh, future wife."

"And the child?" I asked.

"Child?" he echoed.

"You said the woman and her child were very ill?"

"Oh, yes, the child." He looked bewildered, as if the child were a figment of my imagination.

"Do they have malaria?" I asked. Just a guess, but since it was a common disease, it seemed a good one.

"Yes, malaria." Lebon nodded, looking morose. I'd seen him wandering around town with his buddies the day before, not looking in any particular hurry to attend to a sick woman, but he seemed disturbed now.

"Does she have medicine?" I asked.

"Oh, yes," he replied enthusiastically.

"Nivoquine?" I prodded, knowing that I was breaking one of the first rules of Third World communication: Never suggest the answer you are expecting. You will almost inevitably get that answer, and then you'll know nothing. In this case, though, my slip didn't cost.

"No. Aspirin."

"Aspirin?" I repeated, dumbfounded. Aspirin is medicine for malaria? "Is there no nivoquine in Maroantsetra?"

"Oh, yes, there is nivoquine. . . ."

I didn't pursue this, understanding that if it was available and she didn't have it, it must be too expensive for them to buy. It occurred to me that I might buy it for them, but if her malaria was chronic, how much would I buy? I certainly couldn't afford a lifetime supply.

The conservation agents were a mystery to me. Sometimes they reminded me of Stoppard's reimagining of Rosencrantz and Guildenstern. But in this case, Lebon and Fortune were not dead, only highly ineffectual.

After several weeks on the island, I had never seen the conservation agents enter the forest. They frequently walked along the coast down to the fishermen's camp when there were boats moored there. But they didn't go inland. Partly, they were afraid. Every day at lunch, in almost reverent tones, they asked Jessica and me if we were going back into the forest. Sometimes they made excuses, asserting that since we would be in the forest, it was not necessary for them to go. They eyed chameleons warily, too, unnerved by these marvelous lizards.

One day, I found Lebon and Fortune giddy with joy, jumping off the dock into the pale green bay, splashing with excitement. Each time one of them hit the water, the other would laugh like a little boy. Most Malagasy don't swim, so this was a surprise, not least because they were so carefree and exuberant. It was also inconsistent that they should be afraid of the mostly harmless forest but feel at home in a sea known to harbor sharks and barracuda.

Even though I understood that they suffered from forest fear, I had little sympathy. It was part of their job to clear trails and keep people without permits off the island, and they weren't doing either. At my research sites, particularly in the bamboo stands, I began to notice clear signs of human intrusion—ax marks on bamboo, trees gone missing. There were often boats of all sizes and types moored in the little bay. At lunch one day, we asked the conservation agents why there were boats here.

"Because they are too big to dock in Maroantsetra, so they come here with their cargo."

"But . . ." I began, then stopped. Protesting that this was a nature reserve wouldn't do any good. Lebon understood that I was annoyed. That afternoon, I watched as the crew of one boat unloaded hundreds of bags of cloves onto land. They then sat around smoking, strolled through the forest looking for fruit, terrified one another with chameleons, and chopped down trees. From the bowels of the spice boat spilled jarring, garbled Malagasy rap music, which permeated the forest. Some of the men spent the day in camp with Lebon and Fortune, where the smell of marijuana was thick. Fortune's eyes were glazed.

The next day, the spice boat was still in the bay. A wholly different breed of seafarers, a family of fisher people, floated past in their pirogue, making landfall to smoke their fish. Fisher people, unlike sailors, are always local, and they often travel in small family groups. They are also extremely poor, and usually landless, needing just a small dugout canoe, and their own ingenuity, to survive. The fisher family made a fire, and the smell of aging fish smoldering slowly wafted through the forest. Much more pervasive was the sound of chopping wood near the spice boat, the yells of sailors on land echoing back to us. That night, over our bowls of rice, Lebon announced that he had made the fisher people leave. He thought I would be pleased. I was ashamed.

The spice boat was leaking gasoline, leaving a rainbow sheen on the water. Earlier, a tanker had spilled oil in the bay, and for a week I went to sleep in my tent with the acrid taste of oil in my nostrils. Lebon's position is that the bay is not the reserve and is therefore outside of his jurisdiction. When wealthy Frenchmen arrived in a yacht, cruising the Indian Ocean and wanting to walk the beaches of Nosy Mangabe, Lebon welcomed them onshore without permits. These tourists, like me, were exactly the people who should have been paying for access, but Lebon didn't want to upset them. Besides, he argued, the beach is not the forest, and Nosy Mangabe is only a forest reserve. The border between protected and unprotected nature is fluid.

To Lebon and Fortune, this was a job to be taken advantage of at every opportunity. If they didn't follow the instructions, it was just the ungrateful and stingy boss who was losing a few pennies over his employees' behavior. But the bribes didn't cost Projet Masoala, CARE, or WCS—all of the larger, faceless organizations—a few pennies. These bribes ran against the very philosophy of conservation. As Jessica and I had daily interactions bordering on dangerous with sailors, Lebon and Fortune sat back at camp, lounging.

"It is lonely here, with just the two of us," Lebon explained over rice one evening. "The work is hard, and the island so big, it is impossible to do everything that an island of this size requires. We are always patrolling. And we do not even have a boat. And there is no radio, no music. Now that you are here, though, things will be a little better." Lebon smiled at us.

It was true that they had no motorboat. They had a pirogue, which Lebon sometimes fished in. But the island isn't that big, and they put in no effort. Every time I returned to camp, expectedly or no, the two of them were there. Sailors frequently brought them gifts of fish and marijuana; in exchange, they looked the other way when the island was abused.

They *were* lonely, though, and this made their jobs more difficult than I could understand. Across the water from their families and friends, all they had was each other, the two distant *vazaha* women, and whoever came by boat. They had little in common with the fisher people—of the lowest class, uneducated—and so it was these people they kicked off the island when the mood struck them.

Fortune did even less than Lebon. Every morning, he got up and raked the camp, leaving parallel lines of sand among the water apple trees and tent platforms, totally incongruous in the forest. He reminded me of the children's poem about an old woman who rakes the beach, keeping things neat and tidy until the tide comes in again, but making no difference in the larger world. After raking, he was done for the day. A potbellied, quiet man, he sat on a rickety bamboo bench and stared into the middle distance. He wore a pair of old shorts, ripped at the hem. When he went into town for vacation, he put on a shirt and flip-flops. On the island, he wore just shorts, and sometimes, a flowered hat.

Women in town weave baskets and hats out of plant fibers. The most decorated hats have plastic flowers on them—a pink rose, a white carnation. In town, men don't wear flowered hats. But on the island, Fortune wore one adorned with a large pink bloom. Rooted and stoned on his bamboo bench most days, he scowled, watched Lebon cooking rice or chopping wood, and wore that flowered hat.

One day, Felix came to the island with a tourist. Fortune wasn't feeling well, and he languished on the bamboo bench, looking stricken. Returning to camp after focal observations, I found Felix on his knees, giving Fortune a foot rub. Fortune, still wearing his flowered hat, was looking much better.

While Fortune hardly interacted with us at all, Lebon tried to impress us with his knowledge. His French was about as good as mine, although we had largely nonoverlapping vocabularies, but he wanted to learn English. One day he sat in camp on the bamboo bench with a book in front of him. He looked studious, turning the pages at appropriate intervals. The book was in English. It was also upside down.

At night, when there were boats in the bay, Lebon and Fortune waited until they thought I was asleep, then sneaked past my tent platform to the fishermen's camp to cavort with the sailors. They would come back an hour or two later, trying to stifle their laughter, tripping over themselves, high as could be. When the sweet smell of marijuana hung over their cabin during the day, Fortune would sit on his bamboo bench and stare, watching time pass.

12

Naked Sailors

The flora and fauna of Nosy Mangabe coexist with me when I am here. The people of Maroantsetra, though they no longer visit very often, allow me to stay. The fisher people who sometimes camp overnight, during storms or good fishing runs, grant me access. I have no such power to grant, as I carry no authority. But I do share the space with a variety of people, some of whom, I feel, given my perspective as a foreigner and a Caucasian, don't belong; others, I know, belong far more than I ever will.

My parents treated me to a cruise with them down the Nile a few years back, just after New Year's. We all began the week expecting cushiness and little real interaction with local people. I was pleased to find that the itinerary on our frequent stops, with the advertised goal being to see ever more fantastic ruins, was flexible. If the ruin of the hour seemed just like the last, or if the number of tourists who had gotten there before us was too stifling, we could wander about the streets of whatever town we were in.

We were exploring Edfu together, but my mother was suspicious of those we encountered, registering her distrust by scowling at them. She didn't love my choice of streets to drift down, finding them a bit daunting by virtue of their narrowness, the number of children playing with metal shards in the middle of them, the domestic air of laundry hung out to dry in the sharp heat. She allowed me to drag them down these streets, but her discomfort showed on her face. We were not interacting with anyone. The locals backed off a bit when we passed by, and no laughter served as backdrop to our slow conversation.

"If you smile at people, they often accept you as an ally and smile back," I gently suggested. I was surprised at how easily this point was made. My mother began to smile, and our joy increased immediately as locals greeted us, children ran about, and native conversation ceased to halt in our wake. We quickly acquired a guide—a little girl named Sylvia, who spoke some English and seemed to enjoy skipping along beside us. The lesson was simply this: Why not expect good things of people, until they have given you reason not to? This is especially valuable when the stakes are low, or your initial hostility gives you no real advantage anyway. In Madagascar, the lesson is critical. When I act distrustful and nasty, I get the same in return; with just a bit of courtesy on my part, everyone, including me, receives more respect in the end. Positive feedback is a powerful thing.

About half a mile south of camp on Nosy Mangabe, along the coastal trail, is a bridge over a rocky stream. Gushing out of the side of the mountain is a waterfall, shorter than the one in camp, but still quite forceful. When boats come to the island to moor, the sailors on board come on land to get fresh water or to bathe. Though their activities frequently go beyond these legitimate ones, while the boats stay three, four, five days, in which time the tide gives them countless opportunities to leave, I try to appear gracious and unperturbed when I run into groups of sailors at this small waterfall. Unlike fisher people, sailors do not include women in their ranks. Most of these men have rarely seen white people, much less a white woman.

My first interaction with naked sailors was late one afternoon, when I was returning to camp after a long day. I was tired, dirty, and the gear on my back was heavy. I just wanted to get cleaned up, have a big plate of rice, and lie on the dock watching the stars. I wasn't paying particular attention to my surroundings when I got to the bridge, looked down, and saw four naked men staring up at me. They looked so utterly harmless that it didn't occur to me to be worried about the situation, so I continued on after nodding in a universal human sign of recognition. Shortly, though, I heard rustling behind me, and when I sneaked a peak, I found the men, still naked, tiptoeing behind me on the forest trail.

At least I know they're not armed, I thought, glad to be grateful for anything at that moment. They seemed merely curious, and the situation simply silly, rather than dangerous, so I kept on at the same pace, every now and again looking back, to find them still tiptoeing along, trying to be silent while crunching through the leaf litter. When I arrived back in camp, Lebon was there, and as I strode past his cabin, naked sailors in tow, he called them to him. Would he reprimand them? No—he just wanted company. For the rest of the afternoon, they sat on the stoop of his cabin and chatted with him. One of them was draped with Lebon's only towel, while the others remained naked.

The following week, I came upon approximately fifteen men in the same place, some in little bikini briefs, some totally naked, half of them soaped up already, the other half just getting into the action. I walked over the bridge wearily, hoping merely to shock them by my presence and then be gone. The quickest among them recognized me as human before I passed, though, and yelled a hearty *"Bonsoir!"* He was quickly joined by others among them, so I responded, if not with much enthusiasm.

"Bonsoir," I muttered, knowing that the cultural differences between us were so great that I could walk on my hands with a banana up my nose and it might not surprise them more than my mere presence already had. This large group of almost-naked men concerned me a bit, as they might simultaneously regard me as not quite human (the essence of *vazaha*) and as very female. Not a combination to make a woman feel at ease. Still, this group of naked and bikini-clad men did not follow me back to camp, but remained in the stream, washing the grit and grime of sea travel off themselves.

Three days later, I ran into another naked sailor in the river. Walking down to take data on the contents of the wells at stands four through six, I stopped abruptly a few yards from the bridge under which sailors tended to wash, seeing what looked like a man in the act of removing his last bit of clothing. I stopped, squatted, and waited. Private baths being quicker than communal ones among Malagasy sailors, it wasn't five minutes before he finished and went strolling down the path, still naked, heading toward some boat I hadn't known was there.

Sometimes legitimate boats arrived, as one had earlier in the year, just after Ramadan. It bore an extended family of high-class Muslim folk from Maroantsetra. They may have been shopkeepers, like most of the Muslims in town, though their station seemed to be higher than that. Perhaps they also exported vanilla. They had come to have a celebratory picnic and to show the holy man accompanying them the island reserve of Nosy Mangabe. The women consisted of a lovely matriarch, who spoke to Jessica and me with indulgence and warmth, and five younger women, who might have been her daughters, or perhaps sisters, all immaculately groomed and coiffed and dressed beautifully in swaths of colorful fabric. They were not veiled. Most of these younger women were not notably attractive, but one was gorgeous, and she held herself apart from the others. There were two children, a boy and a girl. Both of them ran around and played in the water, not being asked to distinguish themselves by their genders at their tender ages. There was a patriarch with a gray beard and a white cap, and several younger, middle-aged men whom I found hard to distinguish from one another.

They wandered about for a while, discreet and charming. Although they did not say anything, I was embarrassed to be wearing a bathing suit, in light of their propriety and well-dressed sophistication; it felt disrespectful, so I retreated to the lab to put on some clothes. This was one of our afternoons off—every third afternoon, I gave Jessica and myself the option of taking off, although one or both of us often chose to continue focal observations, especially if the weather had provoked an abundance of frog activity. Otherwise, we worked from dawn until dusk every day. It was hot and dry that day, and the frogs were not in evidence. I was still having great difficulty discerning pattern in their behavior, and when, as on this day, it was also hard to find a single frog, it was an easy choice to devote the afternoon to swimming in the sea that shimmered pale green at the peak of hot days, and drying out on the dock with a book.

The very idea of having a picnic on an island to celebrate a holy day and to show Nosy Mangabe to the holy man seemed utterly civilized. My gut reaction to these Muslims, whose families had long ago traveled from the Indian subcontinent, was one of great respect. The women, in particular, were so poised, so involved in enjoying the experience they were having— this was a motivation I could identify with.

With them on the family boat was a Malagasy crew, all of whom lacked sophistication by comparison. The Malagasy men wore only shorts, and they stared at Jessica and me as if we were the first women they had ever seen, lust in their eyes. As I walked through camp, I encountered the Malagasy men in the water apple trees, picking all the fruit they could. They began stashing their hoard on the boat, having picked more than they could possibly eat. They were making a ruckus while they did so, yelling and running through camp. One of the Malagasy was very young, maybe fifteen, and he exuded the strained sexual authority of teenage boys, walking around bare-chested, with tattoos on his belly.

After they were done depleting the island of water apples, the Malagasy men began hunting for large sticks to throw into the mango tree hanging over the bay. Unlike that in other parts of the forest, this fruit was still green. It would ripen during our stay, and we would devour it joyously— fresh mango from the tree, what heaven. But the Malagasy men had no patience. They intended to force the fruit down with sticks hurled at great speed. These badly aimed spears often fell within feet of the little Muslim boy playing in the sand. Meanwhile, some of the older Muslims walked their holy man to the waterfall, pointing out a chameleon and some lemurs. He was delighted.

After a couple of hours, the family left, the women establishing them- selves comfortably in the back of the boat, talking among themselves as I watched them leave. I wished desperately that we could communicate, that I could learn from them what their life was.

Coming back from an afternoon of fieldwork a few days later, Jessica and I found seven mostly naked men hanging around camp, sitting idly on the stoop of Lebon's and Fortune's cabin. Lebon was in Maroantsetra for his vacation, and Fortune was in the kitchen shack, attending to the rice, so the mostly naked men did the only thing remaining to them: They stared at the *vazaha*.

Perhaps they were collecting data on us, as we so patiently had been attempting to do with the frogs just an hour previously. They observed us coolly, but with a certain amount of opinion thrown in, albeit in a language neither of us could understand. These men could do little besides watch us languidly. I walked past them, wondering exactly what they were thinking about. When the *vazaha* walk past, they are silent. As soon as we pass, they break into raucous laughter, laughter that would cause much angst if it happened in the school yard. What was strange was not merely that I didn't understand what they were thinking, what their lives consisted of, but that when I had tried, I had been left more befuddled than in the beginning.

Earlier that day, walking along the coastal path to the bamboo stands, I had crossed a bridge and noticed a Malagasy youth beneath it. He was a boy of about thirteen, wearing ripped shorts, hunting for crabs, jumping from rock to rock. He must have seen me as I passed, but out of the corner of his eye only, a ghost. I didn't give my usual greeting of "*Salama*," for I didn't think he had seen me. I continued walking. When I had gotten one hundred feet down the path, I heard him yelling at me.

"*Bonjour!*" he called. I ignored him but slowed my pace. "*Bonjour! Bonjour!*" I looked back and saw that he had scrambled up to the path. "*Salama!*" he cried. I called back, "*Salama!*" and continued walking. He yelled something else in Malagasy, which I failed to understand, and then was out of earshot.

Later, as I sat in the bamboo stand and watched frogs, two crew members from one of three boats then moored in the bay saw me as they strolled along the beach. The sailors stood and gawked, literally openmouthed. I gave them a long, hard stare. I don't speak when I am watching frogs, as it disturbs them. It is best that I blend into the background, be utterly still and silent, so they forget I am there.

These men made me desperately uncomfortable, turning me into the object of a focal watch myself. Of course they were curious. But I felt like a zoo animal—on display, unable either to communicate my discomfort or to walk away. I realized I should not complain too much about the persistent scrutiny—it was what I was doing to the frogs, after all, and an impulse I understood. But being viewed as prey was something else, and too often I was unable to tell the difference between mere scrutiny and predatory impulses.

The stare I gave the intruding men did not dissuade them, but once they tired of me, they went into the forest, not twenty feet from where I was trying to conduct focal watches of frogs made nervous by human activity. The men began foraging for mangoes and breadfruit. I was infuriated by the interruption but realized that, unlike myself, these men blended right in after a few minutes in the forest, and the frogs resumed their lives.

Sometimes the sailors weren't so quietly curious. Much later, three men in shorts from a loud, ugly wooden boat were trolling around the island. I ran into them in the stream by stand six, where I'd been finishing off a female-choice experiment. I heard their laughter, and though my impulse was always to run in the other direction in such instances, that would have led me deeper into the forest, with no way out, so I put on a relaxed but firm face and strolled out to meet their eyes. These men were different. They didn't contemplate me with that distance I usually get from Malagasy of all ages and both sexes. They regarded me with hunters' eyes, and this difference made me jittery. I said, "*Salama*" to the one nearest the bridge I was walking across, but he and the others only stared at me, then cackled as I strode past into the forest. I considered the real possibility of these men chasing me down, though I was but a kilometer from camp. The look in their eyes was hard and mean, and I was *not* not-quite-human but definitely female to them, as I often seemed to be to the sailors. To them, I was only female.

Later, I ran into the charming fisherman who had once given me two mangoes as a gift. He now greeted me warmly every time he passed by the bamboo stand. I wondered if the wolfish sailors and the gentle fisherman might, upon meeting, not recognize each other as the same species.

My own recognition of species was becoming honed, and I had discovered some sort of wormlike thing that lived in the wells that the frogs used and ate their eggs. I called them worms, though I suspected they weren't actually worms, but without a resident entomologist or the appropriate reference book, I had little hope of figuring out what they were while in the field.

During one hot, dry spell, I set up an experiment to determine what limited the population density of my frogs. I suspected that viable wells are limiting for *Mantella*. Having picked two swaths of forest, we established three plots in each, which we scanned visually for frogs every three days for three weeks. Then we added artificial wells—brightly colored plastic cups—to four of the six plots, and continued monitoring them, predicting increases in frog populations in the plots with additional wells. Within weeks of establishing those artificial wells in the forest, where *Mantella* were rare, I found a mating pair in one of these wells, and *Mantella* eggs in another. The very next time I visited those wells, there were worms inside, devouring the frog eggs. There seemed to be a war on between these two species, whatever the "worms" might be: The worms sought out wells containing frog eggs, so they could eat; the frogs sought out wells with no worms, so that their eggs would survive. Given that both species still existed in the system, there were probably regular successes and failures on the part of both.

Some intruders to my bamboo stand hardly disturbed me at all. One man came and stared at me with quiet eyes, seeming to ask if it was okay to come closer. I nodded yes and smiled, and my intruder friend came closer, looking in wonder at my gadgets. That day, I had a microphone and tape deck in the bamboo, a camera with a long lens set up on a tripod, and a notebook filled with words and numbers. It being clear, somehow, that we had no language in common, we said only a few words to each other. He peered into the thicket where I'd set up the microphone. A marked male frog was sitting there, but he wasn't particularly obvious to the uninitiated. I pointed to the frog, as he wasn't doing anything that I was going to disturb, and said, "*Sàhona.*" The man nodded, his eyes glittering. I sat, trying to appear hard at work, but given that this unmoving male was the only frog visible, and he was just sitting there, I probably gave the impression of being a lunatic instead.

I took a picture of the frog, then let the friendly intruder look through the camera. He didn't get close enough to see clearly—most Malagasy have never handled a camera before, so they don't know how to interact with one—but he saw enough to gesture that the frog was very much larger when viewed through the lens than in real life. He stood in back of me for a few more minutes, then investigated well one, which didn't hold water and was thus utterly boring, although it did have a snazzy piece of pink-and-black-striped flagging tape tied to it for identification. He then peered into one of my newly installed artificial wells, which was empty. Finally, he wandered off. He did not regard me as a museum specimen, a cultural oddity, but, rather, as a human being doing something strange in the forest. Because he dealt with me as another cognizant being, I had fond thoughts of the mute visitor for many weeks.

Having been dealt with as human by a Malagasy man that morning, I got naked-sailored again in the afternoon. Often, I was merely treated to the sight of soapy men in bikini briefs, a sort of lead-in to the full-blown naked sailor saga. Walking along, I decided that this time I would not stop for potentially naked men in my path, would not duck down and wait for them to finish their bathing, but would stroll through. I crossed the second-to-last bridge before the remote camp, the one under which most naked sailor incidents occurred. As I crossed, I could not fail to see the rounded orbs of a naked ass beneath me, the man attached to them facing away from me, so our eyes did not meet. I merely continued walking. Afterward, I thought that perhaps I should have yelled some nicety at him in French, as they were always doing to me. Suddenly, the island seemed crowded with sailors every other day, though thankfully this proved to be a temporary situation.

After I left the bridge, I took data on the contents of wells, then sat and watched frogs do nothing for an hour. When I was ready to leave stand six, which was a bit off the main path, I heard disjointed laughter and what I took to be sailors' voices—there were two boats moored just offshore. I paused, and decided to let them pass, not wanting to come out to the path in the middle of a group of them. The late-afternoon sun slanted through the slim trees of secondary forest, dappling me and the undergrowth with light and shadow. I couldn't see their movement, but I had heard them and knew they were there. Even when they looked right at me, not ten feet away, they could not see a human form in the trees.

They passed, their laughter dying away as they proceeded up the path, in the same direction I intended to go. Wanting to avoid an interaction with a large group of energized sailors, I chose to walk along the beach, rather than the forest trail. I planned to take the path only for a brief section, where large rocks precluded a beach route. Stomping along on the beach, annoyed not to be alone in my forest paradise, I thought that I had passed them and perhaps could beat them to the length of path that we both would have to take. As I turned to join the path, though, I recognized my error. It was at exactly that point that the stream flowed out to the sea and the bridge spanned the small waterfall—the place where the naked sailors did their thing.

The totally naked sailor I had come across earlier in the afternoon was probably gone by now, but he had been replaced by ten or so others. I slogged up the muddy slope to the main trail, uncomfortable, wishing agitatedly that they would all go away. I had almost escaped, when three of them came to the path to greet me. These three were bikini-clad rather than naked, but all looked voracious, as if there were some critical component of their diet that they'd been deprived of for weeks. They stared at me as I climbed the hill to where they stood, all of their compatriots pausing to watch silently. They did not utter any words of greeting, an ominous sign from the usually garrulous Malagasy. As I crested the small rise, I indicated without words that I wished to pass, but they stood there immobile, blocking my path. So with force, arms swinging, muscles tensed, I pushed through them, making two of them crumble in their display of manly strength as they looked at me with their hungry eyes.

"*Bonjour,*" I muttered as I pushed and squeezed past them. The man in bright blue bikini briefs spoke—the color stays with me; perhaps it was the only thing I really saw of any of the men. Blue Bikini Briefs, their spokesman, asked me in French how things were. I couldn't tell if the situation was escalating or deescalating, now that I had pushed my way through their aggressive united front. I avoided his eyes and replied as if we were sitting down to tea.

"Things are good. And with you?" I offered, trying not to betray my fear. Then, continuing my exaggerated display of strength, I walked swiftly down the path. Two of them followed me briefly but then stopped, and I grumbled to myself all the way back to camp. This was the only time, in all my months in Madagascar, that I had ever felt true sexual risk in that country.

13

Vigilance

Time passes on this rich green island, this soft, distant island, this verdant tropical island afloat in expectation and history, this big blue island, this *nosy mangabe*. Days slide past, almost identical in their schedule, varying only subtly in detail, and there is no future to imagine but more like these. I wake in my tent, to the faintest hint of pink coming through the gossamer walls, and lie still, listening. Night frog song ceding to day frog song, nocturnal mouse lemurs nesting, brown lemurs rising. They do not worry if today is like yesterday, nor even if somehow today were indeed yesterday.

Time continues to pass, and I become wary, convinced in my less lucid moments that my personal vigilance is all that keeps time moving forward here in this forgotten world. I must be fully aware that today is Tuesday, for if I do not keep track, tomorrow may also be Tuesday, and I will be forever here, cycling through endless Tuesdays. Even the smallest cues can remind us of what day it is. In Maroantsetra, the market bustles more on Wednesday, the doors of the church are open on Sunday. In the west, Monday has a palpable reluctance, Friday an exuberance, and Sunday drags its heels. On Nosy Mangabe, these names identify nothing—lemurs and lizards have no concept of a week, every day like the last, sleeping, eating, waiting.

Sometimes, thankfully, I lapse in my vigilance and pass a moment, even hours, without pondering the passage of time. But then I am reminded, and

I wonder if the time I live now might come back to be lived again, erasing the first life. Or perhaps that mirror time will compound the first life, reminding me of time already spent, but ruthlessly demanding that I relive moments, rather than giving me new ones. So many of my thoughts are the same each day that I might not know if I had gone through an entire day with exactly the same complement of synapses firing in my head.

March arrives, and the countdown continues: nine more weeks in the field. Nine more weeks of ethereal sky, the moon veiled by a faint mist, its border soft and imprecise. Tiny slivers of pale yellow slip through the thick clouds, crowning the mountains. The sky overhead is a middling blue that has no name, not *sky* and not *midnight*, as those names evoke noon, and night. There is no color called dusk, for dusk changes with the season and the climate and the number of people dwelling in your midst. This dusk is a steel blue with no end, gray clouds wisping at the edge, as if there are margins. But dusk has no borders; it goes far, continues out of the atmosphere into dark, and once there, dusk is gone, and you cannot name the place where it first began to disappear.

In Jamaica, one of Bret's friends asked him, "Is our Jamaican moon the same moon that you see in America?" Just think what it would be like if each place on this Earth had a different sky, if we could not link ourselves with the constellations and moon phases and the rising and setting of the sun. We are already so small and insignificant. How much more so if we were in smaller boxes yet, and could not see out of them into other people's skies.

As in all lives, food provides a regular diversion from thoughts of eternity and echoed days. Meals break up our days at noon and at six, plates piled high with rice. Jessica was writing to her parents one day, intense, focused, when under her breath, she muttered, "I meant to write *bread*, but I wrote *rice*. . . . That says it all, doesn't it?"

Our diet is rice. Rice with beans, sometimes. Rice with potatoes and carrots if we'd just been to town and there were vegetables to buy, and if they haven't rotted yet. Rice with ramen noodles. Rice with fish broth. Rice with more rice, finished off with a glassful of *ranon' ampàngo*, essence of rice.

Some mornings, I find evidence of rats in the lab. There is no way to keep them out. They gnaw through the bindings of some of my books, beginning with a theoretical book on sexual selection, then moving on to

Updike. They leave a few rolls of flagging tape strewn around the lab like party streamers. I ask Lebon if it were possible to buy rat poison in town. He looks dismayed.

"If you poison the rats, the things they leave in the rice will also be poisoned."

"What do they leave in . . ." I begin, then catch up, a bit too slow for Lebon's generous interpretation of rat droppings.

Later, he produces an old rusty rat trap. We set it. We catch two giant rats over the next three nights. These aren't fascinating rodents known only from Madagascar, but the same big rats humans have been transporting around the world in cargo ships for centuries. After this effort, our rice is a bit cleaner, and my books suffer fewer bite marks.

The previous year, when Bret and I were on Nosy Mangabe with Emile, he came to us one day and asked what we had in mind for dinner, though there is but one thing to eat.

We hazarded a guess. "Rice?" Emile was annoyed.

"Yes, rice, but what about the *broth*?" he persisted. Broth? Perhaps he was making soup?

"Broth . . . hmm, yes, well, we do have those bouillon cubes."

"Jumbo cube for broth?" Emile repeated, invoking the name blocked in large letters on the wrappings of these cubes.

"Yes, jumbo cube," we agreed. Seeming satisfied, he left to attend to the making of the broth. Only as we sat down to our meal did his meaning become clear. We had the usual heaping plates of rice. And we had "jumbo cube" broth to spoon over the rice.

"No beans?" I asked quietly.

"You said you wanted jumbo cube for broth."

Emile was peeved. If the *vazaha* had a normal, Malagasy understanding of food, none of this would have happened. Rice is a constant. If you choose to put something on top of your rice, that is okay. But it is secondary, usually trivial. There is rice. And there is broth.

By the time Jessica and I were being graciously fed by Lebon and Fortune, at least I understood this much. For broth, the conservation agents have a predilection for fish. Almost every day, our broth consists of a weak fish stock, fish heads swimming in pale red water, eyeballs viscous and staring. The fish, though caught every day, is not eaten fresh, but smoke-dried, then reconstituted to form broth. It is not good. Sometimes, as a treat, there are crabs on top of the fish heads, their asymmetrical claws dangling loosely outside of the bowl, their flat bodies stewing in the same pale red broth. Crabs that have sat in a fisherman's pirogue for two days, steaming dead in the sun.

"We can't eat this," we explain apologetically to Fortune as he insists, like a good mother, that we eat, eat. "The *vazaha*, we have strange ways, and one of them is to avoid feasting on long-dead crustaceans." He looks betrayed, saddened by our rejection of this special meal.

"More rice?" he asks, hopeful, plying us with fresh mounds of the sticky white morsels. We nod enthusiastically, for we are falling in line, slowly coming to require enormous quantities of rice in order to feel full. A smile spreads over Fortune's lethargic face. We have brought him some joy, by feasting on rice.

One day, a package arrives from Ros, Jessica's mother. She has sent us a hunk of cheddar cheese, now slimy and molded from the trip. We are in ecstasy. I find real macaroni in town, and we ask Fortune to boil it for us. We spend our free afternoon cleaning off the cheddar, washing it in the stream, admiring it, anticipating its sharp bite atop pasta. At dinner, we carry in, triumphantly, a bowl containing small hunks of cheddar cheese. Fortune is in agony as we drop cheese on top of macaroni, and swoon.

"More rice?" he asks, scared that tonight we might say no. And we do.

"Tonight, we have pasta, Fortune. Do you want to try it?" He backs away from the table, terrified of our cheese.

"Lebon, would you like some? It's delicious." Lebon, though unconvinced by our plates, wants to be heroic in our eyes, so he bravely takes a bite. This is all he can manage. We can read his thoughts: What is this cheese, this curdled milk product? And why won't the *vazaha* eat fish eyes when they are offered?

And so this life continues. I am, alternately, stunned by the beauty of this island, the serenity and odd twist on luxury that living in a rain forest affords, and bored, counting the days, eager for new diversions, craving foods, information, entertainment. The weather, even when it is reminiscent of past motifs, provides mystery, something on which to focus.

Rain falls in patches across the bay. At the farthest point, bright yellow lights the horizon, a thin cloud layer letting through the sun's last pure rays before they color with their slant. So cool here, calm. The distant laughter of Lebon and Fortune, replete and satisfied after dinner, is the only human noise. Organic sounds of the night begin to emanate from the forest, frogs and insects mostly, clicking and pulsing with life energy. The bay laps the coarse sand beach. High tide, which can be rough, is tonight tranquil, the water barely undulating with the ripples that end on shore, surges of soft water on receptive sand. The large gnarled driftwood that usually rests underneath a tree overhanging the bay has been pulled out by the tide, freed by the water to do nothing in particular. I feel like that often, that my freedom here is laughable because there are so few options. It is such a feeling of endlessness.

At night, when I am trying to sleep, the rain is a gift; it secludes, gives privacy, and I cannot hear the muted conversation of Lebon and Fortune, rising softly, now falling, as they sit on the steps of their cabin. I have with me my headlamp, my only remaining source of electric light. All others having succumbed to the persistent wet. The only thing that wakes me, so often, throughout the night is the need to pee, that urge brought on by the antimalarials.

One dark, drizzly night, I get up around one in the morning, the third time that evening, feeling the pressure from my bladder. I grope around for my headlamp and, having secured it to my head, leave my tent. Because there is always so much rain and the soil is so sandy, I never need to go far, for the smell of urine is gone almost as soon as it is made. I squat at the edge of my tent platform, holding on to one of the wooden poles that holds the thatched roof on. My head falls slowly forward as I near sleep again. Before I wake and snap it back, my headlamp is sliding forward off my head. It falls off, directly into my stream, and goes out.

I am left in complete darkness. For a few moments I remain there, squatting, considering the situation. I will certainly need the headlamp in the future. Hopefully, it will dry enough to work again. I have no other working light sources—candles aren't useful in the forest, or in a tent. Since there are no poisonous snakes in Madagascar, rooting around in the dark for a urine-soaked headlamp won't be particularly dangerous. So I do just that.

The weather is on my side, and it is hot and dry the next day, and before I leave for the field I rinse the headlamp off, and leave it in the sun to dry. When I come back from the morning's work, the headlamp works, and if anything, I am pleased to have had the distraction. Small things break up the coming and going of dawn, of rain, of new moons and full.

Periodically, a strange cyclic weather pattern emerges, in which clear, cloudless skies in the early morning yield to high clouds and hot, oh-so-humid late mornings and early afternoons. By mid-afternoon, a variation in the cloud pattern acts, rumbling constantly in the distance, moving a single patch of blue around the sky, thunderclouds moving gustily against thick wispy gray. It begins to rain, the thunder increasing in volume, and I feel that this will be a great storm, a storm that, if it were possible, would warrant staying indoors, positioning myself in comfort to hear and watch. But this is not a great storm, it is only a few strong gusts, some brief downpours, and then before the sun has gone very far toward the horizon, the rain has stopped, and the clouds are thinning. The thunder, too, recedes. Alas, I cry, the storm that wasn't. By dinnertime, however, it is brewing again, and as I sit in the little cabin and eat, it begins to rain again, lightly at first. Then, suddenly, the sky opens up, and swallows the island we are on in its entirety, lightning breaking the sky with jagged cuts, thunder by turns simultaneous with the light and almost minutes from it. The winds come again and tear at trees, dead wood falling, the lemurs hanging on, whimpering softly in the rain. And then, sometime deep in the night, calm returns. The rains stop, the winds die, and though the sky does not clear enough to bring moonlight back until very early morning, it is almost as if there was never any storm at all.

But the animals know. When I go out to watch frogs at 5:30 in the morning after such weather, under a bluing sky showing no clouds, they are exuberant, singing to the world. The males call for mates and to taunt their competition, because an important resource has just fallen on them in abundance, equally on all, and it is now up to them to define who can best take advantage of this windfall.

There is a coup in the works, a hostile takeover of the territory of the alpha frog, whom I call Frank. He is a successful frog, if perhaps greedy, defending five of the seven viable wells in the entire bamboo stand. This leaves most of the other males with no chance to reproduce. I have given these principal players names only for ease of reference, because their marks are various and inconsistent, so the only other way to identify them would be "left anterior two scars, right posterior one scar," or "pink-orange-green waistband."

Two other contenders to Frank's throne are making him fight to retain his preeminence. George came in from the east, Caesar from the north, both courting females and looking as if they intended to mate in Frank's defended wells. Frank attacked both of the males, and the five of them scrambled around, jumping on one another and fighting. Whenever one of the females tried to leave, Frank jumped on her and thrust at her in agitated amplexus, until she succumbed and sat still, ready to be trampled in the fray again. In the end, Frank lost everything, as both Caesar and George ended up mating with females in wells that were in Frank's territory. He sat in the middle, mute and still.

But even in defeat, Frank is not vanquished. All is not lost, as Caesar's hard work may have gone only to provide lunch for Frank's child. Previously, I've observed that these tadpoles rely for their nutrition on the eggs of their own species. Sometimes tadpoles get fed by their mothers, and often tadpoles cannibalize eggs not meant for them. The well in which Caesar was mating already had Frank's tadpole in it, so any eggs Caesar pried from a receptive female might promptly get eaten by Frank's offspring. Caesar, the worthy competitor, would have his efforts parasitized after a long battle. While Frank, the male who looks to the horizon, who defends wells at all costs—he may be the one who wins.

Every two and a half weeks, we go into town to replenish our provisions, to get a decent meal, to reset the clock and establish a baseline vigilance again. Once we go specifically to buy a chicken. Jessica and I no longer stay at the Coco Beach, as Clarice allows us to sleep in a room on the second floor of Projet Masoala. It is free, and central, if a step down from the Coco Beach in terms of cleanliness and charm. It has two rank foam mattresses, on which are draped single sheets, and holes in the wall called windows that look out on the streets of Maroantsetra. The mosquitoes are thick, the bathroom foul. But across the dirt road, under the thatched roof of the open-air market, a young Malagasy man sits and strums his guitar, two friends by his side. The music lilts, smooth and light. This scene lingers, seeming to hang in time whenever I come to town, the men no older, the music no less enchanting.

The restaurant that we frequent, now that we are away from the Coco Beach, is across the street from an establishment advertising wine and rum, the prices scrawled on the outside wall. At the table in front, a beautiful, slinky young Malagasy woman is arrayed in tight-fitting clothes, with a fashionable purse, ready to take off at any moment on a scooter parked in front. Also, an odious white man: a dwarf with a serious stoop, no neck, and a Napoléon complex. He chats with a Chinese man, eyes the woman, and speeds off on his scooter, only to return shortly and resume the cycle. We imagine that there is a rental agency in town, one that loans out scooters and lush young women, perhaps both, for the price of one.

This woman who works across the street from us is stunning, bearing curvy hips on long legs, and an angular jaw with pronounced cheekbones. She holds herself with what appears to be confidence and self-admiration. Has she really kept her pride, when she is being bought by grotesque white men for a few dollars? Perhaps she has managed to retain those human emotions, even as she has necessarily turned off the physical responses of her body, sliding only partway into an automated existence.

We leave town quickly, as always, after getting our fill of *poulet au coco* and views of the village prostitute's life, and after acquiring a chicken. When we arrive at Nosy Mangabe with this bird, Lebon and Fortune grow excited, ready for a good meal. But this is an experimental chicken.

Mantella laevigata, my frogs, are brightly colored and toxic. They probably get the building blocks for their poisons from something in their diet, as it dissipates when they're kept in captivity. Lacking both teeth and bad attitudes, they don't use their poisons offensively, only as defense. They are fine examples of aposematic, or warning, coloration, which is also found in coral snakes, monarch butterflies, and many species of caterpillars. Being toxic is very well and good, but if your predator has already eaten you before he realizes you're poisonous, your personal toxicity does you no good at all. Best if you can warn the predator before he takes a bite out of you. Bright coloration is one way to warn predators, but for the unfortunate fact that many potential predators don't see color. Some lizards and snakes do. All birds do. But among mammals, only primates and a few scant others see color.

I want to determine if potential predators are actually discriminating between the aposematically colored *Mantella*, and nontoxic, probably tasty, but cryptic (drab, camouflaged, brown) frogs. And now we have a color-seeing chicken. We also catch a slew of zonosaurs, since we saw one of these lizards eating a *Mantella*. Then we round up three species of frogs: some *Mantella laevigata* (bright and toxic), *Mantella betsileo* (drab and toxic), and *Mantidactylus betsileanus* (drab and edible). Meanwhile, the chicken is becoming acclimated to forest life, where it wanders on a long leash, picking seeds off the forest floor. We use tarps to turn the unused tent platform into a large arena. Using homemade collars and leashes on both the chicken and lizards, we tie them inside the arena, drop in the various species of frogs, and wait for predation to happen.

All the frogs hunker down in one corner of the arena. The chicken takes one flying leap and escapes from its walls. We return her, but she is intent on perfecting that leap. The lizards make repeated run-ups to the slick sides, always falling backward into the arena at the last moment, before attempting their getaway again. Nobody eats anyone else. Lebon and Fortune huddle in the far corner of camp, frightened by our newest game, occasionally shooting wistful glances at the persistently escaping chicken.

Finally, we unleash the zonosaurs, return the frogs to their homes, tear down the arena, and convey the chicken to the still-trembling conservation agents.

"Here," we say, disgusted with the chicken's behavior, "we have no more use for it. Why don't you make a nice broth?" Our experimental forest chicken proves extremely tasty.

The southern summer is ending. On the fall equinox in northeastern Madagascar, the days will soon begin growing imperceptibly shorter. So close to the equator, day length never fluctuates widely. There are not the wide swings of long, lazy summer evenings, warm with light, ceding to short winter days that darken before five. Back home, in the northern temperate zone, the same moment is the spring equinox. On this day the sun passes over the equator to bring more rays, longer days and stronger light, to a northern hemisphere now tilted toward the sun. There the days grow, not shrink, in length. Here, I spin into a mild tropical autumn.

When, as now, it has not rained for almost a week, tadpoles and eggs are drying up, the frogs hide, and none of them are interested in sex or fights. I am left to ponder the shimmering bay, until a change in weather reinvigorates the frogs. It is impossible to tell if I am working too hard, or not hard enough. There is no gauge. There is nothing to compare to, only mounting boredom or panic at moments when I'm not working.

Jessica keeps me on track, keeps me sane. She has begun to hypothesize about what she is seeing, which is wonderful, for two brains are more likely to arrive at truth than one. She goes out to watch frogs even in ridiculous weather, always eager to help carry gear, to talk about what we are seeing. One stormy morning, when I had not gone out because of the weather, and assumed she was still asleep, she bounded into the lab, dripping wet, full of frog stories to recount and interpret. Between her enthusiasm and the various projects I have going now—daily focal observations, taking data on well inhabitants throughout the forest, experiments under way to assess female choice and population limitation—I should be confident that all is well. But how does one know for sure when there is no authority nodding approval from a comfortable chair?

A comfortable chair. This becomes one of my most persistent cravings.

We sit on wooden stools in camp, three-legged pack stools when observing frogs, and rocks and leaf litter in the forest. Our backs become twisted, sore, and tight, from never being able to recline except in sleep. How much I would give for a bit of comfort in this forest paradise.

Four days of solid rain, four days boxed in by a cement bunker while outside it pours down, mocking my scientific intentions. Four days is an eternity. I take a long wet walk, slipping down trails, up hills, across the forest, sighting miserable lemurs huddled in the trees, the flash of a tail as a snake slides out of sight. I reflect on this nonlinear forest world where one hour flows into the next hour and then becomes tomorrow's hour. Again I worry, concerned that time will begin to cycle, and I will relive this day endlessly, never being any closer to an end, or a reprieve.

Finally, I realize that the vigilance is not necessary, that paying heed to passing time or no, it will indeed pass, and will not return. I sit, mindless, waiting for a new today.

14

The New Hotel

As my days turned in upon themselves, the rest of the world spun forward, recklessly. Back in the States, a plan to bring luxury to Maroantsetra had long been in the works, and by April 1997, the plan was complete. Maroantsetra gives access to the natural wonders of the Masoala peninsula and Nosy Mangabe, but this town is not for the fainthearted Westerner. There were two tiny but impossibly cheap pensions in town, sporting flea-ridden straw beds, chickens, and no privacy. There was the Motel Coco Beach, a quiet place, mostly clean but never luxurious, falling slowly into disrepair. And for intrepid researchers, there was a room at Projet Masoala, replete with the noises and smells of town, and a dank mosquito-filled bathroom.

Then the new hotel arrived. The brainchild of a woman who ran what was until very recently the only travel agency giving reliable service to Madagascar from the States, the new hotel was expected to capitalize on a future influx of tourists to the region. Indeed, Monique, the woman behind both the travel agency and the hotel, had begun planning organized tours from the States, thus ensuring that the hotel would receive business. The problem remained, though, that aside from the new hotel, there were essentially no services in the region. Twin Otters still landed only twice a week on the decrepit runway, after bouncing through the air from Tana. There was little to buy or eat in town; nothing for a palate requiring subtle or varied tastes. And the two private motorboats that would take people out to Nosy Mangabe or the Masoala, though not expensive by tourist standards, ran on Third World schedules, with little deference to the expectations of tourists only in the region for two or three days.

In March, before the new hotel officially opened, Jessica's parents came for a visit. Hearing that an important UN diplomat was arriving in town, Monique opened her doors early. The Relais de Masoala was proud to welcome as its first guests Peter and Ros Metcalf. Jessica was excited to see her parents, and though I protested weakly at first, I accompanied the three of them to the new hotel, welcoming a brief respite from the endless days on Nosy Mangabe.

Situated well out of town, thus free from the noises of children and chickens, from the dust and the dogs, the Relais was a picture of serene escapism. On the edge of the bay, it offered views of Nosy Mangabe and of the sporadic flow of spice boats. Coming down the long private drive, itself already rutted with the rain, after leaving the main road, a badly damaged dirt track, one first arrived at the central building. This was a large one-story structure sporting a few large rooms, including a kitchen and dining room, with a tiled open-air patio. Everything gave the impression of utter cleanliness. Plaster walls were a bright white. Nothing was constructed of plant material, though just outside of the Relais property, all of the dwellings were tiny shacks with walls of bamboo and roofs of thatched leaves. At the Relais, the architecture mimicked reliance on native materials, but this was just a facade. Everything was under control.

From the main building, sandy paths emerged, tentaclelike, leading to several bungalows, which were separated by improbable expanses of organized green grass kept in check. Each bungalow had its own lacquered wooden veranda, looking out to the bay and the big blue island. Entering, I found a world of exquisite cleanliness, surfaces entirely of lacquered wood, gauzy white crepe billowing in the slight breeze. Two beds—First World beds—were hung with immaculate white mosquito nets, soft and filmy. The linens were smooth, bright, white. At the windows was hung more dancing white, swaying back and forth with the wind, the rustling of palm leaves barely audible. Those trees meticulously planned and planted, just so, to bear down slightly but not ominously, providing an illusion of tropical life.

The bathroom was the pièce de résistance. After months of life in a tent, I at once noticed three items that stood out: a flush toilet, clean, functional, with a seat, and no standing water on the floor; purest white sinks and counters of—granite, marble?—immaculate, perfectly flat, cool; and, most astounding, a wall of mirrors. I almost did not recognize myself. Living without a mirror for months, you nearly forget the desire to assess yourself daily. Whatever image I had been presenting to Jessica, to the conservation agents, to the naked sailors, and to my frogs was an image that they had to interface with, but not me. I am inside this visage, not responsible for it. Suddenly, I knew, again, my face, my body, from the outside. I was immediately drawn in, then as quickly wished it gone—oh, it was easier without the reflection, without that knowledge. But once attained, it was not returnable and, living with a mirror again for those three days, unable to walk into that austere bathroom without facing it, I came to depend upon it again. Try walking into a public place, or indeed starting any day, without once glancing in a mirror. For me, it was an easy, comfortable habit to lose in the rain forest, a world without human expectation. But when the mirror was again an option, it was impossible to turn down.

Nothing was coarse or loud in the world of the Relais. There was nothing to suggest dirt or grime, or the lives lived just outside the boundaries of this fantasy realm. Those lives were explicitly kept at bay.

The people living those lives were brought in as the help. They looked on in utter bewilderment at this hotel, and though there was a thin veneer of sophisticated luxury on the *stuff* of the hotel, that shell cracked whenever the staff appeared on the scene. Local, rural, Malagasy had no reason to understand what staff were supposed to do, and Monique made it even more difficult by demanding that they do everything as *French* as possible.

On our first night at the Relais, we had drinks on the patio, gazing out to sea, while pretty young Malagasy women dressed up as French maids hovered nervously nearby. We moved on to dinner with no decrease in the nervous energy, as the staff perpetually peered around corners at us, looking fearful. We were not given menus, nor offered a choice of meals. Instead, after a long pause, Ros and Peter were delivered large plates with a handful of sad-looking *pommes frites*, and ungarnished, bunless, cold hamburgers. After about ten minutes, the waitresses arrived again, bearing four large plates of buttered pasta, each with a slab of overdone duck in the middle.

"There's been a mistake," they said. "These are for you." They took the hamburgers and backed away.

"I understand that Monique is arranging for tours of blue-hairs from Southern California to begin arriving soon," said Ros, looking around at the scared would-be French maids peering from around corners, then back to her plate of rumpled food. "I can't imagine everything will be running smoothly enough for sheltered old ladies anytime soon."

Ros, who, with her husband, has lived all over the world and endured all range of indignities, was absolutely right. But she didn't know all that Monique had up her sleeve.

On Easter Sunday, Monique arranged an excursion for us, and we spent the day on a small island inhabited by eighty people. We were told that it was rich with chameleons and lemurs, and that it was partially cultivated around the perimeter—manioc, vanilla, cloves, cinnamon. Monique hoped to make this the next Nosy Mangabe, a place to take *her* tourists, where she could continue the controlled experiment. In truth, there were few trees or animals, and the small community cultivated rice for food, not spices for export. We traveled to this small island in two long canoes, accompanied by an odd assortment of people. Just before lunch, Monique's plan became clear.

A beautifully appointed spread of freshly grilled tuna steaks and skewered shrimp, halved avocados and orchids, was arranged in the center of a large woven mat placed in the sand. Artful but impractical banana-leaf place mats and a centerpiece of tropical fruit completed the stage. Then she placed us all, not boy-girl-boy-girl, but Malagasy-*vazaha*-Malagasy-*vazaha*, around the scene. Sternly advising us not to touch anything, Monique began taking pictures. Jessica and I tried to hide, but she would have none of it. Then it dawned on me that these pictures would be used ever after to sell exactly this spot, and the hotel, to little old tourists from California. The picture would probably be captioned with a brief explanation of who each person was, as she had introduced us all to one another on the boat ride here: "A UN diplomat and his wife and daughter; a local Muslim shop owner; a young researcher working on her Ph.D. on Nosy Mangabe; the most important Air Mad representative in the northeast; a *vazaha* teacher and her husband, from Tana; several relatives of extremely important Malagasy; a charismatic old Malagasy man, and his counterpart, the charismatic old French guy." We had the same number of Malagasy and *vazaha*, and though most of us had never met before, and would not meet again, the image was one of racial and cultural unity and friendship.

I did not want to be used to sell Monique's "adventure tourism" scheme. Her island would be a farce if it were labeled any sort of intact ecosystem, and I believed her motives to be entirely financial, which is often at odds with conservation. Later in the day, on the boat ride back, Monique began talking about the Web page she was setting up for the new hotel and how these photos would be on it. There was nothing to be done.

The following day, when Jessica and I were due to return to Nosy Mangabe, and Ros and Peter were flying back to Tana, we spent a final lazy morning at the Relais. Monique approached Jessica and me, making sure that Ros and Peter were within earshot, and invited us to come stay at the hotel whenever we were in town, gratis. Ros was, as always, the perfect image of grace during this, but suitably sardonic afterward.

Meanwhile, seemingly overnight, all of the employees had donned new duds. The men raking the paths were all sporting baggy yellow overalls; the women, previously made up to look like French maids, now wore orange-and-black miniskirts and had yellow flowers in their hair. These costumes were designed, I expect, to look ethnic. Instead, they all looked like escapees from Oompa-Loompa land in *Willy Wonka and the Chocolate Factory*.

The next time we went into town, Jessica and I accepted Monique's kind offer and stayed at the Relais. I knew that I would not be included in such generosity were it not for Jessica, and she understood that Monique was merely trying to ingratiate herself with Ros and Peter, but we enjoyed the privilege anyway.

We entered our bungalow, expectant, ready for a relaxing day of luxury away from both our tents and town, but as I entered the bathroom, the mirrors held a surprise. Bright white circles had appeared on my shoulders, back, arms, and chest and were creeping up my face. In less than two weeks, I had broken out in spots.

"What *are* these?" I asked Jessica, wondering vaguely if she had noticed them before. She looked surprised when I pointed them out.

"Fungus?" she asked, hazarding a guess.

I thought her guess a good one but decided to try to obtain a professional opinion. The good doctor, who had lectured me on the gentle demeanor of lemurs, would surely know what kind of creeping ick I had. So we headed to town.

On our way, we ran into Armand, one of the naturalist guides who was trying hard to learn English. He was with a loud Austrian tourist, blond and sturdy, who was cultivating an image of one who has seen the world and is mildly bored by it.

"Armand," we called to him, thinking that he, a local who spent a lot of time on Nosy Mangabe, might have encountered the spots before. "Armand, take a look at these. What do you think they are?"

The Austrian, answering for Armand, said that it was from the sun. He, a tourist who had been in Madagascar all of a week, decided that I was foolish to worry; I had merely burned my skin. Armand was in the unfortunate position of being employed by this bombast, so he agreed with whatever proposition was put to him.

"Do you think it could be a fungus?" I asked Armand.

"Oh, yes, probably," he agreed.

"No, just the sun. It blistered and then the skin came off and these white spots were underneath," the Austrian blustered.

"Oh, yes, the sun," agreed Armand. He was going to be of no use to us in the presence of his Austrian, so we excused ourselves to go find the doctor. This sun hypothesis made no sense in light of how much time I had already spent in the sun without spots, how tanned I was, how localized and pain-free the spots were. We left as Armand began explaining the mysterious ways of the aye-aye to the Austrian.

Carrying my two tubes of topical antifungal cream, we strolled to the doctor's house, which also served as his office. He was pleased to see us, welcomed us, and asked us for the news. Malagasy courtesy demands that all conversations begin this way.

"Inona no vaovao?" ("What's the news?")

"Tsy misy vaovao. Inona no vaovao?" ("No news. What's the news with you?")

"Tsy misy vaovao."

Then the conversation proceeds to encompass the news.

After a few moments of small talk, in which he revealed that he had just been in Tana visiting family, he asked after us. This seemed a good opening, so Jessica said, "Well, Erika thinks she's got mushrooms." (In French, the same word is used for any fungus, be it edible mushrooms or mold, and my English-trained brain always hears *mushrooms*.) The good doctor's eyes opened wide and he came around the desk to investigate. Within seconds, he'd come to a decision.

"Yes, definitely mushrooms. It's quite common here, actually." He turned to Jessica, saying, "And you don't have it?"

"No, no," she replied.

"Oh, be careful, then, for just brushing up against her"—he gestured to me—"might transmit it." He again looked me over. "Yes, it's mushrooms, but no big deal. Probably you got it from swimming in the sea."

Marine fungus? I was doubtful.

"Use your antifungals," he advised after investigating my medicine, "and in two weeks you should be better."

Is it just a Western affection to be relieved once you have a name to call your condition, even though no treatment has yet begun and you don't even have any evidence that the diagnosis you've been given is true or good?

We wandered back through town slowly. Severe storms had again hit the Bay of Antongil, and life was not entirely back to normal in Maroant-setra. Several people had drowned when their pirogues capsized, as most fisher people don't know how to swim. We saw a dead cow in the river. But it was market day, and the vendors were out, each selling their one specialty item—charcoal, fish, rice, baguettes. Troops of well-dressed young men strutted through the sandy streets. And one woman was particularly striking, utterly beautiful and coiffed, wearing an aquamarine skirt and the whitest blouse. Her hair was piled elegantly on top of her head. She wore lipstick, and carried a parasol. I had never seen anyone like her in Maroant-setra before. Jessica, who was in the habit of looking down at the ground, from months of watching terrestrial frogs, saw none of this. What she saw was this woman's feet, which turned inward, ninety degrees askew from the normal direction. The woman placed them carefully, slowly, one in front of the other as she walked. The only piece of her clothing that was not immaculate were the flip-flops she'd thrown onto her feet, made more conspicuous by the lack of attention and care. We were intensely curious about her—clearly wealthy by local standards, she had an impediment that would have made life hard and cruel for anyone born with it, especially here. When she disappeared into a shack selling cooking oil, we continued on.

Shortly, we ran into Armand again, this time without his Austrian. We told him the diagnosis for the spots, and he seemed unfazed.

"Where are you going?" he asked, noticing that we were headed out of town, away from Projet Masoala.

"To the Relais," I mumbled, slightly embarrassed to be staying in such luxury.

"Oh, the new hotel!" He beamed. "I think it is a wonderful thing. The other guides and I, we have been talking about it, and we think there will be more tourists now. This means more work for us."

It seemed reasonable to expect such a thing. The guides were organized, and they had agreed on set rates for a half day's, a day's, and a night's work. All of the guides were to request and be paid the identical amount, so that the only competition among them for individual tourists would be based on skill. And with every dollar earned, a set percentage went to a communal pot, which was used for purchases or projects that would benefit the group. I had never expected to find labor organization of the workers and by the workers in northeastern Madagascar. But among the guides, the most knowledgeable of the local people, there had been a careful analysis of what was best for them in the long run. Now they looked forward to the economic boost they hoped the Relais would bring. I only hoped they hadn't overestimated the integrity of the *vazaha* who ran it.

In the still of predawn, I lay struggling with sleep in white linens, under beautifully appointed, though less than effective, gossamer mosquito netting. I woke into a clean white world, where all was shushed and spirited away before it could make a sound that might disturb the still to arrive guests. A boat bearing cloves, moored nearby, scented the cool early morning air. I came out to the steps of the bungalow, pale sky turning faintest blue overhead, still translucent, shades of pink and yellow near the horizon. The sun had not yet risen. Near the beach, a man with a *coupe-coupe*, a long-handled cutting tool with a sickle blade, hacked at dead wood. It was the only sound in this stillness, except for the sounds of dripping from the palm trees, though no rain was falling. The faintest breeze caused the topmost vertical leaf on each palm tree, the cowlick, to sway slightly, without rhythm. The sand paths connecting bungalows and dining room were raked into orderly arrays of parallel lines. Nosy Mangabe loomed large across the bay, just a silhouette now, the sun coming up behind it. Frogs were determining what they would do for the day.

A large red boat bearing metal-encased stores of cloves was performing a slow and arduous about-face near shore. Finally accomplished, it moved out into the bay, thrice blowing its horn to warn hapless fisher people of its approach. It would be their responsibility to get out of its way, pulling up their nets and rowing furiously before being borne down on.

The clove boat disappeared behind a planted cycad, an ancient cone-bearing tree, which obscured this startlingly modern vehicle, incongruous amid the motley assortment of wooden barges, small motorboats, and the myriad pirogues that made up Maroantsetra's typical marine fleet. Out to sea, south through the Bay of Antongil, the many-tiered clove boat departed, a bright behemoth on cool blue water heading toward a cloudless horizon.

Soon it was time for breakfast, which at the Relais de Masoala was a surreal and ridiculous experience. The night before, the guests advised the staff what time they would like breakfast. In the morning, at the appointed time, the guests—just the two of us, we thought—wandered in from our bungalow and sat down at one of the tables on the covered patio. After a few minutes, during which time we felt alone in the universe, a charming but terrified young Malagasy woman appeared, bearing a plate on which sat three white leaf bowls containing three kinds of jam. A spoon rested beside each leaf bowl, delicately poised, ready to fall off. The scared young woman placed the plate of jams squarely in front of Jessica, then walked off resolutely. This task, at least, was finished, one less thing to worry about. Jessica and I looked at each other quizzically; then she pushed the jams toward a more central spot on the table. Shortly, the young woman appeared again, with an identical plate of jams, and placed it, this time with no hesitation at all, squarely in front of me. She left, and Jessica subtly pulled the first plate of jams back in front of her. We decided not to fiddle with anything else until all breakfast accoutrements had been revealed.

A second but equally young and terrified young woman, in identical Oompa-Loompa wear, came toward us, bearing a bowl of sugar with a spoon inside. Hesitating, she finally placed it just to the left of Jessica's plate of jam. A few moments later, she returned with an identical bowl of sugar and placed it just to the left of my plate of jam. Jessica and I looked wide-eyed at each other, but so as not to scare the waitstaff further, we did not laugh. Shortly, plates, each bearing a spoon and a knife, arrived; they were placed just out of our reach, making a symmetrical, if unuseful, array of china on the table. We now had six bowls of jam, two bowls of sugar, two knives, and eight spoons. We resolutely continued to wait.

A third but still equally scared young woman came out, bearing two white pitchers—everything, as always, was white, immaculate, *un*town. These were placed between Jessica and me. I investigated and found one half full of coffee, the other with tea. We did not yet have cups. Two or three minutes later, one of the first women reappeared with a small pitcher of milk. After much confusion, this was placed at the edge of the table, where one of us would be sure to knock it off. Discreetly, when nobody was around to view this act of defiance, we moved it to a more secure location. Shortly thereafter, yet another large white plate with six cubes of butter on it was brought and placed just out of our reach.

A previously unseen woman appeared with saucers and, positioning herself such that she had to reach in front of each of us, in turn, to put them down where she deemed they belonged, made as much of a nuisance of herself as possible. Still, the appearance of saucers was promising. Perhaps cups, for the coffee and tea, would be forthcoming. Or perhaps not. *Peut-être demain.*

One of the women came out bearing a glass of orange juice on yet another plate. She walked around to the left of Jessica and tried to put the glass down, but, finding this rather difficult, given the array of plates and spoons already there, she reached across Jessica to put it at her right. Exactly the same sequence of events then occurred when my orange juice arrived. Having ample sugar and spoons to stir into the typically acid tropical orange juice, we proceeded with this endeavor, as no other ensemble was yet complete—coffee, tea, milk, and sugar without cups, jam and butter without bread. We sipped our orange juice quietly.

One of the slightly less terrified young women came out to us and took a sugar bowl off our table. She moved the remaining sugar bowl to the spot the first one had inhabited, fiddled with it until she felt it was in exactly the right spot, then walked off to greet a newly arrived guest, who had appeared out of thin air. The waitress was still carrying the sugar bowl she had retrieved from our table. We were left with six bowls of jam, and I realized we'd probably gotten his jam, as well. It struck me that the concept of eating anything without a large bowl of rice was so foreign that upon seeing two neatly arranged plates with three bowls of jam on each of them, they must have thought that this was what the *vazaha* ate for breakfast. Not eating rice for breakfast would be the epitome of odd; it couldn't get any stranger.

Having settled down, the other guest had the same charade played out for him, leaving us with our glasses of orange juice and an otherwise-full table, but nothing else to eat or drink. Ten or so minutes passed, and then one of the young women brought out a basket with four small baguettes in it. We beamed at her, then dug in. Meanwhile, the coffee and tea, carefully prepared and brought to us so long ago, were growing cold in their pitchers.

Jessica finished her two baguettes and, hungry for more, asked the woman who came to spirit away the empty basket if we might have more bread. She looked doubtful. After some coercion, she agreed, and walked slowly back to the kitchen, as if wondering how to steel herself for the cook's rage at this request. Almost immediately, a large plate of freshly baked biscuits was brought to our table by the same woman, who announced proudly that our bread was coming shortly.

"Oh, but the bread is not necessary," Jessica said, looking at the biscuits covetously. "You see, we did not know there were biscuits coming." The woman looked unsure, and she walked slowly back to the kitchen, staring at her feet.

About halfway through the plate of biscuits, the majority of jam now gone, orange juice long since finished, cups arrived. Not only cups but also saucers, leaving one wondering what the first delivery of saucers had been about, and what it was we were supposed to do with them now.

Finally, as the last dregs of breakfast were being swallowed, yet another gleaming white plate was borne out by yet another terrified young Malagasy woman. On the plate sat two nicely folded napkins. The plate was placed in the one spot on the table that was not already covered in gleaming white plates, firmly out of our reach. And so ended breakfast at the Relais de Masoala.

15

A Sea of Moral Ambiguity

Back on Nosy Mangabe, we resumed our routine. The boat dropped us on the island a little after eight in the morning, but since the night had been cool and rainy, the frogs were still active. The island was relatively quiet. There was a clove boat moored just offshore, and some sailors investigated me as I sat doing focal watches. Another man, notable for his extremely bright red shorts, wandered into camp in the late afternoon. Down at the fishermen's camp, six-foot-high cubes of cloves sat on shore—small amounts of cloves packed tight into woven nylon bags, then smacked into squareness and piled high. The massive clove cubes were guarded by two wispy men with squirrelly eyes.

We had found raw peanuts in town and had brought them back in excited anticipation of a bit of variety in our island diet. That night, we had a dinner of rice, lentils, and peanuts freshly roasted over a charcoal fire. After Jessica went to bed, I wandered over toward the dock, where I ran into Lebon and Fortune coming out of their cabin, shirts draped over their shoulders. They had the air of men going down to the boat to get stoned, and they hung back in the shadows as I approached. On the dock, I lay watching the stars for a while, then slowly, as if in a dream, got up and walked back to my tent. I intended to immerse myself further in *War and Peace*, and sleep a deep sleep.

My tent platform, a haven, beckoned. My field clothes, now perpetually stinking from mold and sweat, were hanging on a peg attached to the roof thatch, ready to greet me in the morning. But I had, as always, showered in the waterfall before dinner, and now I was wearing the one change of clothes that never left camp, clothes that did not smell. I took off my shoes and climbed into my tent.

In my tent, I kept very little, as early on Lebon and Fortune had warned us that the fishermen might come and steal things. But upon returning from Maroantsetra that morning, I had been in a hurry to get into the forest, so instead of hiding my money in the lab, I had dropped most of my remaining cash into a Ziploc, then placed this inside an opaque green cordura bag, which I left in the tent. Other than that new addition, my tent contained the usual collection of things: a chocolate stash, a pair of pants, some medicines, and the air mattress I slept on.

That night, the green cordura bag had been unzipped, and the Ziploc full of money gone. As always happens in situations that are too awful to comprehend in one blow, I first denied the obvious and sat looking into space, wondering what it was I'd forgotten. I quickly reviewed my actions over the last several days, wondering if I could have misplaced it, but finally I concluded I'd been robbed. This represented the vast majority of my remaining cash, almost seven hundred dollars, a combination of Malagasy francs and U.S. bills. I had our tickets back to Tana and my international plane ticket home, but no other resources. Losing that money would mean real hardship for the remaining five weeks of this field season, as even though expenses are inordinately low in Madagascar, they are not nil.

What to do? Still disbelieving, I considered trying to sleep. I felt sure that any attempt to recover the money would be futile and would alienate innocent people in the process. Finally, though, I decided that this was foolishness, that I would not be able to hold my head high and admit to having been robbed if I did not pursue the issue. There was only one boat near the island; the culprits had to be on it. So I went to Jessica's tent, pausing outside, not knowing if she was asleep.

"Jessica?" I asked, tentative.

"Yes?" came the prompt reply.

"Uh, Jessica, I've been robbed." My voice cracked.

"Oh shit," her disembodied voice said, "I'll be right out."

———

We decided that since Lebon and Fortune were already down at the boat, we would go down there and demand restitution, hopefully with their help. We considered several plans, including the one we preferred most: talking to the captain, allowing him to somehow receive the money anonymously, then having him give it back to us; that way, nobody would pay for his thievery if the money was returned immediately. As we were wandering around camp, somewhat dazed, trying to get our wits together, Lebon and Fortune returned. We explained the situation to them, and they stared at us, silently, in the dark. They were probably stoned from their expedition down to the boat, but rose to the occasion admirably. Jessica asked Lebon what he thought we should do.

"Well," he said, puffing himself up, happy to have his opinion asked, "we must go down there."

So we did. The four of us walked, single file and silent, down the dark path. When we were almost within earshot of the remote camp, Lebon told us that there was a problem.

"The boat is docked out in the bay, and there are no pirogues here to take us to it," he noted.

At the remote camp, the high piles of cloves, silhouetted against the moonlight that glinted on the sea, sweetened the air. The two guardians sat against them, smoking. Lebon and Fortune talked to the guardians for a while; then one of them whistled for a subsidiary boat to come, which would take us to the larger, clove-transporting boat.

"We will go out there and accuse everyone who seems suspicious," Lebon told us, then added conspiratorially, "and we think we have an idea about who it might be. There are a guy and a girl, whom nobody likes. They seem like the types to steal money."

We soon realized that this couple was very young, very middle-class, and out on their first trip together, having paid the captain of the clove boat to take them south to Tamatave. She was the only woman on the entire boat, and they both came from a higher class than the crew. Plenty to make sailors jealous—the perfect scapegoats.

Meanwhile, other pieces of news had floated our way. The clove boat was leaving for Tamatave that night, so we needed to go out now and deal with this. The man in red shorts, whom I'd seen entering camp earlier, became another prime suspect, though I only mentioned him as a possibility. Lebon asked me repeatedly if I could identify Red Shorts man, and I said, no, absolutely not, for I couldn't accuse someone simply because he had made the mistake of walking through my field of vision. As we were standing around at the edge of the forest, waiting for the boat to come get us, Jessica and I began telling stories to fill the time.

"You should be quiet," Lebon advised us, "and get low, as the thief, hearing *vazaha* voices on shore, might panic. Then he will throw the money overboard."

Getting low seemed gratuitous, but we did stop talking. "The other thing," Lebon continued, "is that a woman visited from Maroantsetra today in a pirogue—to visit someone on the boat—and she has already gone home. Maybe she took the money with her then."

I despaired of ever seeing my money again.

Finally, the smaller boat arrived and we waded out to it and clambered aboard, getting thoroughly drenched in the process. It took us to the clove boat, which, still having a full load of cloves aboard, smelled wonderful. It was twenty-five feet long, and bore a vague resemblance to a Chinese junk—the hull was made of wooden planks, and a small wood shack sat perched at the stern. On the top, where we stood, most of the surface was covered in huge flat bags of cloves. The boat was taking those cloves to Tamatave, then returning for the load onshore.

Lebon indicated that Jessica and I should stay out of the fray, so we sat down on a clove-filled mattress and watched the goings-on. Lebon, apparently quite a diplomat, stood on the center of the flat-topped boat, where all the crew had assembled, and explained the situation in Malagasy. A single flashlight illuminated him and the assembly; Jessica and I were outside of its sphere. His address went on for five minutes, then ten, and I found myself lying back on the bed of cloves, listening to the waves against the wooden hull and Lebon's melodic but indecipherable voice, and gazing up at the indigo sky pierced with stars. Sailors furtively stole glances at Jessica and me, more often with wonder than with animosity. I was growing concerned that this would turn ugly, but we never felt in any danger for ourselves, only for other people and their reputations.

Lebon finished his speech, and the captain stood up, holding the flashlight. He shone it into everyone's face in succession, demanding of them what they knew. Everyone who was known to have gone onshore was hauled out, and all whom Lebon and Fortune had seen in camp were given special scrutiny.

The formalities disintegrated for a few moments, as if by fiat, and the captain approached Jessica and me. Speaking in a low French that the sailors most likely did not understand, he gave us his opinion of the situation.

"The cook is your man," he confided, pointing at a little man with skin darker than the rest. "He is new to my boat, and I don't trust him."

We didn't respond to this newest accusation, and the captain sidled off.

"In Tana," Jessica told me after the captain left, "a woman had her purse stolen, and the thief was brought down by so many angry men that he was hospitalized for his wounds." She paused and looked at the cook, who was sitting alone in a dark corner of the boat. "Everyone's enemies are being named in this witch-hunt." She looked gloomy.

As people began to settle down again, it seemed that a plan had been arrived at without consultation of the two *vazaha*. We were to take the four most suspicious people to shore, with their bags, and search them thoroughly. If we found nothing, we would take them to the police the next morning (for which privilege, I would have to pay, with money I no longer had). Meanwhile, the boat would go to Tamatave as scheduled that night.

"But we just want to get the money back," Jessica explained to the group, though most spoke no French. "Please, if the money is returned anonymously, there will be no retribution."

Nobody but the two of us seemed pleased with the option she proposed. We had no choice but to go along with the group plan, and so we reboarded the smaller boat and, with several innocent people, and, at most, one guilty party, went back to shore. We steeled ourselves for an ugly scene.

In the fishermen's camp, the guy and his girl, the cook, and one other sailor emptied out all their worldly belongings for us to stare at. I wanted nothing to do with it. If any of them had stolen the money, it surely wouldn't be in their things now anyway. What were we proving by humiliating them in this way? The girl scowled as she sorted through her underwear for all the men to see, and her boyfriend made a show of demonstrating that he had nothing, absolutely nothing, to hide. As expected, no Ziploc holding 2 million Malagasy francs was revealed.

"If the money is returned," repeated Jessica at my urging, "everything will be fine. We don't need to know who took it, or why. We will be satisfied."

Otherwise, we would, somehow, involve the police the next day. Thinly veiled threats were made by Lebon. We left the four scapegoats and one remaining clove guardian, as the other was leaving with the boat, and walked back to camp.

The walk back was surreal unto itself, as it being a moonlit night, we decided to walk down the beach rather than through the forest. The tide was high, and the moon illuminated the bay. Jessica and I walked in front of the two conservation agents, relieved to be free from the process for the moment, as if the whole incident had been but a dream from which we were now in the process of waking. From behind us, Lebon called our names. We looked back, to find him holding a large nasty-looking fish, long and thin and blue, with many tiny razor-sharp teeth. We stared at him, and asked him the first question that came to mind, though it was also the dumbest.

"Where did you get that?"

"I caught it," he said proudly, and again he had the opportunity to puff himself up. Fortune smiled shyly behind him. He was always the wifely one, supporting Lebon in all his endeavors, never demanding any attention for himself—indeed, shrugging off questions addressed directly to him as if they would cause people to think too much of him and too little of Lebon.

"You caught that?" Though I didn't like to encourage Lebon in his manly pride, this was impressive. The fish, still struggling, looked downright dangerous. Knowing very little about fish, but knowing there were barracuda in the waters here, I thought it might be one.

"Is it a barracuda?" I asked.

"No," Lebon stated, as if he knew what he was talking about, "but perhaps in the same family." I just stared at him. To our sounds of encouragement, Lebon strode into camp, carrying his prize, which he had somehow managed to catch with his bare hands in a pounding surf.

Before going to bed, Lebon told me to check my tent thoroughly for the money. I did, and also rechecked every inch of the lab. Finally, near midnight, I fell into a fitful sleep. It was starting to rain.

In the morning, it was still raining and, anticipating a day of misery with the police, I slept in. At 7:30, I trudged to the lab, found the door closed—which meant that Jessica was still sleeping—and pushed it open. There on the table was the Ziploc full of money, intact. I was stunned. Looking around as if expecting to see gnomes, I picked it up and felt it to make sure it was real. In a daze, I walked over to the cabin, where Lebon and Fortune were just having breakfast, the first of their three daily rice meals. They, too, had slept in after the late night on the clove boat. I showed the money to them, not knowing what to say, and they, too, were flabbergasted. They asked me where I had found it. "No," I replied, "I did not find it. It was returned. It was on the table in the lab this morning."

They looked at me, unsure, seeming not quite to believe me. Having intended to tip each of them with a 25,000 FMG note, I peeled off the bills in front of them. Lebon murmured, "No, no" to my effusive thanks, but I said, "Yes, yes," and then wandered back to the lab. Briefly, I thought the whole debacle might be over.

But what of the five hapless folk down at the remote camp, four of whom were innocent and had been delayed by one thief? I thought it necessary to give them *cadeaux* as well, but I decided to wait until Jessica got up before broaching this subject with the conservation agents.

Sitting in the lab, having put on my field clothes just as it started to rain again, Lebon and Fortune came to me. They seemed to have something on their minds but were not eager to say it. I tried to encourage them, but they stammered and mumbled. I couldn't make any sense of it, except that they wanted to know what to do about the people down at the remote camp.

"Normally," Lebon began, as per usual, turning utterly unique situations into everyday ones, "we would radio for the police this morning and let them take care of the problem. But the money has been found. So shall we radio the police?"

"No, no," I hastily replied. "The money has been returned, so I am happy, content. I do not want to involve the police." They looked at me, silently. "Is there something else you want to say to me?" I asked, truly curious what it was that was so difficult for them to address. After a few more minutes of stop-and-go conversation, we decided that before I went down to my stand, located near the remote camp, Lebon and Fortune would go and tell the people who had been detained that the money had been returned, that the police would not be called, and that all was well. As they began to leave, Jessica emerged from her tent, and I called her over for help with communication.

The stickiest part of the conversation was when I introduced deception into the mix. I suggested that if it was better for these detainees, they could tell the captain of the boat they'd been on that the *vazaha* had found her money and that none of them was implicated. This didn't translate well at all, and Lebon seemed intent on pursuing a witch-hunt. The money had been returned in the night by someone on the island, which rather severely limited the possible culprits, but taking any of those people to the police would have been a cruel thing. I reiterated our position.

Jessica and I headed off in the opposite direction, down trail F, to take plot data. When we returned in the pouring rain, all seven people were in camp—the detainees, the clove guardian, plus Lebon and Fortune. I didn't know what this meant, but I thought perhaps we should go over and address them, thanking them for their cooperation and for returning the money. Jessica said no, the woman was taking a shower, and the men were all sitting around being manly. "Let them be," she said. So we did.

Later, Lebon came over to the lab to talk with us.

"What will become of the people down there?" he asked.

"Do they want to go to Maroantsetra?" I suggested, thinking for some reason that the boat that had left last night would be returning for its cloves sometime soon. No, they didn't want to go to Maroantsetra.

"Where do they want to go?"

"They were going to Tamatave," Lebon replied, "but, normally, you would not pay for their trip on the boat. Perhaps just a small gift for each of them?"

Thankfully, he had brought up the issue of *cadeaux*.

"Yes, yes, of course," I agreed. Jessica and I conferred, thinking that ten thousand each was generous. We rummaged about and found the appropriate number of FMG notes, which I then tried to hand to Lebon.

"No, not yet," Lebon mumbled. "After lunch, we will all go down, and you will present the gifts to them then."

"Always a ceremony in this country," Jessica muttered. I found the idea quaint, if somewhat unnerving. A ceremony to present gifts to people whom we had detained because one of them stole all of my money? Let it happen, just let it happen.

Later, but still before lunch, after the four detainees had left camp, the clove guardian came to the lab to speak with us. He suggested that I give him a gift for his troubles. In fact, he was the only one of the five who had not been troubled by this incident, as it was his job to stay with the cloves anyway. Jessica told him that there would be a ceremony after lunch. He wasn't satisfied. He suggested an additional gift for himself, for his particular efforts in coming to our aid. He reminded us that he had whistled for the boat the previous night. The man was a wolf. And, I concluded then, the thief, as well.

During a lunch of rice and barracudalike fish, Lebon chastised me for keeping valuables in my tent, and I practiced contrition. Afterward, we headed out in the pouring rain again. With Lebon and Fortune in massive green ponchos, we trudged down the flooded path, finally emerging at the remote camp. Much to our surprise and dismay, we found there more than thirty people, and five boats moored right offshore, and the huge tarp-covered pile of cloves. All present stared at us unabashedly.

"Do you suppose they came to see the spectacle?" I asked.

"Oh, quite probably," Jessica responded.

Lebon led the five people from the boat, the two *vazaha*, and Fortune down to the beach, where our old friends the fisher people were just pulling up. The man who sometimes sought me out in the forest to give me mangoes was there. Meeting his eyes, I felt comforted. He and I both knew that this was more our home than the sailors', even if they did outnumber us at the moment.

Jessica and I stood facing the five, and Lebon made a long pronouncement in Malagasy. It quickly became apparent that one of the many boats here was going to Tamatave and would take the three who intended to go there—the cook no longer wanted anything to do with his old boat. It seemed that full fare was required for the passage of the remaining three, and this had become my responsibility. Jessica asked how much, and the captain emerged from the woodwork to say that usually it cost eighty thousand per person but that he would charge us only seventy thousand FMG. I gasped and tried to look faint. Meanwhile, I was trying not to stare at the captain.

The captain. A corpulent man with deep black skin, he wore a tattered white T-shirt that didn't cover his potbelly. The English words printed on it made no sense: AMERICA PARTY DANCE 100% EXCELLENT. Around his neck hung a gold chain with a shark-tooth pendant; on his fingers were chunky gold rings. His lips twisted into something between a sneer and a snarl. An evil-looking man, and clearly a crook.

We quickly came to an impasse. Poor Jessica, always caught in the middle, was trying to make it clear that this was absurd, that it was not our responsibility to pay the exorbitant fee for these people to go to Tamatave, especially when all of this had happened because money had been stolen from us. We were not the culpable ones here. The captain wasn't buying any of it.

"If these kids," as he referred to the guy and his girl, "aren't your responsibility, then they should be sent to the tribunal." He grinned at his own logic.

"No, no," Jessica answered emphatically. "We have gotten our money back, and besides, we don't know who took it, so it is out of the law's hands."

The kids, a sweet young couple, whom I was convinced had had nothing to do with the theft, stood silent throughout, except for one moment of hilarity on the girl's part when she discovered a chameleon behind Lebon. It was a female *Chamaeleo pardalis* engaged in the laborious process of digging a hole for her eggs, and it seemed oblivious of the crowd. By this time, all of the thirty or so onlookers had surrounded our ceremony-turned-charade. Once the Malagasy were alerted to the chameleon's presence, however, we had to move the animal to allay their ancient fears of these slow, harmless, if otherworldly, lizards.

After carrying the chameleon to a hidden spot where she could bury her eggs in peace, we resumed our negotiations. Jessica was struggling to act as both interpreter and mediator in the dispute, and I, not knowing consciously what I was doing, invoked a kind of good cop–bad cop routine. Jessica, who was fluent in French and understood some Malagasy as well, was trying hard to make everyone happy, as was apparent to all. She was eager to please, presenting their proposals to me with swiftness and skill, then mine to them with the same efficacy. Meanwhile, playing like I spoke no French, I listened to what I could understand with an impassive face, then, upon having it translated, regardless of the content, scowled and cursed and said "No!" sharply several times. I stood with my arms crossed and a distant look in my eyes, except when I glanced toward the young couple, when I had to soften.

I suggested several plans of attack to Jessica, including that the corpulent shark-toothed captain and his henchmen be reminded that we were not culpable, that it was we who had been robbed, not the other way around. Still, the most effective strategy I had was to stonewall. I wouldn't respond to Jessica's entreaties with anything but a shrug, waiting to see what kind of response that would produce in any of the other players. I didn't hope for much from the shark-toothed captain, but I thought that perhaps one of the other boats might be going to Tamatave and would propose a more reasonable price. I knew from some details I had managed to pick up during this negotiation that any money we gave Shark Tooth was going straight into his pocket, as there were no more taxes to be paid for additional passengers, and his boat was already going to Tamatave.

Ultimately, the tactic of standing around, looking grim, worked. The captain turned to us and said, "You are students, eh?" A very good sign. Everyone knows students are poor.

"Yes, only poor students, so you see, it is not that we don't want to give you the money; it is that we don't have the money." Half true, anyway. In the long run, I could probably afford to hand over the sum he was demanding, and wouldn't miss the cash much once I returned to a First World economy. But I was living in their economy now, and I felt that I needed the buffer of the relatively small amount of cash I had with me, in case some true emergency struck and we needed to escape or bribe our way out of a nasty situation. Perhaps more to the point, I was stubborn, and I knew I was being taken advantage of. Why did this crook deserve my money? That logic, though, wouldn't get me anywhere with the captain. He needed to believe that we were impoverished *vazaha*, an oxymoron in this land where white skin always signaled relative wealth. The shark-toothed captain rubbed his massive belly and drew his tongue across his lips. He seemed almost contemplative, yet fiendish—the Antibuddha.

"Well, then, propose a price," he offered. Jessica turned to me, not betraying her surprise at this turn of events.

"What's your best offer?" she asked me.

I considered. Was this to be real bargaining, where I lowballed and he highballed and we ended up at the mean? Or was he going to take my offer seriously? Knowing the answer to this would have altered my response significantly, but I could not know. Finally, I settled on offering a total of 100,000 FMG, which was double the *cadeaux* I had earmarked for the detainees. Because of the public way this ceremony had progressed, I would not have the opportunity to offer the young couple or the two detained sailors their *cadeaux* separately, and I did not retain much hope that the captain would share his plunder with them. Jessica was deeply uncomfortable even suggesting this number to the captain, thinking that he would consider it an insult. But when she did so, the captain readily agreed.

"Just remember me next time," he said, with a wink.

"Now, what does that mean?" I asked nobody in particular. "Are we selling our souls here?" I thought the shark-toothed captain would probably appear at some later date, expecting Jessica and me to fan him while feeding him peeled grapes in our underwear. Jessica clarified with Lebon that the 100,000 was everything and that there were to be no more gifts. He assured her that the captain only wished to be remembered by us the next time he was on Nosy Mangabe, recognized with a smile, perhaps a joke.

16

The Dread Rosalie

To work in Madagascar, every *vazaha* researcher must help train a Malagasy student. This enforces a moral obligation to give something back to the country—in this case, an enhancement of the knowledge base. The Wildlife Conservation Society, as the administrators for the protected lands of northeastern Madagascar, had a student they wanted trained, and they were sending her to me. I didn't know if they wanted her to learn particular skills, but I doubted it, as they themselves didn't know what field skills I possessed. Jessica and I had both heard horror stories about researchers who had been stuck with uninterested "trainees" who learned nothing and, worse, required constant supervision, thus preventing the research from getting done. Rosalie Razafindrasoa was due to arrive for the final three weeks of my field season, when I was finishing my experiments and tying up various loose ends. I feared that her presence would compromise my ability to finish my research. Before her arrival, Jessica and I knew nothing of her, except that she was a graduate student at the University of Tana. We worked ourselves up by fabricating atrocious personas for her, such that we could only refer to her as "the dread Rosalie."

At dinner a few nights before Rosalie was due to arrive, we asked the conservation agents when the boat would come next. We were both hoping for mail, and though getting letters to Maroantsetra from the States took several weeks, and many just disappeared into the system, if they did arrive in town, Projet Masoala sent them out to us with the boat. Uncharacteristically, Lebon was in a bad mood.

"I don't know the schedule," he said, glowering into his plate of rice. Then he added, "Probably sometime next week. Fortune and I are leaving to be trained."

"Trained—has this happened before?" Jessica asked.

"Every year, two or three times a year." He seemed proud of this.

"And will someone be coming to take your place here on Nosy Mangabe while you're gone?" we prodded, curious as to our fate.

"Someone from Eaux et Forêts, yes." Ah, a bureaucrat from the Department of Water and Forests come to oversee us.

"And what about Rosalie?" asked Jessica, introducing the Rosalie question for the first time. Lebon looked at her abruptly. "You know Rosalie?"

"No, but we've been told that we must work with her," Jessica offered. "Do you know her?"

"Yes, we know her. She worked here, doing observations on animals."

"Observations? Behavior?" Our interest was piqued.

"Yes, behavior."

Jessica and I looked appreciatively at each other. To our knowledge, nobody had studied in depth the behavior of any Malagasy animals but lemurs before.

"On what kind of animals?"

"Oh, lizards." He paused. "And snakes." Then another pause. "And frogs," he concluded. It wasn't sounding like a behavioral study after all, given the investigation of so many unrelated species. More likely, she had been conducting a survey of the fauna of Nosy Mangabe.

"And she also did conservation," Lebon offered.

He seemed to know a lot about her. So we threw him a softy, a question to which you can never say no, at least not if you're Malagasy.

"*Est-elle gentille?*" Jessica asked. *Is she nice?*

"Oh, no," Lebon responded quickly, "not nice at all."

Jessica and I gaped at him, then laughed uproariously. We had never before heard him disregard the rules of etiquette.

"Why not?" Jessica pursued.

"She captured animals without permits, and when I told her to stop, she wouldn't, so I had to call in the authorities, and we had a trial, here on the island."

"A trial?" This was sounding like a fantasy, or a nightmare, it was hard to tell which.

"Yes, and she was not very nice at all." He was sure of this at least.

"So you're going to be gone when she's here?"

"Yes, both of us," he said, motioning at Fortune.

The faceless Rosalie irritated the usually unflappable conservation agents so much that they were being protected from her very presence. My curiosity was growing.

Lebon and Fortune were whisked away to their training early one morning, and we had received word that Rosalie and an interim conservation agent would arrive within hours. Instead, fog closed in around our little island, and by early afternoon, we were alone in the Universe. Jessica and I were all that remained in a gray, drizzly world, with only the surf softly reminding us of a moon, somewhere. The boat that was supposed to arrive bearing Rosalie failed to materialize. For two days, our little island lay suspended in fog. There was no world outside of us and the forest, and all it contained—frogs, chameleons, kingfishers, ruffed lemurs calling from the summit, a troop of brown lemurs overhead. All was insular. A paradise flycatcher flitted overhead. Lemurs leapt from one tree to the next, greedily grabbing water apples as they ripened. In the night, wild pigs arrived in camp, grunting, digging deep holes everywhere. I hadn't believed before that there were any pigs on the island at all.

Finally, the dread Rosalie arrived. With her came Yves, the boat captain, who was to act as conservation agent until Lebon and Fortune returned. Rosalie, we quickly learned, was thoroughly middle-class. She was an educated twenty-four-year-old from Fianarantsoa, on the *haut plateau*, where her father directed the normal school, the equivalent of an American junior high. She had been training to be a teacher before deciding that biological research was her true passion. Jessica and I remained wary of her, even as she flashed her big smile, busied herself setting up her tent, and quickly made herself available to be taught. It was still utterly unclear to me what I was supposed to train her to do.

"How many species have you collected?" she asked us the day she arrived.

Among the scientifically inclined in Madagascar, it is a common misunderstanding that all biological fieldwork must inherently rely on systematic collections. This consists of finding as many different species within a particular group as possible, then preserving them in alcohol (pickling) so that you or others may later look at them at your leisure. It was not Rosalie's fault that this was all she knew, but it is difficult to overcome the belief that fieldwork and herpetology are comprised exclusively of collecting and pickling. I realized that one service I could offer was to show her a different kind of fieldwork, another line of scientific inquiry, one that did not involve accumulating vast numbers of species. Instead, I would show her how one comes to understand one or a few species very well.

I began by explaining the basics of behavioral fieldwork to Rosalie, including the concept of the focal watch, during which the observer watches just one animal for a period of time that can seem to go on forever. Part of the problem in training someone in this kind of fieldwork is that it is necessarily solitary and silent work—to learn anything of the animals, you must be still for long periods of time and let the patterns of what they do reveal themselves. This is not an activity easily taught—either you have the patience and observational skills to discern pattern or you do not. Unlike the surveys Rosalie was used to, where teams of people moved through the forest catching animals, then reconvened to "key them out" (identify the species), this work did not involve chasing, collecting, or identifying of species. I couldn't include her in my experiments, as they were already well under way; their integrity would have been compromised had I inserted a new researcher into the mix now.

But as I explained the focal watch to her, she became visibly excited, so I suggested that she go out to a bamboo stand we were monitoring and conduct a focal watch of a marked frog to see what she could see. Returning to camp an hour later, she was excited. She had seen a female rebuff an attentive male.

"People should study the behavior of everything," she said.

I had made sure to warn her that this work can at times be quite boring. Watching frogs can feel like a never-ending task. But she took to it. Both Jessica and I were beginning to like and respect her, and thereafter I dropped the moniker: Dread Rosalie no longer, unless she should earn it.

In addition to patience and observational skills, a good behavioral biologist also needs a solid theoretical background. I asked Rosalie what courses she had taken in evolution or ecology, either as an undergrad or as a graduate student. She seemed stumped by the question. In her experience, there were no such courses at the university. Rosalie had never been introduced, formally or informally, to the basics in her own field, and she claimed no knowledge of evolution at all. I decided that this, at least, I could try to teach her.

Because my French wasn't up to the task of giving lectures, I asked Jessica if she would mind translating a short lesson every day. When I asked Rosalie if she would be interested in such a thing, she was exuberant.

For our first lesson, I began not with Darwin, for Rosalie had heard of him, but with the modern synthesis, which was an ambitious and successful attempt by biologists in the 1930s to combine evolutionary theory with new advances in genetics. I then introduced her to the four forces of evolution, all of which have the power to alter gene frequencies in a particular gene pool: mutation (direct genetic change), gene flow (movement of organisms into or out of populations, thus changing the frequencies of genotypes in those populations), genetic drift (differential reproduction of particular genotypes due to chance events), and selection (nonrandom differential reproduction). Previously, Rosalie knew only of mutation.

The next day's lesson was on natural and sexual selection, where my own interests were focused, and Rosalie's enthusiasm and wit turned it into a conversation.

"Selection shapes the forms and sounds and rituals of all organisms," I began. "From the very beginning of humanity's study of evolution, Darwin was talking about two different kinds of selection. Every living organism must survive, which is accomplished through a process he called 'natural selection.' And reproduce—that's sexual selection."

"You have to survive, obviously, but reproduction?" Rosalie asked, seeking clarification.

"Without reproduction, the individual's gene line stops, and won't be represented in future generations," I explained. "Selection can't act on those genes anymore, so they are lost forever."

Rosalie scribbled in her notebook.

"The two selections are often viewed as distinct because they cause animals to do different things," I continued. "Under natural selection, we expect both sexes to attain their goals in similar ways, through acquiring food and shelter. Under sexual selection, though, there is marked sexual dimorphism—the two sexes may accomplish their objectives by different means."

"Like how?" Rosalie asked, looking up from her note taking.

"Think of the peacock," Jessica suggested, invoking a classic example of sexual selection. "Its tail attracts peahens, but it also makes it more difficult for the peacock to escape from predators. That big bright tail makes him more likely to reproduce, but less likely to survive."

Rosalie didn't look convinced. "If the tail isn't good for him, why do females prefer it?" she asked.

She had hit upon a central question in evolutionary biology: How do sexual and natural selection reconcile with each other? I smiled, in part to hide the fact that I had no idea how to answer her question in a way that would satisfy her.

"We really don't know," I admitted. "Females do prefer larger tails on peacocks, and those larger tails do have a survival cost. But why females have that preference has been hotly debated for years, and there's not one good answer that everyone can agree on. We're still trying to work it out."

"Really?" Rosalie asked, stunned to hear that Western science still had some things to learn.

"Really," I confirmed. "But we do know some things. For starters, in most animal species, females are limiting for males."

"What is 'limiting'?" Rosalie asked, pen poised.

"It means there isn't enough of something, like females. In this case, it means that males could reproduce more if there were more females."

"Why is that?" she pursued.

"Because the more matings any given male can get, the higher his chance of successfully reproducing. Increasing the number of matings a female gets, however, doesn't significantly increase her chance of reproducing. From the males' point of view, there aren't enough females to go around," I concluded. Rosalie had stopped writing, and was just looking at me.

"Consider humans, before birth control," Jessica said. "A man who has sex with twenty women in one year has a chance of fathering twenty children; a woman who has sex with twenty men in one year can become pregnant only once."

This made more intuitive sense, and Rosalie nodded and picked up her pen again.

"So," I continued, "the asymmetry between males and females, regarding how many offspring can result from multiple partners, leads to similar asymmetries in behavior and strategy, as well." Rosalie was writing furiously. "Because females are limiting for males, females are likely to choose among potential mates. Males, however—except for human males—are not usually apt to be choosy. Instead, males tend to compete among themselves, to impress females, or to control resources, like food, that females need."

"So," Jessica summarized, "costly traits like the peacock's tail can be maintained in two ways: by female choice or by male-male competition."

"Male-male competition tends to be showy, with big or loud displays," I said. "Male moose butting heads and antlers. Roosters crowing at each other. Male elephant seals viciously attacking other males who come near their harem."

"But what about female choice?" Rosalie asked, intense. This, she wanted to hear more about.

"Female choice is just as, if not more, important than male-male competition. It's not as photogenic, though. That makes it harder to identify. Typically, females choose mates by approaching the one they've identified as their favorite, then making it clear that they're sexually receptive," I said.

"How do females identify their favorites? What do they look for?" asked Rosalie.

"Females may make their choices based on some resource that the male is offering—a food source he defends, or paternal care he will give to his offspring," I explained. "But more frequently, females seem to choose mates on the basis of their genetic quality."

"How does a female recognize genetic quality?" Rosalie asked. "Humans can't assess that, can we?"

I smiled. She was identifying so many important questions. "Genetic quality usually can't be gauged directly," I conceded. "But an animal's genotype—all of its genes—produces its phenotype—all of its observable properties, including size and color."

"So," Jessica explained, "assuming a good correlation between observable, phenotypic, traits, and hidden genes, females can assess a male's genetic quality on the basis of his size or his call. In many frogs, for instance, the most complex calls, or those at a particular frequency, are the most attractive to females."

"Female gladiator frogs choose males on the basis of both their calls and their nest, which the male builds and maintains," I said. "And in some poison-dart frogs, females choose males that defend the best territory, because those territories contain bromeliads, which are necessary for their tadpoles' survival."

"About those poison-dart frogs," Jessica interjected, "why did you stop working on them?"

"What are these frogs? Where did you work on them?" Rosalie asked me, curious.

"They're toxic, brightly colored little frogs, like *Mantella*, but found in

Central and South America," I answered. "I switched partly because the poison-dart frogs were already quite well studied, but also because they provide an example of just one lineage that has evolved many complex behaviors in response to being poisonous, colorful, and diurnal. I knew that if we found similar behavior in the *Mantellas* here in Madagascar, that would provide a wholly new data point, and suggest convergent evolution between the two groups."

"Interesting," Rosalie reflected, nodding to herself. "But are frogs the only animals that have female choice?"

She was chiding us for our preoccupation with the leggy critters. We laughed.

"No, of course not," I said. "Most animals have some sort of mate choice, although a lot of it is difficult to understand. In some bowerbirds, females choose males on the basis of how many blue things they have acquired."

"Blue?" Rosalie asked, unsure she had heard me right.

"Blue," I repeated. "You might wonder, Why blue?"

"Yes," she said, looking at me intently.

"Well, blue things are rare in nature, so presumably more difficult to find than, say, green leaves, at least in the forests where these birds live. It's difficult to acquire and keep blue things, because they're rare, so females can look for males with the most of them as a way to assess their quality."

"But it seems so random," objected Rosalie.

"It does, doesn't it." I agreed. "Again, how these processes get started is still a bit of a mystery. Why do females like blue if it doesn't help them survive or have better offspring?"

"Doesn't one line of thought suggest that males who have the skills to acquire a lot of blue things have sons who can do the same thing?" Jessica asked. "So the sons, like their fathers, will be sexy and attract mates."

Rosalie smiled at this. Like father, like son; if senior is a catch, so, too, will be junior. After a pause, she tried to bring some of the theory she had learned back to real organisms.

"So what do you think *Mantella laevigata* is choosing?" Rosalie asked.

"That's a large part of what I'm hoping to figure out," I said. "A couple of months ago, we didn't know anything about these animals. I think," I said cautiously, "that females are looking primarily for good wells in which to lay their eggs. But they might also be looking for some aspect of male quality I haven't found yet. These males fight a lot, and call, which begs the question: Why? Fighting and calling, like all activity, are energetically costly, so if they weren't adaptive in some way, they would be lost."

"Why is that?" Rosalie asked.

"If fighting was really nonadaptive, the animals that conserve energy by not fighting would thrive more than those that wasted energy with fights. Given that animals do call and fight, then, there must be a reason. Why call? Why fight? That's what I'm trying to figure out," I said. Rosalie seemed satisfied with that answer, but she later approached me with a question that had apparently begun to plague her.

"Why do you have to bring selection, or evolution, into this at all? Why not just study behavior?"

My multipronged answer included a discussion of the importance of a theoretical background to all empirical work, having a framework in which to interpret the pattern you observe.

"Okay, then if you're going to study selection, how do you know what traits to look at?" she asked.

How indeed? She was hitting on all of the land mines that were salient to me, as someone engaged in this research. "That's a large part of defining your research question," I admitted, "and one that we don't talk about much. It helps if you can find an obvious morphological trait, one that the animal uses to interact with its environment in food acquisition, territorial defense, mate getting, or the like. Basically, you need to watch animals for a good long time before you form an idea of what to monitor for the effects of selection."

Rosalie continued to go into the forest, mostly to bamboo stand six, and watch frogs. Early on, her disbelief that this was really what we did led to an interesting mistake. I had suggested that she try to observe a single frog in stand six all afternoon. I was trying to get her used to what it is that students of animal behavior spend most of their time doing. Apparently unable to believe that this was what I was suggesting, she remembered that one of the other things we did in stand six was take data on all of the marked bamboo wells. Every three days, we took data on water level, frog activity, and numbers of eggs, tadpoles, and parasites in each well. On this day, Rosalie walked from well to well in stand six and repeatedly took data on all of them.

Her persistence proved valuable. The following day, Rosalie told me that for three days she had been watching a well in stand six and that it had more eggs in it every day. It had been raining almost constantly. I knew that five days earlier, just before she started her observations, there had been a large, almost fully metamorphosed tadpole in that well. It had left just before she arrived, and now she reported that eggs had been showing up in great numbers ever since. Two things were probably in play. The tadpole had been eating some number of eggs, so those that would have been eaten were now free to develop. More interesting was the possibility that females may be unwilling to deposit in a well with a tadpole. Once the tadpole metamorphosed, though, what had been a very bad place to lay eggs now became a very good place, for it had a demonstrated ability to produce young frogs. Perhaps selection had enabled females to discern the difference, and the newly hospitable well became a place females descended upon to mate in. That Rosalie was a good observer was but one more piece of evidence that she was going to be an excellent scientist.

She was concerned, though, that she wasn't working hard enough to please me. I found it difficult to explain that I had no such expectations, and that if she was learning, that was success. At lunch one day, after she lowered her head for her customary moment of silence, she asked if we would be working the following day. Jessica, well familiar with the schedule, explained what wells we would be taking data from and which experiment we would be working on, before noticing that Rosalie looked a bit shocked.

"You work on Sundays?" she asked in a small, plaintive voice. That stopped Jessica short, as she, like me, has no religion, and we worked every day the weather allowed.

"Yes, we do, but you don't have to," I interjected.

"Are you sure?" Rosalie asked, clearly concerned that I might think her lazy.

"Yes, of course," I assured her.

Later, I was sitting on the dock with my photo equipment, trying to capture some of the magic of the midafternoon light over the bay. I had a camera with a zoom lens mounted on a tripod. Rosalie seemed interested, so I had her look through the viewfinder. I zoomed the lens in and out, then swiveled the camera on the tripod so she could see a variety of views.

"Does it use film?" she asked me.

I didn't know how to answer. I'd been interacting with her as if she had seen cameras and knew of their basic functioning. This was well before digital cameras were common, even in the developed world. Now I wondered if this was the first camera she had ever seen, but I didn't want to make her uncomfortable by asking. By this time, Jessica had joined us on the dock. Rosalie, pointing at my hair, asked Jessica another odd question.

"Is this blond?" she asked, referring to my usually distinctly brown hair, which was now a bit lightened from the months of tropical sun.

Jessica looked unsure for a moment, then responded. "No, definitely not."

Rosalie looked slightly disappointed. "I've only seen blond people in photographs," she said. "I thought Erika might be blond, even though she doesn't look quite like the pictures."

Our lessons continued, and Rosalie persisted in surprising me with her intuition for the material. She kept me on my toes with her questions, asking about the evolutionary origins of the sexes one day, the nature of sex determination the next. Jessica, of course, was a natural at this material, and between the two of them, my brain was tested regularly.

One day, we discussed the impact of ecology on mating systems—what determines if a population of animals is monogamous, say, or polygynous? I based this discussion on a seminal 1977 paper by the biologists Emlen and Oring. One of their main points, revolutionary at the time, is that females choose their level of association with one another based on parameters such as distribution of food resources. The social system that results is largely a matter of how individual males respond to female spacing—if females are clumped in space, a single male can often control multiple females, and polygyny evolves. If females are all fertile at essentially the same moment during a brief mating season, however, polygyny is less likely—one male cannot monopolize all fertile females simultaneously. At the end of my lesson, Rosalie, as usual, had questions.

"Is the implication that as parameters of the environment change, then so, too, might the mating systems of animals that rely on those parameters?"

After hearing a cursory review of their arguments, she had identified the take-home message that I believe Emlen and Oring wanted their readers to intuit. Here was a woman who was a natural at the logic of evolutionary biology, but she would never have the opportunity to truly explore that talent, simply because of where she had been born.

Rosalie continued with her questions, asking about sexual versus asexual organisms, and we discussed hermaphroditic and clonal species. We talked about trees that, when isolated, can self-fertilize if they don't receive another individual's pollen, and about polygynous fish, in which the dominant female turns into the resident male when the male dies.

At the end of all these questions, Rosalie said, "I'm not very good at biology." It was such a ludicrous statement, I had to laugh.

"Oh, that's clearly not true at all."

She shook her head. "No, really I'm not. I never remember the names of things."

What a common and sad misconception this is: That it is the drones, who make the mind-numbing effort to memorize all the terms as soon as they are uttered, who are good at science, whereas the people who think conceptually and creatively, as Rosalie clearly did, are somehow inferior. I had to correct her impression.

"No, it doesn't take much intelligence to memorize things. With time, when you've heard the terms enough, you will remember them. What takes intelligence is to really understand the concepts, and that is what you do so well." She looked down, slightly embarrassed. Then, abruptly, she asked a wholly different sort of question.

"What is homosexuality? Is it a disease, or a choice, or . . . what?"

She was very nervous about this, and it seemed to weigh on her. I wanted to know where her interest came from, so we pursued it. It soon came out that Rosalie had a friend at university who was a lesbian. Rosalie was concerned that the woman's group of friends were at some risk of turning into lesbians, as well. She seemed to have created a schema for homosexuality that involved an infectious agent. I tried to allay those fears, and we discussed some of the scant evidence for genetic bases for homosexuality. We also talked about the fact that people tend to be very adamant about it not being a choice, often saying they have known since they were very young.

"I think with her, it was a choice," Rosalie said.

I shook my head. "When you say that to many homosexuals in the States, they say to you, 'Why would I choose this? Look at all the difficulties it causes me. What are the advantages?'" Then I asked her more about her friend. She said they're not still friends, but only because the other woman moved away. When they first knew each other, during Rosalie's first year at university, her friend wasn't out yet. The concept of coming out was new to Rosalie, which probably contributed to her viewing her friend's apparent transition as a choice. Then Rosalie revealed the most awful part of the story, as if the naïveté of the college girls wasn't sad enough.

Several elders in the community began asking all of this woman's friends, including Rosalie, why she had become a lesbian.

"What happened to her?" they demanded of Rosalie and others. "Why is she doing this now, to herself and to everyone around her? You should tell her to stop." The elders demanded that these students explain why a comrade was homosexual, and they encouraged them to confront her. This only confused Rosalie and her friends more. She understood so little about what any of it meant, even what a lesbian was, that she hadn't been sure what to believe.

After months in the field, the season was drawing to a close. On my last Friday night on Nosy Mangabe, the sky put on another show. Looking at the horizon, I saw large clouds tinged with yellow, wispy flat clouds in pinks and blues, the thinnest line of bright yellow-orange lying atop the thunderheads to the north. Surrounded by all of this beauty, I was itching to get out of there. I wanted to be home, where I wouldn't have to face my moldy tent or cuts that refused to heal or naked sailors in the forest.

But even now, I was discovering fascinating new elements in my system. I had established artificial wells in the forest to assess whether wells were limiting for my frogs. A limiting factor is any critical resource that exists at a suboptimal level, thus slowing the growth of either individuals or populations. If, in this forest, the number of frogs was restricted by the number of wells, then wells were limiting for these frogs.

In my artificial wells, we found several unexpected species moving in, including a tiny little frog called *Anodonthyla boulengeri*. After a male and female *Anodonthyla* mated inside a well, almost filling the space with their eggs, the father remained with the eggs until they hatched, then stayed with the tadpoles until they metamorphosed. On several occasions, I saw attending fathers somersault around the eggs in their wells, cycling over and around the eggs. I suspect this served to aerate the water and keep the eggs breathing.

Back in camp, though, relationships were getting more difficult. Lebon and Fortune had returned, and the animosity between them and Rosalie was clear. I didn't want to take sides, even though I had made a friend of Rosalie in just a few weeks, while the conservation agents had remained enigmas for months.

It was my birthday a few days before we were due to leave, a fact I made little of, but one that Jessica and Rosalie took seriously. When I got up that morning, I found a carved wooden dolphin and a poem on the table in the lab. Jessica had whittled the dolphin while doing focal watches, and written the poem about our life on Nosy Mangabe, as personal a reflection of those months as I could imagine. Every nuance was perfect. Soon our time together would be over, and I had pangs of regret about leaving, even though I was glad to be going home. Then, as I returned from brushing my teeth at the stream, Rosalie stopped me in my tracks.

"Happy birthday!" she announced, and proceeded to kiss me in the Malagasy (French) way—on both cheeks. She had a small speech prepared about how she hoped very much that I would be successful and happy in finishing my doctorate. Then she presented me with a music tape of a band from Fianar, her hometown. I was touched, and a bit embarrassed, by her generosity.

Later, Rosalie took it upon herself to make me a birthday treat. Having but one egg, some flour, sugar and oil, and a wood fire, she managed to make things closely resembling doughnut holes. They were extraordinarily delicious, although Lebon made a point of denigrating them, and Jessica and I both made ourselves slightly ill gorging ourselves after months of rice and fish broth.

As we made preparations to leave over the next few days, it became clear that Rosalie would shortly be seeing her *sipa*, the Malagasy word she used to describe her longtime mate but not husband. She never used his name, just called him her *sipa*. What a wonderful word, I thought, and we don't have an equivalent in English. *Boyfriend* sounds juvenile, and underrepresents the seriousness of the commitment after a while. *Partner* is more often used to describe a romantic interest of the same sex. *Significant other*—too clinical.

"How do you say *sipa* in English?" Rosalie asked me.

"I don't think we have such a word in English." She was dubious, then surprised, once she realized that I hadn't simply misunderstood her question.

"Why not?" Her simple questions were often the hardest.

"I think some concepts are best described in particular languages, and the attempts of other languages to describe the same thing are never quite as good. *Sipa* is a good example of a Malagasy word that is perfect, sounds beautiful, a word the whole world could use comfortably. Also, *tsangatsangana*—a walk, a stroll, a little hike." Rosalie laughed. She couldn't believe that I thought there were words in Malagasy that were better than the alternatives in other languages. But Malagasy, in particular, often uses on-omatopoeia to convey meaning—*tsangatsangana* almost sounds like a slow lope, an easy gait.

"How about *bon appétit?*" she began, rifling through her language stores now.

"Yes!" I agreed. She was always a quick study. So many times people in Madagascar had asked me how you say *bon appétit* in English. At first, I searched for words, but now I know: it's *bon appétit*.

"Also *bon voyage*," she continued.

"Another one—in Spanish: *macho*. Swaggering men trying to prove how manly they are. No other language I know has as good a word." She wasn't familiar with *macho*, but she later used it to describe Lebon as he chopped wood. Now she owned the word, just as she owned so many biological concepts previously unknown to her.

The day before we left Nosy Mangabe, I took pictures of Lebon and Fortune to send back to them, and they proved to be complete hams in front of a camera. Lebon posed with a book, looking pensive. Fortune giggled under his flowered hat. They broke out equipment I had never before seen—a transect tape, some flagging—climbed a boulder with it, and pretended to be hard at work. After the photo shoot, I gave them a few things I would not be taking home with me, for which they might have some use, but I also offered them real gifts.

"When I come back, next year, or the year after, is there anything you would like me to bring for you?" Lebon considered this seriously for a while, but Fortune knew immediately. He pointed to my hiking boots.

"Shoes, like yours." Fortune didn't have anything but flip-flops, so we measured his feet, and I told him I would get him boots. Lebon, always the showman, wanted a couple of nice shirts, "ones with collars."

Finally, we left Nosy Mangabe, but it would be a long time yet before I saw home. That first night off the island, I took Rosalie, Jessica, and the good doctor, who turned out to be an old friend of Rosalie's, out to dinner at the Coco Beach. We talked of birth control and AIDS, and the good doctor admitted that though the Malagasy government denies the existence of AIDS in their country, it is there. He sees it, even in the small hamlet of Maroantsetra, especially in the women rented by infrequent white tourists. We talked of the children who result from these unions, and Rosalie and the doctor were surprised to hear that single women have babies in the

States, too. Rosalie and Jessica both insisted on flattering me with compliments, which embarrassed me, but I also felt proud that I had impressed on these two young women what you can do if you try. They both had such enormous potential as biologists, which Jessica would surely realize, but Rosalie might not, simply because of where she was born. She was aware of this injustice but felt powerless to combat it. It is simply true that it is easier to "do what you want," as she put it, if you happen to be born American than if you are born Malagasy.

17

Descending to Reality

The next morning, Jessica and I rose at 5:30. Air Mad sent a vehicle to take us to the airport, and we spent an hour or so driving around town, occasionally picking up an additional passenger, mostly stopping so that the driver could chat with passing acquaintances and argue over the price of peanuts. Finally, we were deposited at the Maroantsetra airport, the single room that still had no doors. There were flights to and from Maroantsetra twice a week, and when the tiny Twin Otter planes landed and shortly took off again, people from the surrounding villages came out to watch. Air travel is rare throughout Madagascar—so rare, in fact, that in the south, where the graves of important men are usually decorated with zebu horns, a patriarch who had once taken a flight has a large replica of a plane atop his grave. Even before the plane arrived, there was an air of expectation and activity in the airport on flight days, so that though there were at most twenty passengers flying on any given day, there was bustle and excitement at the decrepit airport.

When we arrived, a mass of people swarmed around the large scale. There was no one behind the counter. We dumped our bags in a pile as close to the scale as possible, then arranged our tickets in a decorative fan shape on the counter next to the others, similarly prepared. Sitting down in the plastic chairs, which were surprisingly reminiscent of those in airports in the midwestern United States, we began to wait.

On this day, the other travelers included a couple of would-be courtesans. A bit past their prime, they were dressed in black lace and external red bras, coiffed and made up and bedecked in gold necklaces and thick gold bracelets. But they were a little older and heavier than most of the women you see consorting with tourists and expats. There were two young Frenchmen we hadn't seen before, probably short-term tourists. They were the only other *vazaha*. Several people carried large baskets, sewn up at the top so as not to spill their precious contents. Although it is a very select group of people who travel by air in Madagascar, it's still not unusual to get on a plane and see sewn-up baskets being used as luggage.

One man had a massive white block that was crumbling at the edges, probably salt. Another carried gnarled pieces of driftwood. A third was lugging an immense cardboard box filled with coral. Most of the women over forty—many of whom were not flying, just observing—wore two straw hats at the same time, stacked so neatly one on top of each other that you had to look very closely to perceive that there were in fact two hats there. Some wore five or six—an efficient, if peculiar, way to transport them.

A well-dressed gray-haired man, who, by his bearing, conveyed his supremacy in the Maroantsetra airport's social and political hierarchy, began making the rounds. He bore bad news. This was not unexpected, given that our plane, which was supposed to leave in less than an hour, was not yet in evidence.

"I am quite sorry, but the plane will not arrive until eleven-twenty this morning." He apologized. The level of precision made a further mockery of Air Mad—he might as well have said it would arrive at 11:23, for in the four hours between now and then, anything could happen. "Would you like to return to town?" he asked. The Frenchmen and slinky young women, as well as the owners of the various marine art, were all going back to town. We chose to avoid dragging our heavy equipment through those dusty streets one more time, staying instead at the airport, which was at the end of a ruined dirt road, far removed from the relative bustle of Maroantsetra.

To occupy herself, Jessica took a walk. She reported later that she had been wandering down a footpath near a small village, where she had been surprised to hear an old woman, standing behind a rickety fence, speaking in French to her.

"The raging bull coming up behind you is in some danger of goring you," the woman advised. Jumping nimbly aside, Jessica thanked the old crone, then paused to watch the agitated antics of this beast as it pulled the man who was trying to calm it. Softly, a new voice arose at her side.

"*Bonjour, vazaha,*" it said. Jessica pretended not to have heard this too-typical introduction. The man was persistent, though, and finally she muttered, "*Bonjour*" in reply. He took this as encouragement, and embarked on the story of the bull's fate.

"This bull will be sacrificed today for a celebration of the turning of the bones of the ancestors." This got Jessica's attention. One of the most renowned and fascinating cultural traditions of many of the Malagasy tribes is the ritual *retournement*. In the animist tradition of ancestor worship, the bodies of the ancestors are dug up every few years, dressed in new shrouds, and, if they are fully decomposed, moved from the body boxes they were buried in to smaller stone bone boxes. Even after the remains are in bone boxes, the tradition continues, and the ancestors receive new shrouds on a regular basis. While the ancestors are above ground, the current village elders speak to them, recounting the events of the previous years.

"Isn't this the wrong season for the turning of the bones?" Jessica asked.

"No, no, this is the right time, for it is in accordance with the rice harvest." He embarked on a detailed, hard-to-follow explanation of the importance of the rice and the ancestors being in harmony. Then he added, "You may come to the ceremony, if you would like, and participate with me and my family. If you bring a camera, that would be wonderful, for we have never had photographs before." Enthusiastically, Jessica told him that she had a friend with a camera and that we would return shortly.

Having hurriedly gathered my camera equipment after Jessica had told me about her interaction, I returned with her to the site where the frenzied bull had almost taken her out. We found nobody. I wondered briefly if we hadn't been conned, realizing that right now our bags were sitting unguarded in the middle of the mostly empty airport, where they could easily be taken. Despite my earlier experience with the clove boat's guardian, I generally had little suspicion of the Malagasy, finding them far less likely to steal than their need might predict. I didn't want that impression to change.

We turned and walked down a side road, and shortly came upon a crowd. Several women wearing bright, matching *lambdas*, the traditional fabric skirt wrap, were disappearing behind some thatched-roof houses off to the right. We stood around being *vazaha* for a few moments, looking vaguely confused, and the trick worked. Out came Knick (pronounced *Kuh-nick*), the man Jessica had met earlier. He was, it seemed, the master of ceremonies for this *retournement*, which was now beginning its second day. The villagers were preparing the zebu for sacrifice, and waiting to listen to the speeches of the elders.

Knick led us in through the crowd and sat us down in front of several rows of men and children. The women had all dispersed. Repeatedly, we suggested that perhaps this wasn't the place for photographs, saying that we would be honored to sit and watch only, but he insisted, and it became clear that he wanted documentation of the event. I would send or bring copies of these pictures back, and this tiny village would have a permanent record of their sacred ritual.

We were in an open area with no trees, the village buildings of thatch and bamboo encircling us. In front of us lay the zebu, feet tethered, lying on its side, groaning intermittently. It frequently raised its head enough to look truly menacing, causing the crowd to recoil. In front of the zebu stood a low tray of banana leaves, on which were three glasses of pale liquid, the ceremonial rum. Also, a saucer with clear liquid in it, the purpose of which remained unclear, though Knick explained most aspects of the goings-on. An extremely dark young man in a brimless straw hat scurried to and fro, adjusting the angle of this banana leaf, filling that glass just slightly more, looking askance at the zebu when he had to walk near it. He didn't interact with the other participants, and I asked Knick about him.

"To do the actual killing, a Comoran man is needed. Otherwise, the ancestors are displeased." He nodded in the man's direction. "That is the Comoran."

So bloodletting was performed by outsiders. How they had found a Comoran, a native of the Comoro Islands to the northwest of Madagascar, I had no idea.

It came time for the elders to address the ancestors and tell them how the villagers had spent the time since last they were disinterred. The crowd, perhaps a hundred people, circled around the zebu, and a distinguished gray-haired man stood up. His hat in his hands, he spoke clearly and, it seemed, eloquently, though I understood none of the words. Sometimes he drew laughs from the crowd, more rarely brief applause, and as he finished, it was clear he had elicited great joy. Then a second man rose, tall and gaunt. The sun was rising in the sky and shone fiercely down on him. A villager raised a palm leaf over the man's head to shield him. This man had the air of a stand-up comic. He delivered lines deadpan, producing great laughter from the crowd. The barest hint of a smile played at the corners of his mouth, as if he had rehearsed for weeks and was finally getting to orate.

When the elders were finished, a woman poured rum over the zebu, then slapped its stomach. Villagers gathered around and held the zebu's tail in their hands.

"What is the significance of this?" I asked Knick, curious.

"It is important for the villagers to hold the zebu's tail in their hands," he answered, leaving any further explanation to my imagination. After a few more iterations of pouring rum and holding parts of the zebu, the animal was dragged ten feet away by several men. A little girl with a pale, torn dress walked by, but she was indifferent to the proceedings. Bracing himself out of reach of the zebu's sharp horns, the Comoran slit the animal's throat while additional men tried to hold it still. The blood was collected in a small vat.

As the sacrifice was happening off to one side, women began dancing, all color and swirl. They danced in a long, bending line, following one another. Soon they were singing as well and clapping their hands as percussion. The sacrifice of the zebu marked the end of the solemn portion of this long ceremony, and the beginning of the celebration. The rum, previously reserved for small ritual-laden sips only, began to flow freely. Banana leaves were ornately folded into cups with long, curved sides, as the few available glasses had apparently been reserved for the ancestors. The living drank from banana leaves. Jessica and I were handed leaves containing some of the potent liquid, and it was made clear that we must drink, or risk displeasing the ancestors. One old man, who had apparently been nipping at the rum before the appointed time, danced among the women.

After the Comoran killed the zebu, he beheaded and eviscerated it. A platform of banana leaves was laid out where the speeches had taken place, and proper glasses of rum were placed at the corners for the dead to imbibe. A middle-aged man and woman, who, Knick said, had been specially chosen for the task, were seated on low wooden stools in front of the display. They were handed umbrellas to shield themselves from the hot sun. Slowly, piece by piece, the head and organs of the zebu were brought and placed on the leaves in front of them.

"These two people must keep watch over the zebu's organs," Knick informed us, "and if they protect these parts from evil spirits until midnight tonight, then we are free to feast on the meat." I glanced in the direction of the organ guardians. The man was eyeing the ritual rum covetously, while the woman shooed away a curious chicken with a palm frond. "Please, if you can, stay with us for our feast." Knick was a gracious host, but we had been there for two hours, and we had a plane to catch. I felt sure that both evil spirits and chickens would be kept at bay, and the feast would commence as planned. Until then, dancing and drinking would be the order of the day.

"Before we leave, Knick, might I take a picture with just you and your family?" I asked. He had been so generous, encouraging photos of particular people, but I had not seen him with his own family. He grinned widely.

"Yes, please, I would like that. Wait here—I will go get them."

We stood in the shade of a hut, watching the women dance, their *lambdas* blinding as they twirled. Several children stood near us, eyeing us curiously. Folded banana leaves were being passed among the men, who now lounged on the ground, occasionally tipping a leaf too far, spilling its precious contents.

Knick reappeared, and he arranged his family in front of the organ display. He had gathered more than thirty people. I had forgotten that in Madagascar *family* refers to a more inclusive yet more close-knit unit than it does in America. These were not distant cousins he saw once a year, but the people he lived with and among, on whom he relied for friendship, labor, and advice, and who relied on him.

Returning to the airport after the *retournement*, we unwittingly played the pied piper, a long line of festive children in tow. I felt a need to record some observations about the *retournement*, so I opened my computer, to the delight of the amassed youngsters. They crowded around so closely—mine was the only computer for hundreds of miles, and surely the first they had seen—that I wished I'd had tricks or games to show them. But to reduce the risk of incompatibilities and crashes in the field, I had stripped the thing of most of its obvious pleasures. But even a spreadsheet was scintillating to these children, and when I simply typed text, one little boy actually sounded out some of the words he saw. His literacy was stunning, given the poverty he came from, the lack of schools or books, and the fact that I was writing in a language that was, at best, his third, after Malagasy and French.

Finally, it was time to be processed for our flight, so we reunited ourselves with the bags we had dropped by the scale, waiting to be called up to the counter. The sequence in which we were called seemed to follow an algorithm that included the order in which the tickets had been laid down, as well as how pleasingly they had been fanned out into their decorative display. Shortly, it became clear that the scale was not just for our bags but also for us, the plane being so small that everything going on board had to be weighed. We were more massive than any of the Malagasy being weighed, and gasps of incredulity could be heard as Jessica and then I clambered up on the platform and the needle flew upward. Apparently, we were light enough, though, for soon we were on our way.

We were not going directly to Tana, but to Antalaha, a town on the east coast of the Masoala peninsula. Antalaha is unlike other Malagasy towns in that a few of its residents have become extremely wealthy from exporting vanilla, although most of the townspeople are impoverished. While even middle-class Malagasy, such as Rosalie, could never conceive of being able to afford a plane ticket out of Madagascar, some of the residents of Antalaha have private jets, in which they fly to Paris for weekend shopping sprees.

The Wildlife Conservation Society had its regional headquarters in Antalaha, and I was to meet Matthew Hatchwell, the head of WCS in Madagascar, with whom I had been in much communication. I was also due to give a short presentation on my research to the WCS staff. We were welcomed into the Hatchwells' home, which had once been a building used for processing vanilla, and there spent a truly enjoyable, if odd, few days. Just days before, I had been living in the rain forest, sustained on rice and fish broth, washing myself and my clothes in a waterfall and sleeping in a molding tent. Now, suddenly, after a brief foray into a traditional Malagasy ceremony, I was having tea with Matthew and his wife, playing with their inquisitive towheaded son, sleeping in a real bed, and eating chocolate chip cookies. I didn't know how to grapple with so many changes this quickly. Wistfulness for the calm of Nosy Mangabe hit me for brief spells, while I also remained wistful for the First World, although our time with the Hatchwells offered a good approximation of the comforts I craved.

We flew back to Tana, where Jessica was reunited with her parents and I stayed in their house for the last time. Oasis though their house was, it was in Tana, and the ubiquitous fumes, beggars, and curbside food stalls seething with naked children and rats were still in evidence when we moved through the city. Ros had been doing my homework for me, and she informed me when we arrived that Air Mad had changed its schedule. My flight to Paris was leaving thirty-two hours *earlier* than my ticket indicated, and it was overbooked. As irritating as this glitch was, the Metcalfs, true to form, made everything comfortable during my last day in Madagascar. Jessica and Peter took me on a walk to a hillside outside the city, on which an old tomb lay partially obscured by weeds. What lay before me on this breezy, gorgeous afternoon—clouds high above the hills, rice paddies far below—would be my last image of the vastness of Madagascar, until I returned again.

As I waited in Ivato airport, the international gateway out of Madagascar, I realized that the day I had fantasized about for so long had finally arrived. No more naked sailors. No more sitting on my blue three-legged stool waiting for frogs to act. No more clumped white rice and questionable fish heads.

At last, the plane was ready. As I boarded, I felt a different kind of gaze fall upon me. This was not the "There's a *vazaha* in our midst" look I had been receiving all of these months. Now I was back in the land of white people, for even though this was an Air Mad flight out of Madagascar, only the wealthiest Malagasy ever fly out of their country, and most of the passengers were white businessmen, male expats, and tourists. What I felt now was their gaze, made curious by circumstance. Many of these men who had been in Madagascar had taken advantage of the slinky Malagasy misses for rent, but few considered such women wife material, although such women specifically seek marriage. These men were returning to their country, to women of their same class and education, to resume their acknowledged relationships. During their foray into a reversal of mate choice and sexual politics in Madagascar, these men had seen few if any white women. White people are rare in Madagascar; white women are but a tiny fraction of that already-small minority. I had been free of mirrors for many months. Now I realized I had also been almost entirely free of the male gaze.

Our nighttime departure from Tana meant that almost as soon as we took off, Madagascar had disappeared into memory. Only around Tana were there any lights at all. Even where they existed, they were sparse, separated by rice paddies, dimmed by frequent power outages. I slept fitfully, my rest interrupted by touchdowns in Nairobi, Munich, and finally Paris. I was heading to London, where my parents were living at the time. I knew I would be surrounded with the trappings of the First World, which I craved, but I was not prepared for my reaction to being back in a land where I spoke the language; where commerce was constant, fast, and efficient; where nature was relegated to parks; where there were so many things available to buy, and eat. Walking down a busy London street, my mother lost me to reverie. Forcing her way back through the crowds, she found me gazing at the window display of a Baby Gap.

"Our children are so pampered," I began, then looked around at what they grow up expecting—lots of goods, but also heavy doses of anonymity, stress, and urban sprawl. "They have all these material things. But few of them have a family to compare with Knick's." We are nuclear, tight in upon ourselves. Looking out at the world from our small cocoons, we have a narrow vantage point that offers little insight into the breadth of possibilities for human life.

Sensing my tension at being dropped into the big city after so much time in the rain forest, my parents took me to the countryside. We visited lovely English ruins, which sat in rolling fields covered in wildflowers. Walking up the spiral stone staircase in the ruin of a castle once lived in by royalty, I realized that I had been in ruins like this as a child, and that it had not occurred to me then to imagine what it implied about people's lives. It was a ruin, a historical artifact, not something to be interpolated into a modern understanding of human life. But now, the comparison seemed obvious. The very richest and most pampered English of the four-teenth and fifteenth centuries lived surrounded by cold, dark, thick stone walls. Their beds were made of straw. The kitchen staff kept fires burning always, because they were so hard to start. Filth crept in everywhere, and even many royals made no attempt to stop it. Bathing was an occasional occurrence. The rich had more trees and woodland animals around them than the average middle-class person from any country today. And already the poor had even less, living in urban pits with few laws or public health policies to protect them.

How utterly foreign I was among the Malagasy, just half a planet away. I could barely comprehend their expectations for their lives, as there were so few parallels with mine. But move me back in time, just five hundred years in time, and I was equally at a loss. Hearing about the lives of the fifteenth-century British royals, or of famines in North Korea, plague in Africa, abject poverty in America—this is not sufficient to evoke empathy. One must truly see people living in ways other than one's own. Better yet, one must live differently for a while, with other people's rules and history.

PART 3

18

A New Launch

A year and a half later, Madagascar beckoned again. I had not gone back the following rainy season, choosing instead to live in Panama with Bret for a few months, where he was conducting his own dissertation research on tent-making bats. At the time, before the United States had turned the canal back to Panama, the country was an odd mix of First World and Third World. Most of the trappings of the United States were for sale. We lived on a small island in the middle of the Panama Canal, at a research institute run by the Smithsonian. This island bore almost no resemblance to the small island I had lived on when in Madagascar. Here, researchers from all over the world gathered to study ecology and evolution, and the facilities reflected the prominence of this island in tropical biology research. Air-conditioned labs, modern sleeping quarters and bathrooms, a cafeteria open all night, public computers with an E-mail server, and frequent, reliable boat service to the mainland left one with the impression of a well-oiled machine. Nothing in Madagascar had ever evoked such an image for me. In Jamaica, once, a friend of Bret's, upon being discovered greasing his bike chain with coconut oil, advised Bret that "the wrong lubricant is better than no lubricant." Such practical wisdom serves well those people with limited access to resources—a valuable asset in Jamaica or Panama. But in

Madagascar, there is rarely a choice. What do you do when there's no lubricant at all?

Bret returned from Panama after eighteen months, just in time for us to get married, celebrate our nuptials in Turkey, then spend a few months in the United States before heading back to Madagascar. I was enjoying the comforts of being home with our cats and our things, but I knew I always appreciated them even more after I had tweaked my reality by living in a different world for a while. I began the months of paperwork, procuring equipment, making travel arrangements, and packing before finally going to the field. As I assessed what I had learned during my previous season, and what I hoped to discover on this one, I realized I would have a much better chance if I could find someone like Jessica to work with me. Bret would be there and could help with data collection for one of my experiments, but his role would be mostly as intellectual and emotional support, for he would be writing his dissertation while we were there. I needed a field assistant.

Enter Glenn. At the time, Glenn was an undergraduate hanger-on in the Herpetology Division of the Museum of Zoology, where I was based at the University of Michigan. Glenn had been one of those children who was always bringing home snakes, lizards, and frogs that he had captured. As a college student, he had collected several more herps, which he was living with. (By contrast, I had only a couple of frogs at home.) Back then, he was vying for the title of world's most obscure herpetologist. Since then, he's obtained the lowly rank of graduate student. He jumped at the opportunity to go to Madagascar. He had the time, I found the money, and we were set.

As soon as we landed in Tana, I was Erika again. The officials who occupied various booths at the airport were still there, dressed in military uniforms, receiving money, looking at passports, handing out forms, and conducting customs checks. Something had clicked in me, though, and now I had an easier time accepting the inconsistencies and swallowing the indignities dished out by these uniformed men who wielded only enough power to annoy unsuspecting *vazaha*.

We went to our hotel, a clean, inexpensive affair near the zoo in the center of Tana. Arriving well past midnight, there was only one room free, so the three of us packed ourselves and all of our baggage into that room and fell into exhausted sleep. We all woke several times during the night, though, as the tourists in the adjacent room engaged in loud carousing with prostitutes. In the morning, when I went to use the communal bathroom, I found it occupied by them, as well. Bleary-eyed from jet lag and the tasks that loomed before I could extricate us from Tana, I went out to the balcony. I was reacquainting myself with the bustle of morning commerce on the street below, and the relative calm of the rice paddies just a few yards farther away, when one of the tourists spilled out of his room.

"Oh, we have company!" the young Frenchman, cigarette in hand, exclaimed in French. "I do hope we weren't too loud last night." His hand swept over the evidence of the night's debauchery—an empty bottle of liquor lying on its side, a pair of pants flung over a chair. I just looked at him. I had no interest in pretending to be this man's ally. He assumed that we were on the same side because of the color of our skin; I assumed we weren't, because of the broken look of the woman in the doorway.

That morning we began the arduous task of getting research permits, visa extensions, and plane tickets, and making air freight arrangements, all of which needed to be done before we could leave Tana. Benjamin Andria-mihaja, who had helped me with logistics on earlier trips, was a godsend. The organization he ran was now independent. It had changed its acronym from ICTE to MICET, now including a reference to Madagascar in its name, and was largely devoted to helping researchers such as myself wade through the morass of rules and requirements necessary to work in Madagascar. I had brought Benjamin a small gift, a Leatherman-type tool, but I had qualms about giving it to him, for *gifting* was a standard euphemism for *bribing*, which was rampant in many government agencies. Benjamin had previously worked in the government, and he had apparently been disliked by many of his peers: His rigorous refusal of bribes made them look bad. Mine was a true gift, but the last thing I wanted was to insult his integrity.

We spent several days playing cat and mouse, the game of contrition demanded by the system. But I was getting better at this, and as my frustration diminished, the interactions went more smoothly. The Département des Eaux et Forêts, the first of two agencies requiring input on the permitting process, made us wait for several hours the first day we showed up, then told us to come back the following day. The next day, we received the same treatment. Occasionally, we were called up to someone's office to sit in front of their large desk and answer questions that seemed unrelated to the task at hand. "Are you Americans? Do you like Madagascar?" At the end of the second day we were dismissed again and told to return in the morning. Glenn, unfamiliar with the schedules and red tape of the developing world, voiced his concern that we wouldn't get our permits at all. He hadn't bargained on the long delay between leaving for a field season and actually getting to the forest, and he was annoyed with the people in charge. Each trip to these offices was an adventure unto itself, a long, winding taxi ride through remote Tana neighborhoods, often taking half the morning.

The next morning, we returned, but the group mood was deteriorating. I knew we needed to keep up the appearance of eager hopefulness, so I encouraged Bret, who understood the importance of the facade, to keep Glenn occupied and out of view. I had suffered through my own intolerance with the system for years, and I didn't want the bureaucrats reacting to Glenn's, which was still in its early stages.

A few hours after we showed up, I was invited into yet another office. A smartly dressed young woman told me that our permits had been granted. I voiced my approval of this outcome and thanked her for all her help, though I had never seen her before. Then she explained that the permits were in a locked room and that the man with the key was not here. In fact, he was on vacation. Perhaps I should come back the following day. All acquiescence and smiles, I thanked the woman again for her efforts on our behalf and promised to return the next morning.

I did, but the man with the key did not. By midafternoon on that fourth day, another copy of the key was discovered, the room was opened, and the papers were delivered to us. Now we had to take them to ANGAP, the second of the two agencies, to be processed; once that was accomplished, we would receive the actual permits. After four days spinning our wheels at DEF, ANGAP gave us our permits within five minutes of our arrival. The weird calculus was apparent again—the agencies issuing permits take precisely as much time as you have budgeted, whether that's three weeks or three days.

Arranging to get our bags to Maroantsetra was similarly complex. Air Mad had changed its rules somewhat, and the four hundred pounds of gear that we could not carry with us on the plane had to go by freight, a service operated by Air Mad.

"We can't guarantee when your freight will get to Maroantsetra," we were told at the Air Mad office in Tana, "but if you want to go to Sambava, we can promise it within a week." This is rather like being told, "We don't know when we can get your wedding dress to Poughkeepsie, but we can get it to Boise by Friday." As my research program was based in the rain forest outside of Maroantsetra, this option did not appeal.

The woman at Air Mad thought it "likely" that our freight would get to Maroantsetra before it was time for us to return—a date three and a half months in the future. Not comforted by this, we went instead to the airport, which was several miles outside of town, to talk to the Air Freight people directly. The problem, they explained, was that the planes to Maroantsetra were so small, it was impossible to know when there would be enough room to get the freight on board. The man in charge, though, seemed convinced that it would not take more than nine days from the time we left our freight with them. In fact, he guaranteed it. And he repeatedly refused my offers of monetary incentive to smooth and speed the process. Somehow, we'd entered a wholly different Madagascar.

I also had to check in at the Wildlife Conservation Society, which meant getting to their offices. To do so by taxi always involved describing to the taxi driver what part of town I needed to go to. The driver, predictably, scratched his head, not quite understanding my pronunciation, and never having heard of WCS. Finally, inevitably, I succumbed, admitting what I knew all along but didn't want to say. "It's near the paint store, Gamo." At this, the driver's eyes lighted up with recognition, and we were off. Paint stores are rare, and precious. Conservation organizations, on the other hand, have no apparent function, at least to taxi drivers in Tana.

Finally, we flew to Maroantsetra, where we found the airport much changed. It still consisted of a single weedy airstrip, one wind sock, and a shell of a building, with no equipment inside but a large scale. But there was glass in the windows, and the roof, previously caved in, was once again at ceiling level. Most significantly, the single door, the one that Bret had knocked off its hinges three years earlier, had been replaced.

Upon arriving at the airport, we were bombarded by men asking us where we were staying, then suggesting we stay at their hotel. Matthew Hatchwell at WCS had told me that a new hotel had opened in town, the Maroa, and that it was clean, cheap, friendly, and a short walk from Projet Masoala. The Coco Beach had raised its rates, and though twenty dollars for a bungalow is cheap by First World standards, the rather decrepit huts on the outskirts of town didn't warrant the price. Furthermore, Projet Masoala had turned the room Jessica and I had slept in in 1997 into a storage area. I certainly couldn't afford the Relais de Masoala, the luxury hotel outside of town, which had opened its doors to Jessica and me. There were two other hotels in town, both extremely cheap. One, the Vatsy, charged by the hour. The other, the aptly named Hôtel du Centre, was directly

across the street from the market, and in desperate shape. With so much
money tied up in equipment, I didn't want to risk staying in a place without
some degree of security. Besides, in years past, when Bret and I had traveled
as backpackers through Central America and Madagascar, we had stayed in
such places. I felt we had done our time and now deserved to graduate to
the next level. Glenn, who had never before traveled in the developing
world, would get to skip the bottom few rungs entirely.

I engaged the men vying for our business. The most persistent of the
lot was a fat man, sweating profusely. I thought it a bad sign.

"Where do you want to go?" he asked slyly.

"I don't know. Projet Masoala at the moment." I hoped to avoid being
tricked into some hotel I wanted nothing to do with.

"Relais de Masoala?" he repeated in error back to me, taking us for
wealthy tourists.

"No, no. *Projet* Masoala. We are researchers." He looked blankly at me.
There wasn't any money for him in Projet Masoala.

"What hotel? I have bungalows for twenty-five thousand FMG." About
five dollars.

I was exasperated with this guy and wanted the decision to be over with.
"Give me ten minutes," I told him. He laughed in my face. Then he scuttled
over to the only other *vazaha* in the place, a smarmy French guy in his
mid-thirties, who had a slinky young Malagasy woman draped over him.
The foul hotel man repeated what I had said to the Frenchman, and they
both had a good laugh. The Frenchman grabbed his sweet young thing by
the ass, causing her to topple off her platform heels. I called the sweaty
hotelier back over.

"What's the name of your hotel?" His mumbled answer came back
sounding like "Maroa."

"What?" I persisted.

"Look it up in the guidebook. Very recommended. You will see."

I knew he was lying, but I didn't have the strength to resist. "Okay."

"So, you will come stay at the bungalow for thirty-five thousand a
night?"

"You said twenty-five."

"There is one for twenty-five, one for thirty-five."

"What's the difference between them?"

"No difference."

Of course. "There is electricity? Outlets?"

"Yes."

"And a private bath?"

"Yes," he lied.

"Hot water?"

"Everyone asks about hot water; everyone thinks it is good."

It wasn't an answer, but I didn't care. I now remembered where I was, and realized that hot water was, to say the least, unnecessary. I was tired of the discussion and just wanted to get going.

"Okay, we'll take both." So we collected our bags, stuffed ourselves into his car, and trundled into town. We passed the sign for the Maroa, and just as I was going to protest, he pulled into the Hôtel du Centre.

"You said we were going to the Maroa."

"No, no, this is the Hôtel du Centre."

Yes, I thought, I know what it *is*, but it's not the advertised product. But since we were here and had taken his car, we had to look at the place. The sleazy French guy and his sweet young thing were already camped out in one bungalow. The door was open, and they were mostly naked. The sweating proprietor showed us to the one next door, which was drowning in filth, the air stagnant and fetid. In the tiny room was a torn and stained foam mattress, over which a crusty sheet had been partially thrown. The wood floor was rotting. There was no fan, a critical element in the tropical stillness. Through an open doorway was the private bath: a closet-size enclosure with a spigot hanging loosely from the ceiling, a rusted drain in the cement floor. There was no sink or toilet. He led us outside and motioned to the building next door, out of which was oozing something akin to water, but wasn't quite.

"Voilà, la toilette."

I was not pleased. This was hardly an auspicious reentry into Maroantsetra. We told him we would stay one night, then left our stuff and headed into town. We went immediately to the Hotel Maroa. It was miraculously clean and had eight or ten individual bungalows. The bungalows had thatched roofs, bamboo walls, and wood floors, as well as electric fans, porches, and private bathrooms with sinks, toilets, and showers. Simple by First World standards—as usual, there was no hot water—it was paradise after the Hôtel du Centre. There was the usual complement of geckos and bugs sharing the space, but after all, it was basically open to the air, so nobody had expected hermetically sealed quarters. Soon we would be living in tents.

The family who owned the Maroa was accommodating, friendly, and eager to help. There was a restaurant serving mostly faux Chinese dishes in the main building, where the owners lived. The bungalows surrounded the main building in a small dirt courtyard, in which the chickens ran free. A wooden fence separated the Maroa from the rest of town, and I felt that our things would be safe here and that we would be content. We went back to the Hôtel du Centre and engaged in a short argument with the owner over exactly how much we owed him. He wanted full price for the two bungalows, as if we had spent the night, plus an "inconvenience fee," so named for the inconvenience we had caused him by leaving early. Finally, we came to an agreement, retrieved our things, and moved to the Maroa the same day.

We had several days to kill in Maroantsetra as we waited for the bulk of our baggage to arrive from Air Freight. During this time, we habituated the new employees at Projet Masoala to our presence, and made some new friends. The office staff was now comprised of two women, Edwige and Laurence, who had not been there in 1997. Our relationship, like mine with their predecessor, Clarice, began on a hostile note, and had to be massaged into harmony. As in previous years, the local staff had not been alerted to my existence before my arrival. I had completed all of the paperwork required of me by WCS, and we were to be the only foreign researchers in the area for months, but nobody had thought to tell these women we were coming. Understandably, they were a bit suspicious, and set out to make my life difficult. Finding Clarice gone, however, and having brought a few pretty items of clothing for her, I distributed them to Edwige and Laurence, which smoothed away some of the distrust.

The captain, too, had been replaced. The little boat with two outboard motors was the same, but Yves, who had always had a frantic look in his eyes and seemed none too stable, was gone. Pascal was the new captain. Shy, intelligent, and curious, Pascal was a beautiful man with rich insights about life and those he saw around him.

"I love the sea," proclaimed Pascal early in our acquaintance, adding that there was nothing he would rather be doing than driving the little boat across dancing waters.

Projet Masoala had also acquired a vehicle, an old but not decrepit Land Rover. Heloise was the only person authorized to drive this beast. As such, she was the chauffeur. Maroantsetra is a small town, and there are neither many places to go nor many people authorized to go anywhere, but it was Heloise's job to be at the ready, should someone need to go someplace.

My friends Felix, Armand, and Emile were all still around and working, and there were several more guides we quickly became familiar with on this trip. To a person, all were skilled, personable, quick-witted, and full of humor and goodwill. Whenever we were in town, I sought out the guides, and they sought me out, identifying kindred spirits, I think, in our shared love of the forest and its inhabitants.

Our time was primarily spent lounging in the small yard at Projet Masoala or at our bungalows at the Maroa, watching people come and go. But we also wandered through town, acquainting ourselves with the expanded lot of consumer goods now available. PVC pipe was being sold in a limited number of sizes, though most of the connectors were not. Metal files and soldering irons were available. And, as always, the diversity of handwoven products was immense. Malagasy artisans are highly regarded, the products from various regions including intricately carved wooden furniture, handmade papers, batiks and other fabric arts, and semiprecious stonework. In Maroantsetra, the artisans work in straw.

Bret decided he needed a hat to protect his fair skin. For about seventy cents, it is possible to commission a hat from the women who sell straw baskets in the market. The hat lady, sharing no language with us except those few words of Malagasy we knew, measured lengths of raffia around his head. The next day, we went back and picked up a hat that perched nicely on top of Bret's head, as is the Malagasy custom. Unfortunately for Bret, it is not his custom. So he commissioned another one, specifying with hand gestures that he would like it a bit larger in every dimension. The following morning, he picked up his sombrero. It came down to his eyes, and would act as an umbrella in a downpour. He and the hat lady were developing quite a rapport by now, so when he went back, somewhat abashed, desiring a third hat, some middle ground between his two existing hats, she was ready to comply. That third hat would last him several months.

Wandering around town during those slow days, I found a greater diversity of flip-flops than had been available two years earlier. Desperately cheap, these were rejects of the First World. Some bore a picture of a fat, jolly animal on the instep, with the words FRIEND MOLE. Others, with an improbably thick sole, carried a tag that read, in fancy, misspelled script, MODREN. When typos or other errors in the prediction of consumer desire happen to products designed for the First World, they get shipped to people without choices, people in places like Maroantsetra.

We were still in town on Sunday, a special day in Maroantsetra. Missionaries had once been here, so even many of the locals who retain their animist beliefs go to church. Everybody strolls through town in their Sunday best after going to church. Some stores close entirely, but most just close during the hottest part of the day, the *sieste*, as during the week. Glenn was suffering his first bout of tropical indigestion, so Bret and I went looking for food alone. We found a building with a sign reading LEBON CAP, but it didn't seem to be open. A young boy carrying a bucket of eggs on an immense rusty bike pulled up to the gate. He saw us standing at the closed door, looking confused, and gave a shout. Smiling, a heavyset woman let us in. And, unlike many restaurants in Madagascar whose doors *are* open, this one had food and juice. In the developing world, products sold as juice are primarily sugar and water, with a hint of fruit. *Jus naturel* is the magic phrase in Madagascar, and the mistress of the Lebon Cap had two kinds: *corocol* (sweetsop) and *grenadelle* (the exquisite passion fruit). Ah, sweet heaven.

The food was no less inspired. Malagasy tomato salads, when you can find them, are made with simply sliced rose red tomatoes dressed in vinegar and black pepper, sometimes with slices of tiny raw onion. In Maroantsetra, my preferred entrée is "substrate of the day" with *sauce au coco*, poured over mounds of rice. The coconut sauce is rich, savory, complex, and bright orange. Usually, the substrate available is scrawny chicken, heavy on tendons. That Sunday, there were fresh tuna steaks, the fishermen having come back early out of deference to a Christian God. I celebrated the tuna, which gave its life for my gustatory pleasure.

After lunch, we wandered through town, stopping to sit on the shaded stoop of a store that was shut up tight. We engaged in the exhausting activity of being *vazaha* in public, saying "*Salama*" to everyone who passed. A few children stopped in front of us, touched us, flashed big, perfect smiles. We were like dolls on display.

"*Sali, vazaha!*" other children cried, streaking past in a furious run.

"*Salama*, Malagasy!" Bret responded, causing mirth and confusion among the children. You are *vazaha*, the logic seemed to go, but we are individuals, with names. Referring to them as Malagasy, although it seemed parallel to calling us *vazaha*, had never occurred to them.

The Peace Corps had arrived in Maroantsetra the year before, in the form of two American women. We had dinner with them, for as soon as *vazaha* arrive in town, the few other *vazaha* hear about it, and we had quickly found one another. Angela was teaching English to the naturalist guides and some others. Linda's job was less clear, but she had an interest in conservation and ecotourism on Nosy Mangabe.

When we returned to the Maroa that night, a small party was in process. Four large tables with tablecloths and matching glasses were set up in the dirt courtyard, with people milling about. Occasionally, they erupted in applause. Then a round of singing, with clinking of glasses and outbursts of clapping. A whistle. Much appreciative shouting in response. Laughing. More clinking of glasses. I listened through the window of our bungalow, wooden shutters open but covered with a sheer drape. Scattered female laughter punctuated the singing and talking that drifted in. A pleasant, rising and sinking hum of content human voices. Never before had I been privy to such a party in Madagascar. I have wondered at such times why I still feel embarrassed about my own curiosity with regard to the Malagasy, when they make no attempt to conceal their curiosity about me. The difference, I guess, is that I am in their home, and they are not in mine. Their curiosity—even hostility, if they have it—is acceptable, but I must be deferential. I owe them everything, and they owe me nothing.

We checked every day for evidence that our freight had arrived. I was anxious, convinced that we would never see our gear again, feverishly coming up with alternate plans: How long do we wait until we assume that our bags are lost? How do I try to conduct my research without tents to sleep in or equipment to measure parameters? How will I explain this to my doctoral committee back in the States? We wandered through Maroantsetra for those first three days, fiercely focused on our bags and their possible location within the system. We were not waiting; we were scheming.

And then, on the fourth day, I woke up in my thatched-roof bungalow at peace. Maybe today, maybe tomorrow, probably sometime—what do the specifics matter? In a small dusty town with little to offer the outsider, I was suddenly content to laze about on the porch of my bungalow, entertained by my companions or my novel of the moment, but most often just to gaze into the middle distance. I had left the world of precious time and entered that of passing time. I strolled through the market, assessing the vendors' baskets of rice, admiring small piles of potatoes, onions, pineapples. I realized that sometime I would be called upon to return to the market and buy enough food to last the three of us two or three weeks, to plan and organize. But I felt that this responsibility, not being immediate, wasn't very real. I wandered back to my bungalow, where the proprietors of the Maroa had recognized my change of attitude and supplied me with a raffia mat on which to sit. When I sat on that woven mat, watching chickens chase each other around the yard, listening to the yells of children splashing through puddles as the rainy season began, I didn't worry about equipment and research and time. I found myself there and, there being no plans to leave, would remain until something else came along. I had finally begun to learn how to wait as the natives do.

No wonder the raised voice and irritated demeanor of a *vazaha* desiring an immediate research permit or plane ticket fail to produce anything but mutual frustration. In my current trance, I would not have been compelled by someone else's insistence that his needs were paramount, either. It will happen when it happens. I began to take the early-afternoon *sieste*, when everything closes down and even the dogs move into the shade. I was getting twelve hours of sleep every day, and why not—what else was I going to do?

Then our bags arrived—all of them, unscathed. Edwige told us that the boat could take us out to the island the next morning, but if we missed that window of opportunity, it would be several days before another came. Jolted out of complacence, suddenly time mattered again. Damn the *sieste* anyway—how could we plan around those two and a half hours when nobody would conduct business with us? We needed to get the bags from the freight office that day, before it closed; we needed to have the permits I had so painstakingly acquired in Tana glanced at and approved by Projet Masoala; we needed to buy provisions, which would involve multiple trips, hauling heavy baskets of rice, beans, and charcoal through the sandy town. Each one of these activities could take an entire day. Why, my newly rediscovered discontent screamed, why must things be so inefficient and slow? Why? Because nobody else here has deadlines of such an immediate nature. People live, people plant and harvest rice, people sit in the market under umbrellas and sell their wares, people sleep and eat and flirt and take care of children. Again, I was the *vazaha* with strange ideas about time.

19

Observer, Observed

Pascal took us out to Nosy Mangabe in the little motorboat, and Lebon and Fortune, onshore, smiled widely as they recognized me coming in. Two years earlier, Rosalie had told us that she thought they were terrified of Jessica and me. I wondered at their apparent pleasure now, and thought these may have been fear grins, of the sort known in other primates.

If they were, it was warranted. The island had gone to seed, a sour, wildly sprouting seed, which left its foul odor on all it came in contact with, and a lingering smell of helplessness. The physical structures of camp were basically unchanged—three tent platforms still prominent, the conservation agents' small cabin, the dank cement-floored lab, the tiny structure housing the toilets—but all was in chaos. In 1997, one of the toilets never worked, but the other one usually did, albeit with a lot of leakage from the tank. There was always an inch or two of water on the floor of this dark room where spiders went to die. The PVC pipe that ran from the waterfall to the wooden shower and then from the shower to the toilets had been wobbly, but secure. When we arrived this year, though, someone had walked into the pipe and knocked it off its connection—no adhesive had been used in its construction. Now a waterfall's force of water was flooding camp constantly, and reattaching it seemed impossible with the huge amount of water now flowing out of the pipe. From the channels the water had formed, it seemed the PVC had been broken for at least several days. The noise was deafening. There were no shower or toilets as a result. The pit toilet was even less appealing this year, for the boards on which you squatted were rotting, lending a very precarious air to the endeavor.

Furthermore, the little pool in which I had been attacked by the lemur, the pool closest to camp, where we got our drinking water and, just downstream, brushed our teeth and washed our faces, had been polluted. It was being used to clean fish, the unwanted parts left to decay in the once-fresh water. Worse, the conservation agents were using the pool to bathe in, now that there was no shower, and the waterfall, though it was my preferred bathing spot, could be reached only by clambering over several boulders. The Malagasy, traditionally, don't use toilet paper—they find the habit dirty and rather disgusting, which perhaps it is. Instead, they prefer to clean themselves after a bowel movement by rinsing themselves in water. This once-pristine water source quickly became known to us as "butt-water pond."

We couldn't do anything about the bacteria now living in butt-water pond, and this left us without an easily accessible source of clean water. Bret set about to fix some of the problems in camp immediately, using his unique combination of mechanical and logical skills, and an intuition that often resulted in him packing just the right combination of required items. Now the two tubes of epoxy putty he had brought saved the day.

Glenn, on the other hand, had never before packed for such a trip. I had given him what background I could think of regarding the living conditions: He needed a tent, something comfortable to sleep on and cheap, quick-drying clothes that could be discarded at the end of the season if necessary. He had to bring all the toothpaste and shampoo and whatever else he might need. I told him what shots to get, and which prescriptions to request from his doctor. Everything needed to fit in one seventy-pound bag plus his carry-on. Except for the toilet paper I packed for all of us, he needed to be self-sufficient.

When the trident emerged, like Neptune's, from Glenn's bag, it made him easy to mock. Did he expect to be sparring with the deities? In what bizarre situation did he imagine coming to rely on a trident? Had he ever needed a trident before? But he had also packed a folding shovel, which was extremely useful before its untimely demise shortly after we arrived, and fishing rods, the likes of which Lebon and Fortune had never seen. He was new to this game, while Bret and I were relatively experienced at predicting the disasters that might befall us, but we had all done relatively well in this test of our accuracy in deciding what we would need to live on in a rain forest for several months.

Bret was doing what he could to elevate our lives above the minimum required for mere survival. After several spectacular attempts to reattach the broken pipe, he realized he would have to block the water source first. He climbed the waterfall and found the pipe's origin in a pool above the cascade. His first choice of plug: a mango. When he laid the sweet fruit at the entrance to the pipe, though, massive suction stripped the flesh off the mango, pulling the remaining fruit far into the middle of the pipe, where it stopped, firmly embedded. All water flow was halted, apparently permanently. In one sense, the plug had worked perfectly, but there was now a mango lodged inside a twelve-foot length of pipe that was not replaceable without a trip to Tana. The pipe had to be cleared of mango plug before any further attempts could be made to reattach the pipe to the shower. Over the course of several hours, Bret effectively plunged the pipe by repeatedly decreasing, then releasing the flow of water into the pipe at its origin, slowly moving the mango downstream until, finally, it shot out the other end, hitting the shower with a welcome thud.

After experimenting with fruit and nonfruit plugs alike, Bret found a stopper that worked, then set to fixing the problem back in camp. He had found a spigot in town; using a variety of adhesives and blades he had brought with him, he fixed the broken pipe and installed the spigot, giving us even easier, if less romantic, access to pure water than we had at the pool before it became butt-water pond. He spent several days fixing the toilets, finally producing two brilliantly functioning flush toilets where before there had been none. The rooms they were in remained dark, dank little places where insects and their predators collected, including both the neon green *Phelsuma* geckos and the occasional boa. Wearing a headlamp into one at night, clutching a roll of toilet paper while trying to stay dry in what seemed to be constant rain, did not approximate a developed world toilet experience, but it was several orders of magnitude better than the alternative.

Bret, however, is a perfectionist. It was clear to him that what was missing was a toilet seat. Few Malagasy have access to flush toilets at all, and those who do have generally never seen a toilet seat. It wasn't surprising that there was no seat. I had spent the previous season strengthening my stomach muscles squatting over the toilet or a hole in the ground, and I expected to do the same this year. Bret would have none of it.

When next we went into town to procure supplies so that Bret could fix the rest of camp, and to get Rosalie, who was going to help me and be trained at the beginning, rather than at the end, of my field season this year, Bret had an agenda. As I languished at the Maroa, my gut reacting to Nosy Mangabe bacteria, Bret took Glenn on a mission. Find a toilet seat. In Maroantsetra, it was now possible to buy three kinds of adhesives, and two or three gauges of wire—hardware stores were diversifying and becoming better stocked. But there wasn't a prefabricated toilet seat anywhere in town. Bret spoke essentially no French, so I had taught him set phrases to use when seeking particular objects. In my daze, I had inadvertently led him astray. He wasted his entire morning walking around town asking for an *"assiette de toilette."* A toilet plate. Finally, I got it right, but he still had no luck finding a seat.

Remembering that across the river there was a place claiming to be a technical college, he went there. In short order, Bret found a man who knew another man, the actual craftsman, who would carve a toilet seat for us. We had taken the measurements of the relevant toilet, and with these, a sharply honed aesthetic, and very little French, Bret described to the middleman what he wanted.

"Oh yes, I understand." The man nodded. "Europeans use these. I have seen them." If true, this suggested a rare sophistication for a Maroantsetran. Because we were headed back to the island the next morning, they arranged to have the toilet seat sent on the next boat. The price for commissioning a toilet seat? Twelve dollars. We expected that if and when a toilet seat did arrive on Nosy Mangabe, it would be a plywood plank with a hole crudely cut in the middle of it.

Several days later, when I came back to camp after a morning watching frogs, the toilet seat awaited.

"This," Bret told me, "may well be the most beautiful toilet seat the planet has ever seen." And so it was. Carved out of a deep red hardwood, two thick planks had been melded together in a perfect seam. All of the edges were rounded and sanded, the grain of the wood seeming to bend as the form itself did. The proportions were perfect. It was a work of art.

The fine workmanship of our new toilet seat did not impress Lebon and Fortune. They were too busy watching us to care much for art. Meanwhile, Rosalie had arrived, and I was busy teaching both her and Glenn how to start a field season. Truthfully, I was distracted by them at this point, as what I really wanted to do was jump into the work myself—I had been away from my frogs for almost two years and was now yearning to learn more about them, rather than teach others how to do so. So I dragged them out to the forest day after day, looking for appropriate spots to set up experiments, and for populations to mark. I wanted to be watching frogs, but Rosalie and Glenn had nothing to do but watch me. I made excuses to wander off and find frogs doing interesting things, but often I would look up from my observations and find Rosalie or Glenn silently, almost shyly, observing me.

This year, I was going to continue the experiment designed to test what limits the size of *Mantella* populations. Part of my aversion to this stage of the process was that I needed to lay several transect lines through the forest to establish grids. Using pieces of neon flagging tape, I intended to mark off areas of the forest that were identical in size so that we could monitor frog populations. Drawing straight lines of thirty-five meters (115 feet), or even the shorter lengths of ten meters (33 feet), in the tangled, viny, steep, and slippery understory proved to be an exasperating, muddy task. It never resulted in grids as accurate as I was hoping for, due to the surprising appearance of large trees or boulders exactly where a line should go. Glenn volunteered frequently for the job of walking the plastic transect tape along the compass bearing I had calculated, and he quickly came to understand why I disliked this particular task so much. Each of us, at some point, ended up facedown in decomposing leaf litter, after an ankle-level vine had tripped us while we focused on compass and transect tape instead of on our own feet.

Another task that both Glenn and Rosalie helped with was finding populations of frogs to watch, and marking them. When Rosalie had been with me during my previous season, she had walked into several populations that Jessica and I had already tried to mark. We had clipped their toes, tied waistbands around them, stitched beads into their backs, but nothing stuck. Before leaving for Madagascar this year, I had consulted a book on field methods for studying amphibians, where I found a reference to tattooing frogs. After dialing a phone number given in the appendix, I was soon listening to a message of a gruff male voice advising that they only took orders late at night, a few days a week. Were those motorcycle engines I heard revving in the background? I called back at the appropriate time, and it became clear that I was communicating with a tattoo parlor in New York, a hangout for bikers.

"What do you need?" the man asked after yelling at a buddy to cut his engine. I hesitated, thinking perhaps I should give up on this line of inquiry altogether.

"Well, I need to mark some very small tropical frogs." I paused, waiting for a laugh, or confusion, or annoyance, to become apparent at the other end of the line. Nothing. So I continued. "I'll be in the rain forest in Madagascar, without access to electricity, so I need a battery-powered tattoo machine that will allow me to permanently mark the wet skin of amphibians." Long pause. I thought maybe he had dropped the phone.

"We can do that," he said finally. "Sometimes we need to tattoo on the road, so we have portable models."

I was incredulous. "Really?" I asked. "Frog skin is wet, so it won't work the same way as a tattoo on human skin does." Now I had managed to annoy him.

"I know *that*," he said, "I'm not an idiot. Just last week, we were down at Sea World tattooing penguins toes." He paused again, thoughtful. "But penguins aren't amphibians, are they? Still, they're in the water all the time, and their skin is wet. I think the same machine will work for you."

I was off to the races.

Glenn took to tattooing the frogs, which I was grateful for, and soon we had several populations of A1's, D4's and P6's. Each of us, Glenn, Rosalie, and I, picked a population and began watching individuals each morning, again using the afternoons to run experiments. Quickly, I began seeing males employ sneaky strategies, avoiding other territorial mates while trying to attract and court females. K2 was a male defending a territory that included no egg-laying sites—no wells—but he often met with reproductive success anyway. He always seemed to be assessing whether or not his nearest competitor, who controlled access to the wells K2 needed to mate in, was present. If not, he would quickly make his move and attempt to utilize a well himself. I tried to stop myself from overestimating what these frogs were capable of, but sometimes it did seem that they were building scenarios, plotting alternative outcomes. But these are frogs, animals with small brains. What really differentiates us from them?

I was not the only person considering this question. Many of the guides were on the island more frequently than they had been in 1997. There were a few more tourists, at least one most weeks, and they always had a guide with them. Furthermore, Projet Masoala, apparently on orders from headquarters in Antalaha, was pursuing trail-building and camp-rehabilitation projects now that Bret had fixed the most egregious problems in camp. In theory, the guides were being paid for their work on Nosy Mangabe, which required their unique combination of forest knowledge and physical skills, but in practice they were being taken advantage of. Since 1997, an exquisite new trail had been constructed up to the old cemetery. The trail was perfectly graded and lined with rocks, with trenches dug at regular intervals to allow runoff down the hillside without the trail becoming washed out. The guides had designed and built the trail over the course of several weeks, but they had been paid for only half their work. Now they were routinely being called out to the island to do camp maintenance. One of the guides told me that he had worked only one day for pay in both January and February, a total of 24,000 FMG (less than five dollars) per month. Many days, he was out on the island doing manual labor, work that, the guides agreed when pressed, was truly the job of the conservation agents. None of them knew what the conservation agents made, but they believed it was around 500,000 FMG a month, or roughly twenty times what the guide had made. I asked one guide how much they got paid for each day of manual labor.

He smiled, the weak smile of a man defeated. "Oh, no, we do not get paid for this work."

I was already friends with Felix, Armand, and Emile, and quickly I came to know Paul, Augustin, and others, as well. Often when I returned to camp for lunch, they were there, which itself was a departure from the isolated feeling the island had had in years past. They were all intensely curious to know what I had learned about the forest. They would ask me what I had found that day, and I, happy to have people as excited about my frogs as I was, would tell them of a new tussle over territory I was watching, or about a mother frog that had fed her tadpole. These stories, so easily interpreted in terms of human experience, were fascinating to the guides. And they, like me, wondered how complex these frogs really were.

Bret, meanwhile, was working on a chapter of his dissertation in which he was attempting to explain the long-recognized but poorly understood correlation between species diversity and latitude. There are more species the closer you get to the equator. At the poles, there are few organisms; in the tropics, there are many. Any rather obvious explanations one might come up with for this—there is simply more sunlight in the tropics, or more resources—fall apart under closer scrutiny. The guides, especially Paul and Felix, frequently asked Bret what he was working on, and they were surprised to learn from him just how unique their home was.

"More species here?" they would ask, curious. "But isn't it just that there are different species here?" The much-discussed endemism of Madagascar was well known to the guides—what you find on the great red island, you can find nowhere else in the world. But they had never before heard that the tropics had more species than, say, a comparable area of land in Europe, or North America. Even Nosy Mangabe, with its conspicuous lack of certain species, was much more diverse than any two square miles of temperate forest.

One of the most difficult aspects of both Bret's and my scientific discussions with the guides was convincing them that the world they knew, the rain forests of northeastern Madagascar, does not look like the rest of the world. This is one of the most formidable aspects of communicating with people in the temperate zone, too. Everyone assumes that their world is *the* world, or at least fully representative of the diversity that is out there. In fact, part of Bret's thesis focused on the idea that one of the common explanations for species diversity patterns, competitive exclusion, seems to hold true in the temperate zone, where the evidence was first found to support the theory, but not in the tropics, where species are most diverse. Competitor species do not necessarily drive each other to extinction in the tropics, although they usually do in the temperate zone. Even scientists, who seek explanation for the patterns we see, are biased by our predominant experiences, which tend to be in First World, temperate zone countries.

Rosalie understood the world's Western bias all too well, but she managed to elude the bitterness many people would have felt in her situation. Instead, as a burgeoning scientist in a country too poor to provide much, if any, support for such a career, she took advantage of joy where she could find it. Even when a large (but nonpoisonous) snake, a *Madagascarophis*, bit her, she was philosophical about it, figuring that she had annoyed it enough to deserve the attack. We had a discussion on the long walk back from the forest one day, just Rosalie and me, about science, work, and ways to define quality of life. We spoke, as always, in French.

"Why do you work here in Madagascar?" she wondered aloud. "What about it do you enjoy?"

Despite their very different perspectives, Rosalie and my mother both failed to understand the appeal.

"It is arduous to work here, to be sure, but also thrilling to glean new information about the frogs and this forest." I paused. This wasn't a complete answer.

"Aren't there animals at the museum in Michigan?" she asked.

The only other *vazaha* she had worked with were collectors, who took animals back to their museums in the United States, France, or Italy, rather than studying them in their natural environment. She had told me earlier that she disapproved of the wholesale ransacking of her country's flora and fauna for the knowledge of First World scientists but also recognized that there was value in that knowledge. It also meant that she knew there were a lot of Malagasy animals dispersed throughout the world.

"Yes," I acknowledged, "but they're all dead. It's hard to study the behavior of dead animals." She laughed. "But more to the point, perhaps, is that I defined a research question that would bring me to Madagascar. That was part of the choice, not an unexpected by-product."

"Really?" she asked, surprised. "I like the idea that you actually enjoy working in Madagascar. Most people do not." She shook her head slowly, remembering.

"Don't get me wrong," I continued. "It's difficult and excruciatingly frustrating at times. But in many ways, Madagascar is more real than the United States. Many people in America are accustomed to having things, and the money to buy them, but they don't have close-knit communities of friends and family. The reverse is true in Madagascar." She was nodding ruefully.

"But sometimes things would be nice," she offered.

"Oh yes, they are," I conceded. "I guess it's very easy for me to think that I would rather have community than things, but how do I know? I like my things, my comforts, but I have never had real community, so I have no idea what we have given up for a few possessions and comforts." I didn't tell Rosalie, but having Glenn with me on this trip was reminding me of my own weaknesses. This was his first time in the developing world, and he was struggling to make it feel like the world he knew and understood, to interpret it in First World terms.

That evening, the four of us—Bret, Glenn, Rosalie, and I—were having dinner at a table on the middle tent platform, where Rosalie's tiny tent was pitched. It was low tide and full moon, and the clear white light bounced off the still bay and onto everything in camp, lighting us up as if on a movie set. With her strong personality only slightly hidden beneath shyness and a soft voice, Rosalie taught us Malagasy words for some of what was so present in our lives then—moon and tide and sun and cloud. I asked her about her name, and she told me she wished her parents had given her a Malagasy name, not the French Rosalie, which evoked colonial times.

What she really wanted to talk about that night was music. Bret had brought some music with him, and a Walkman, and she was intensely curious what kind of music we listened to. We brought out one of my small playback speakers, usually reserved for experiments, and put on traditional Latin American salsa and merengue, which Bret had fallen in love with during his time in Panama. Rosalie had never heard such music before, and it made her want to dance. So, on a coarse sandy shore, Bret taught her to salsa, to merengue. She was tireless, and soon I took his place, though I dance less well than he does, and had never led before and fluidity.

The light from the moon, as well as a few candles we had melted into the table, projected our silhouettes onto the tarp that lined the back of the tent platform. Lebon and Fortune were up at their cabin, drinking, watching our spiraling forms, hearing shards of music and laughter. Soon, unable to resist, they came down to where we were. Lebon danced a little with us, but mostly he and Fortune retreated into shyness, watching from the shadows. Only Rosalie was utterly unself-conscious, the rest of us sliding in and out of embarrassment and fluidity.

The next morning when I got to my stand to do focal watches, it began to rain furiously. I sat there feeling glum, seeing no frogs, then retreated to the fishermen's camp to wait until the onslaught diminished. There were ten or fifteen fisher folk there, smoking fish, cooking rice, and trying to stay marginally dry, just as I was. I greeted them, put my stuff down on one corner of the giant tent platform—not wanting to displace them or their stuff, but feeling that I had a right to use the space, as well—and, after updating some data sheets, began to read. I often carried a novel for just such an occasion. After a few minutes, a small boy came over with a brush and cleaned the area in front of me. After a few strangled words of protest to indicate that this wasn't necessary, I merely said, "*Misoatra*." "Thank you."

After a while, a youth of about fifteen or sixteen came up to me shyly and looked over my shoulder. I smiled at him, then continued reading. Trying for real communication with my very limited Malagasy vocabulary was pointless. "No problem." "What's the news?" "No news." "Rice frog administrative building." "Going for a little walk." "Thank you very much." "Pain. No pain." "You're welcome." Doesn't make for much of a narrative. So I sat reading while he looked over my shoulder for a few moments. Then he said, distinctly, and in English, "Your book is in English." I looked at him, laughing—but I had thought you someone without a second language, and here you have a third!

"How do you know English?" I asked him, slowly enunciating each word.

"I am learning English at the lycée in Maroantsetra." He paused, noticing my surprise. "I fish with my family on the weekends for our food," he explained, then asked, "Are you waiting for someone?"

"No, only for the rain to stop. I study frogs."

"Oh, yes," he said, thoughtful, "I have seen you working in the—I don't know the word in English—in the *bambou*?" He was unsure if I would understand the French word.

"Yes, the bamboo," I agreed. "It is the same word in English." I had slipped into French but wasn't sure why. My French was better than his English, but it was clear that he wanted to practice. His English was certainly not bad for a poor child from Maroantsetra who has to help his family fish to get enough to eat. I told him that it was very impressive that he spoke three languages.

"My English is very bad." I think they teach this as a stock phrase. Every Malagasy says it when you tell them they speak English well. "What country are you from?" he asked, having some difficulty with the grammatical construction, but getting it right before finishing the sentence aloud.

"The United States." He looked confused. Ah yes, the ridiculous name that our country has. If we weren't such a superpower, we'd have to explain ourselves every time we left our borders. *"Les Etats-Unis,"* I added.

"Ah, America." He nodded and smiled. In Madagascar, unlike in many countries, the United States has no history of neocolonial or military activities. But the French have, so we, along with the rest of the non-French *vazaha*, are the good guys, relatively speaking.

"What is the book you are reading?" He changed the subject, then added, "I have no books to practice my English with."

Oh, I thought, I would gladly leave you a book to practice with, but how could you possibly get through what I have brought—Steinbeck and Austen and Twain and my current book, *Tereza Batista*, by Jorge Amado, translated from the Portuguese. How to explain this? I thought of the Sartre novel I had also brought, translated into English. How odd it would be for him, whose second language was French, to read Sartre in English, his third.

"This book is from, and about, South America. It is translated from Portuguese." I couldn't remember how to say *translated* in French, and I didn't think he would know the word in English. Sure enough, he didn't catch that part.

"So, in all of America, North and South, you are speaking English?" He seemed excited at the prospect of all that land available to him if only he spoke English.

"No, in South America, they speak Spanish, and Portuguese. Only in the United States do we speak English." Canada, Mexico, and Central America were too complicated to explain, given my limited language skills and lack of a map. I wished that I had brought world maps to show people. What arrogance we have, calling ourselves Americans. The Mexicans and all peoples south know it, and call us Norteamericanos, which is what we are, though it doesn't describe us as precisely as when we say that we are from the United States of America. But our nationality is American, though Mexicans, Hondurans, Brazilians, and Chileans are equally American. If only language could be revamped once the mistakes become obvious.

By this time, the rain had eased. I began to hear frog calls from the bamboo stand next to the fishermen's camp. In back of me, rice was being dished onto plates, with fish to follow.

"Please," my young friend said, motioning to the gathering group of people, "come eat with us."

"No." I smiled, grateful that Rosalie had instructed me in this point of Malagasy hospitality. When people are eating, they must invite those who are not. This holds true even if there is not enough, and those invited are expected to decline. "Thank you," I said, "but I think it is time that I return to the forest."

20

Now We're Cooking
with Charcoal

As static as many aspects of life on Nosy Mangabe were, it seemed I was often in transit—going to or from the forest, the waterfall, or town. The boat ride from Nosy Mangabe to Maroantsetra is but three miles, but it can take three-quarters of an hour, depending on conditions. Under the rubric "conditions" falls everything from the size of the swells to the mood of the captain. The rich warm greens of the forest recede as Nosy Mangabe darkens to a silhouette, and the only color at hand is blue, the water deep and rich, the sky pale and infinite, the distant mountains an indefinable hue that seems blue, though you know it can't be, really. Seabirds fly by, their gullets hanging low over the water. Flying fish occasionally make an appearance, jumping silently out of the way of the boat. Pirogues pass silently, the fishermen rarely looking hurried as they paddle out of the way of the motorized menace approaching them.

Finally, a turn to the right, into the broad river, which at this point is indistinguishable from the sea, then bank left, and one is amid reeds and water hyacinth. The wholesale general store appears, a one-room barn where you can buy mints in fifty-package bundles, or car batteries, in this region with hardly any motorized land vehicles. The hulls of boats, once brightly painted, are now flaking, streaks of blue and red flashing from otherwise-dull corpses. Interspersed among them are live boats, with crews napping or gazing out to sea.

Town was more full of possibilities this year, with not just more hardware but more food to buy, as well. Lebon and Fortune were not cooking for us, as they had been advised that it was against the rules. Cooking for ourselves added several hours to every day's tasks, but we didn't risk serving ourselves rancid crustaceans. In the market and stalls around its perimeter, I was able to find real cheese, soy sauce, vinegar, hot peppers, potatoes, garlic, cucumber, and even thyme. In one store, there were sometimes outrageously priced boxes of European cookies, which we bought and hoarded. And there was still ample rice, beans, onions, and cooking oil to go around. Not exactly a full pantry, for our American palates, but good enough.

The act of cooking proved to be extraordinarily arduous. We bought charcoal in town, then carried it to the island in massive woven nylon bags. Everything the bags touched turned black with sticky, tarlike soot. We bought small rectangular metal "stoves," into which we poured and arranged charcoal, then tried our damnedest to light. Being extravagant *vazaha*, when we found kerosene in town, we bought lots of it to help light fires for cooking. It still took twenty minutes to get a fire going well enough to cook on, even with copious amounts of kerosene added to the mix. After handling the charcoal, pouring the kerosene, trying to light the thing without burning one's hair, and fanning it furiously for ten or fifteen minutes, the cook required a bath before actually beginning to cook. We tended to work in pairs. While one person was working on the fire, the other would retrieve onions and garlic from the baskets I had strung up from the roof of the lab to keep the rats out. We still found evidence of rats in our food sometimes, but the basket pulley system was an improvement. With one of our lock-blade knives, which was too small for the task, we would peel the tiny onions and garlic and chop them. One of two *cocottes*—cast-aluminum pots we had bought in town—went on the fire, then some oil was placed inside, followed by onions and garlic. If someone had remembered to soak beans the day before, we could start cooking them in a lot of water now, so long as we didn't want to eat within three hours. Rice took about an hour from start to finish. Vegetables to go with the rice, the same.

We ate either rice and beans or rice and vegetables every day, and I came to appreciate more what Lebon and Fortune had done for me two years earlier, even though I was eating better now. It still wasn't worth it. Washing up took another hour, scrubbing the metal pots as clean as possible in a shallow pool with a combination of local sand and a Scotch-Brite pad we had carried halfway around the world.

We did have our small victories with food. One day, after coming into town through water hyacinth and faded boat hulls, we found pineapples, tomatoes, eggplant, and ginger. Oh, luscious ginger. The wonder of the marketplace in Maroantsetra is that, as a *vazaha*, with clear evidence of fantastic wealth, all one has to do is make a fuss over a particular food item, and there is a good chance it will show up again the next time you come to town. We never went without ginger again.

We found peanuts, too, a fantastic, easy source of protein. We commissioned a wooden mortar and pestle, hoping to fashion peanut butter. And so we did, one peanut at a time. Bret, Glenn, and I each tried our hand at it, but none of us had much success. Bret estimated the number of poundings required to fully smash a single peanut at ten. A whole afternoon could be killed making enough peanut butter for a single meal.

One of the family members at the Maroa offered to make peanut butter for us. Our interaction beforehand suggested that they had a blender of some sort, but when the nut butter was delivered to us, it was clear the man had spent an entire day smashing nuts by hand, just as we had. And he would get no benefit from doing so, beyond what we paid him—there was no pride in craftsmanship to be had in smashing peanuts. But he refused to tell us how much we should pay him for his hard work, saying he wanted no money. Finally, we gave him an amount that made him smile and thank us, but it was impossible to get past the layer of politeness at such moments, and we never knew for sure if a gaffe had been made. Although our protein- and fat-starved selves continued to crave peanut butter, we never again asked the people at the Maroa to spend their time making it.

We also found a little old lady sitting on the stoop of an old building with a plate of—could it be?—macaroons! In my First World life, I am not a fan of coconut, but nothing sounded better than freshly made macaroons that sweltering afternoon in Maroantsetra. We bought ten and devoured them all. The old woman spoke no French, but her little granddaughter, who was helping, did, and I managed to convey the idea that no matter how many macaroons the woman could produce by the following morning, we would buy all of them. Early the next morning, we found ourselves in possession of 147 macaroons.

We needed beans even more than we wanted macaroons, so I took another basket, not the one brimming with macaroons, to the friendliest-looking bean vendor, and proceeded with the complex machinations that these transactions always involve.

"How much for the lentils?"

"Seven hundred and fifty a kapok."

"Okay, I'd like ten kapoks." Blank look. Hesitation, a reach for the kapok, a nervous laugh.

"Ten?" She looked at me, doubtful.

"Yes," I tried to say in my most confident voice, not revealing that this number was rather arbitrarily picked, in deference to our decimal world. She delivered the lentils to my basket. I also received ten kapoks of red beans, at nine hundred per kapok, which was going to be difficult for the bean seller to calculate, largely because she had little practice with such enormous transactions (16,500 FMG by my math, about three dollars). Most local people have so little cash that they pay with exact or nearly exact change for a couple kapoks of beans—handing over two or three bills, totaling ten or fifteen cents. The largest currency in Madagascar was still the 25,000 FMG note—less than five dollars at this point—and very few vendors or even shopkeepers could easily give change for that large a bill. The vendor probably wouldn't sell this many beans again for the next week.

I took out my wallet and handed her a twenty-five thousand FMG note, all that I had. One of the difficulties in switching between First and Third World economies is that when I changed three hundred dollars, I had received several stapled packets of 25,000 FMG bills, which few people wanted. But the banks were unwilling to part with an equivalent amount of ten thousand FMG bills, so I was stuck with stacks of these bills, which were enormous by local standards. I had seen local people wait in line at the bank for upward of an hour to take out a total of ten thousand FMG, less than two dollars, and walk away with a handful of bills of various denominations.

Not only would it take the vendor a while to calculate the total; she would then have to find the change for me. Calling on an intricate network of kin and neighbors, she disappeared behind several stalls, where shadowy figures passed, handing off money. Finally, she reemerged with enough bills to give me my change. Often the change given seemed random, bearing little resemblance to what was actually due. I made a point of just accepting what they gave me, unless, as rarely happened, I was given too much, in which case I returned it. It was pennies to me, but sustenance to them.

———

When we returned to Nosy Mangabe, provisions replenished, I made an attempt at forest risotto. This was in the same tradition as jungle pie, which Bret and Glenn had invented. Jungle pie was a mixture of pineapple, bananas, sugar, and crumbled crackers—plus fresh cinnamon and cloves, when the spice boats came in—packed into a *cocotte* and cooked over a charcoal fire. Like the relationship between pie and jungle pie, forest risotto would be the closest approximation of risotto I could make under the circumstances. We didn't have arborio rice, of course, nor stock, nor Parmesan cheese, nor asparagus, spinach, red peppers, olives, chicken, prosciutto or any of the other fine ingredients that can be used to create luscious risottos.

First, I had to get two charcoal fires going. Thirty minutes and a mini-bath later, I sautéed onions and garlic in vegetable oil obtained from a large bucket in town. After a poor *vazaha* attempt at winnowing the rice, I sat down and culled by hand the medium-grain rice, which was the only kind Maroantsetra vendors sold, and poured it into the oil and onion mix. I slowly added the water, which was boiling on the second fire, in small increments. And I planned, at the end, to add some precious Swiss cheese and a miniature can of tomato paste. But Rafidy found me first.

Rafidy was the Maroantsetra radio repairman. There were but a few radios in town, so he sought other work, as well. At this time, Vonjy (pronounced *Voonj*), a Malagasy graduate student from Tana, was living in a tent in the lab on Nosy Mangabe. He was studying wild pigs. In my seven months on Nosy Mangabe, I saw pigs only once. Vonjy had an assistant to help him study pigs—Rafidy. Even the two of them together rarely saw the animals. They did find and collect droppings relatively often, carefully packing them away to look at in a different place, in another time. We were curious about each other's work but clearly didn't understand it, and our attempts to explain it to each other seemed to fly past without comprehension.

Vonjy was extremely shy, and he never talked much, even to Rafidy. Rafidy, on the other hand, suffered from gregariousness on this lone little island. So, though his French and mine were comparably mediocre, and had largely nonoverlapping vocabulary sets, we often found ourselves in conversation, especially when I was doing anything in camp that he couldn't begin to comprehend. An attempt at forest risotto was just such an activity.

"Erika!" he cried, running over to my fires. "You can't make rice that way! Let me show you."

Rafidy was actually a very good cook, and he produced a few meals that were, to my starved palate, quite delicious. He usually wasn't quite as interested in what we made, but he couldn't let me make such a tragic mistake with rice.

"This is a special Italian way," I told him. It felt sacrilegious to liken what I was doing to Italian cuisine, but I didn't have any better words.

"Italian?" He was, by turns, disbelieving, then amused, then curious. "I've never seen rice made this way." He reflected, then said, "I thought I knew all the ways to cook rice." As good a cook as Rafidy was, he, like all Malagasy, cooked rice only one way, the same way, three times a day. He put it in a large pot with a lot of water, then burned the bottom of it, producing a thick black crust, which stuck to the bottom and sides of the pan. The fluffy white rice on the top was eaten with whatever "broth" he had prepared. *Ranon' ampàngo* was then made by adding fresh water to the burned rice shell and simmering it over the dying fire. This beverage was drunk with and after every meal. We *vazaha* were never able to get any Malagasy to eat with us for more than two meals, as we either failed to burn the rice or forgot to make the *ranon' ampàngo* after doing so. A meal without *ranon' ampàngo* is pretty much a meal without eating. Risotto, it occurred to me now, had no chance of producing *ranon' ampàngo* from its dregs.

"Why do you cook it this way?" Rafidy was deeply curious now. As a Malagasy, he wasn't sure he was going to like the end product of what I was doing, but as a cook, he wanted to know.

"To bring more flavor to the rice, to make the broth part of the rice," I suggested. He took a step back.

"Part of the rice?"

"Yes."

"But . . ." He couldn't continue—there weren't any words. Rice is so integral to the Malagasy's being, it is like a god. You don't sully your gods by mixing them with broth, even if you do occasionally pour broth over them. Instead, he changed the subject, returning to territory he was sure of.

"Let me show you how to winnow the rice." His eyes twinkled deviously. I laughed.

"You've shown me so many times already. I just can't do it." It was true. The wide, flat basket used so expertly by women and men alike to separate out the debris from the rice was unwieldy and unpracticed in my *vazaha* hands. With years of experience, I would learn, but for now, I always ended up inadvertently throwing much of the rice onto the ground. At that point, I would give up and just pick through the rest of the rice by hand for the remaining rocks and grit.

"Don't you do this at home?" Rafidy asked as he effortlessly flung a new batch of rice on the winnowing basket.

"No, we don't have to. The rice we get is already winnowed." He stopped winnowing for a moment.

"By whom?"

"Er . . ." I paused. I wasn't sure. "By machine, I think."

"You must have a lot of machines at home."

Before I could parse this bit of wisdom, I had to turn my attention to one of the fires, which was getting low. Ungracefully, I managed to get the *cocotte* off the fire, and wedge in new pieces of charcoal before balancing it back on the fresh, pointy charcoal. The result was barely functional—the pot perched precariously at a wild angle. Vonjy approached as I was doing this, and he and Rafidy watched me in my ineptness. Usually shy and exceedingly proper, Vonjy couldn't restrain himself this time.

"Don't you cook with charcoal at home?"

"No, we don't. Isn't it apparent?" I asked. He nodded.

"But how do you eat?" It was the obvious next question.

"We cook with gas, lit on fire. It's piped into our homes." They both gaped at me.

"You cook inside?" they asked.

"Yes." I thought about this. Vonjy was a middle-class family man from Tana, on the *haut plateau*, where it gets quite cool in the winter. Surely he cooked inside? "Don't you?" I asked.

"No. We have a shelter, attached to the house, with two walls. But not inside. That would be dangerous." Indeed it would.

"We have pipes, which keep the gas contained. It's not so dangerous," I reassured them.

"Is it very expensive?" Hmm. Good question. Dollar for dollar, the natural gas we use to cook with is extremely expensive compared to the charcoal they use. But relative to income, our gas is much cheaper than their charcoal.

"No, not so expensive." I didn't mention all the years of developing an infrastructure necessary to provide such a luxury at a low price.

The concept of gas stoves was remarkable to this educated middle-class man, who happened to have been born into a country with few amenities.

How surprising he would find our lives, so simplified in terms of daily, life-sustaining chores, but so much more complex in order to afford the simplification.

Time is of the essence in America, but we spend it working at trivial things in order to buy those objects that save us time. In Madagascar, time is worthless, so common as to not be worth watching, counting, or saving. People here claim to know how old they are, but I believe that they are estimating. Pascal, the captain, assured us that the large shipwreck off Nosy Mangabe had been there for three years. I knew that less than two years earlier, it had not. In a world where day length is constant, it may be harder to keep track of time passing. More to the point—why should you? Once an adult, you monitor the important events—your life's relationships, the birth of your children, deaths in the family. And perhaps for a while you know how old your children are, but once they are grown, they, too, will forget exactly how many years, or moons, or rice harvests, or rainy seasons they have lived through. They will remember that there was a hurricane, several years ago, when the waters rushed down from the hills, bearing both corpses and the decimated rice harvest. They will remember that this time of year it usually rains, and that in a few months, things should be drier again. They know that two days a week the market is fuller than usual, and these are the days to dress up, walk around the muck and the chickens in one's best clothes, looking and being looked at.

Time does not factor here. At Projet Masoala, they speak of the *programme* with some regularity, although it is rarely followed. The *programme* exists, I presume, to allay the fears of the white people in charge. Without a *programme*, nothing would get done. This is a truism in the developed world: Without deadlines and fear of reprisal for missing them, what incentive is there? But in Madagascar, most people's work directly affects how much food they have in their stomachs. If you are a fisherman, you cannot be lazy and fail to go out in your pirogue for a week. This does not require attention to a *programme*, merely what natural selection gave us—hunger to prompt us to eat. Being scenario-building humans, we can estimate that having been hungry before, we will be hungry again, unless we act preemptively to secure food before the hunger hits.

The guide Augustin explained the Malagasy passion for rice this way: The Malagasy are born and raised on rice, three or, minimally, two times a day. They become accustomed to having full bellies—not just feeling sated, but feeling physically full. To a *vazaha*, eating a bowl of rice as large as a Malagasy eats causes a feeling of deadweight in the stomach. The

Malagasy learns to equate physical fullness with satiation, and when rice is absent, no matter how many nutrients and calories enter his body, he feels he will die of hunger, for his belly does not feel full.

None of us *vazaha* was afraid we would die of hunger on Nosy Mangabe—though we all lost a lot of weight inadvertently—but we had moments of fearing death from other causes. The Malagasy are accustomed to having primarily rice meals. The *vazaha* are accustomed to having constant body temperatures. When Glenn began complaining of fever and weakness in the middle of our season there, I assumed at first that this was another inexplicable tropical fever, the likes of which everyone there seems to get and recover from without the apparent aid of medicine. But as Glenn grew worse, it seemed necessary to take him to town, which Bret did, so that I could remain on the island and continue my work. Shortly, the diagnosis came back: Glenn had malaria. The doctors in town, with the exception of the good doctor, who was now gone, apparently diagnosed everyone presenting with fever as having malaria at first. But Glenn responded to a quinine drip, which was set up inside a bungalow at the Maroa, while Bret nursed him back to health. My emotions at this news were chaotic. I felt horrible that I had brought someone to Madagascar who had never before traveled this way, and that it was he, not one of us, who had fallen ill. I felt responsible for his illness, which I really wasn't, but also for his overall well-being, which I was. I seriously considered sending him home, so that nothing more could happen to him. As much as I wanted a field assistant, it was more important that he be safe. How would I answer to his mother, or myself, if he died in the field?

But Glenn wanted to stay and, as if to prove his increasing strength when he heard that I might put him on a plane home, he recovered quickly. Meanwhile, Bret was in town and had little to do, so he began surreptitiously introducing the word *snorkel* to Maroantsetra. He had brought a snorkel to Madagascar, which Paul, the guide, had seen and admired, so he had an easy jumping-off point. Running into Bret on a dusty path, Paul would smile widely and ask Bret about the news. "*Inona no vaovao*, Bret?"

"*Tsy misy vaovao*, Paul." Bret would respond, as was required. *No news.* But then he would veer somewhat from convention and switch to English. "Will you go snorkeling today, Paul?"

"Oh, yes, today is a good day to snorkel," Paul would agree heartily, enunciating carefully his newfound word.

Bret disseminated the concept of snorkeling primarily through Paul, but he also dropped the word casually into conversations with people who knew only the barest rudiments of English, their third language. As Bret began infecting the town with this concept, snorkels began to appear. Two days after Bret and Glenn came back to the island, I watched a sailor come onshore to get water. Usually, when a sailor was sent from a boat to get drinking water, he jumped overboard with a large hollow plastic canister and swam until he could wade ashore, pushing the canister ahead of him. This time, the man wore a snorkel.

Later the same day, on his way back from washing clothes at the waterfall, Bret found a remarkable lizard. It was on a rock, sunbathing, and when it spotted Bret, it dove into the shallow pool and disappeared. Bret wasn't sure that such an animal even existed, and he briefly convinced himself that he had imagined it. But it did exist, and he caught it and brought it back to camp for all to see. It was the largest, most gorgeous skink I had ever seen. At well over two feet long, it had a long, thrashing tail and a bright yellow underbelly. It was strong and could wrap itself around you like a boa. When it swam, its reduced arms and legs folded back, and it moved like a water snake. *Amphiglossus astrolabi.*

I held it on the stoop of the lab as Glenn retrieved the field guide to figure out conclusively what it was. Rafidy came up to us.

"*Très grave,*" he said, pointing to the lizard. *Very dangerous.* We looked up at him, down at the lizard, and back at him. None of us believed this— poisonous lizards are rare, and between Glenn and me, at least, the nominal herpetologists, we would have heard of one that existed here. Of course, we didn't know this animal existed at all, so it was just possible.

"It's the teeth that will get you," Rafidy continued in French. "They are poisoned." We nodded noncommittally, while Glenn found the descriptor in the field guide. He read: "... Malagasy people are very afraid of this species and told us that they are poisonous." We looked around expectantly, hoping to find the invisible hand that was writing our script just before we read it.

21

A Team of Men,
and Some Cookies

I was tattooing frogs in camp when, fifty yards away, a tree fall almost killed Bret. First there was just noise, a thunderous, splintering collapse of a massive old tree, breaking the expectations of daytime rain forest sounds. Chattering lemurs, frogs calling back and forth, and the drone of the nearby waterfall were instantly replaced with a searing, urgent crack.

Sitting on our tent platform, Bret heard it, too. Having worked long nights in neotropical forests chasing down bats, he knew well the distinct *snap* of a tree fall. He looked behind him, to see improbable movement, a trunk three feet wide bearing down on him. He sprang, ran full speed off the platform toward the shore. As he dove onto the shaky wooden dock, the crashing stopped as suddenly as it had begun.

The lemurs resumed their conversation, the frogs their vocal competition, and the lazy heat of the rain forest pressed in from all sides. All seemed normal. Except that my husband was lying facedown on the dock, bleeding somewhat, but not flattened, and a large tree hung, poised, over our tent platform, caught in the arms of another tree. The downed tree's huge root mass was almost perpendicular to the earth where it had once stood, and an immense mass of wood was suspended over our delicate backpacking tent. Those few hollow aluminum poles strung with nylon mesh couldn't protect us now. At any moment, the tree might complete its path of destruction to the ground, flattening all in its path.

Somehow, despite the excitement, Glenn and I had remembered to put newly tattooed frog T4 back into a Ziploc bag before racing to the scene. Augustin, the naturalist guide, was on the island that day with two Eastern European tourists, as were Vonjy and Rafidy. Lebon and Fortune rounded out our population. It was a very full house. After Bret picked himself up and assessed his damage—not bad—we turned our attention to the tree. Here, we had a problem.

"What we must do," announced Augustin, "is go into town, acquire a team of men and a lot of good rope, and . . ." Bret, Glenn, and I were looking at him in disbelief. After the last few months in Madagascar, we knew without a second thought that what he proposed was impossible. His instinct was surprisingly Western—get the experts and the proper equipment to solve the problem. But the suggestion was meaningless in Madagascar. Augustin, a native Malagasy, who had been there all of his life, a smart man with a quick wit, surely knew his country better than this.

"Strong rope, Augustin?" I asked.

He smiled shyly and looked down at his feet. "They must use good rope to pull boats," he suggested.

"Have you ever seen good rope here?" Bret asked.

"No, but . . ." Augustin's voice trailed off again.

"Where could we get strong rope?" Bret wondered aloud, gently mocking. "Nairobi might be our best bet," he added, bringing home the point to the ever-optimistic Augustin. Nairobi, of course, is in Kenya, a different country, a different world. Strong rope couldn't be found on Madagascar. Certainly not in town, a boat ride away, almost certainly not in Tana, a boat ride and plane ride away, with no planes due for several days. We had at our disposal only what northeastern Madagascar could offer, which mostly amounted to brainpower and a lot of rice. The tent platform had to be saved, solely with our ingenuity and strength. We had nowhere else to sleep, as the wet season was in full swing, making the ground spongy in places. More to the point, backpacking tents aren't made to withstand months of punishing tropical rains and persistent humidity. Already, my tent was rotting, the grommets ripping, another tent pole snapping spontaneously every week. And this was on the platform, a small raised bed of wood with a thatched roof high overhead, and a massive blue tarp we had strung along one wall, to reduce the impact of the weather.

Thankfully, on this trip, Bret was with me. He seems to overpack for every situation, a trait I often resented when we were simply trying to get from A to B, and it seemed unnecessary to drag the *stuff* of our lives along with us. In fact, he is careful, calculated, and largely efficient when he packs, and even the few apparently frivolous items turn out to have use in unlikely situations—such as the fifty-foot length of climbing rope he had dragged with us to Madagascar.

Three months earlier, when our living room floor had disappeared under piles of gear, research equipment, scant clothes, toilet paper—all the necessities for life in this endeavor—I had demanded of him what on earth the climbing rope was for. He wasn't sure. I was feeling peevish, wondering how I could possibly get all of the equipment I needed to conduct my research, including a fifty-pound battery, into the three-bag, 210-pound limit I was up against. Bret didn't have the same needs—his role would be to help me keep my sanity, give me some field assistance, and write his own dissertation, none of which took up room in the backpacks. So his own 140 pounds of gear and clothes ended up including items such as a snorkel and a length of climbing rope. At the time, I'd thought him hopeless.

When we had gotten to my site and set up camp, Bret promptly found a use for the rope. He slung it over his shoulder, climbed a large mango tree overhanging the water, and made us a rope swing. It was one of very few distractions in a life otherwise full of field work and the arduous tasks of feeding ourselves and trying to keep clean and healthy. Most nights, as the sun set over the bay and the mainland of Madagascar, we took turns hurling ourselves on that rope swing, twisting in the slight breeze, escaping momentarily the slow, normal confines of gravity and human muscle that we were otherwise restricted to on this island.

Now that a tree threatened to destroy our home, that little tent platform on which we slept, hung our clothes to keep them from molding, and sat at night talking, the rope became a necessity. It was, we had been telling each other, the best rope in all of Madagascar. Augustin had been right—this was what we needed, and it just so happened that we owned the object in question. Now all we needed were experts.

First things first: Get all our stuff off the tent platform. At any moment, the tree could break through the branch it was resting on and crush the platform. We went back to the base of the fallen tree and touched it, gingerly at first. Would another fifteen pounds of pressure send it crashing to the ground, or would it take a thousand? We couldn't budge it, so we quickly set about vacating the platform, bundling our clothes, tent, and sleeping gear into bags and whisking them away from danger.

"You are all ready. No more danger," Lebon announced. Now that our stuff lay in a pile in the middle of camp, he figured the job was done.

"No, no, we need to try to save the platform," Bret reminded him. Lebon looked a bit put-upon.

"But the team of men . . ." he began. He knew there would never be a team of men. Teams of men never just materialize in Madagascar, and when you try to assemble such a group, it might take weeks, months, or simply fail to happen at all. Lebon knew this. But he obviously didn't want to have a part in deciding what our next move would be.

Bret climbed the mango tree on which the rope swing hung and untied it. He then ascended a tree near the platform, near the tree on which the fallen giant was resting. He tied the rope to the trunk and tossed the rest down to Augustin, who had volunteered for the truly dangerous task ahead. With great hesitation, and the knowledge that any moment the tree could come crashing down, killing him instantly, Augustin climbed the roof of the tent platform, slipping often on the wet thatch. Slowly, with many missteps along the way, and unhelpful instructions from those of us on the ground, Augustin tied the rope to the fallen tree. Bret then climbed another tree, far in back of the tent platform, and tied the free end of the rope to it.

Both of them descended and strolled over to us.

"Here is the plan," Augustin announced. "We will cut the tree in increments, and every time we cut a piece off the bottom, it will fall a little, supported by the rope so it does not fall all the way." By way of explanation, he pointed back to the tree Bret had tied the rope to. "Finally, it will swing around and fall away from the tent platform."

We rated the probable success of this plan at about 40 percent. But we didn't have a better one. If we destroyed the tent platform while trying to save it, we wouldn't be any worse off—we couldn't sleep on it until the danger was gone, so something had to be done.

"Okay, then." We agreed to the plan. Having worked for some years in Central America, where machetes are the cutting implement of choice, I assumed we would use my machete to cut the tree. I had brought it from home, though originally I had gotten it in Costa Rica, where it was indispensable in getting through thick, viny forest. Here in Madagascar, the vines weren't nearly so bad, and most days, the machete hung from a nail, unused. Bret retrieved it now, and received dubious stares from Lebon and Augustin.

"What's that for?" Augustin asked.

Bret was mildly exasperated. Hadn't Augustin just explained this very plan?

"To cut the tree," he said. Lebon shook his head pensively, a sure sign that he thought we were making a huge mistake.

"Why not use an ax?" Augustin asked. Another apparently brilliant but misguided suggestion, as we figured there weren't any axes for hundreds of miles, either. The machete would work, even if an ax would work better, but the point seemed moot.

Bret decided to play along. "Where will we get an ax?"

"Right here." And Lebon pulled an ax from out of thin air, or so it seemed. Bret and I looked at each other, baffled. It was pointless to wonder where this ax had been for the last several months. This was apparently the instrument Lebon used to chop wood for the fires he and Fortune cooked over, and it was a better tool for the present job. The head of the ax was none too secure, but the blade was relatively sharp, and it quickly became clear that Lebon had had extensive practice chopping wood. The rest of us stayed out of the path the ax head would take when it flew off the handle, as we assumed it certainly would, and watched in some awe as Lebon took on the tree. This man—usually quiet and inactive—was remarkably strong, able, and precise; he repeatedly whacked away at the same spot on the tree. Augustin spelled him periodically, and Bret tried his hand at it, but the rest of us sat back and watched. Lebon was the star. Tropical hardwoods have the reputation of being impermeable for a reason: They heartily resist the advances of burrowing pests, fungus, and even the sharp blade of an ax.

Soon it began to rain. The ax began slipping from Lebon's grasp as he attacked the tree, and we decided to call the project off for the day. We moved our pile of belongings into the lab. The lab, remember, was a building of about twelve by thirty-six feet, with a cement floor and porous walls, four windows with broken shutters or no shutters at all, and a door that didn't close all the way. The roof leaked, water seeped up through the floor, it was perpetually dark and moldy inside, and all variety of animals broke in when we stored items of interest in it, such as bananas or chocolate. We had built a small lean-to out of bamboo and palm leaves at one end of the stoop and under this we cooked our rice twice a day.

Still, it was a shelter, the only building we had access to on Nosy Mangabe, a place that was more water-resistant than anyplace else on the island, save perhaps the cemetery cave. Vonjy and Rafidy had set up their small tents in the lab. The Malagasy, as a rule, don't like the forest, and they particularly don't like sleeping in it. Even these men, who spent their days in the forest chasing down wild pigs, didn't want to sleep outside on a tent platform. They preferred sleeping in the lab, which was fine by us, for it meant we had our own tent platform. Until today. The lab served as the kitchen for all of us, the pantry where we hung our provisions, home to Vonjy and Rafidy, and storage place for my research equipment. We sat there some days when the rain poured down and there was no point going out into the field, as there would be no frogs. At night, by candlelight, I might sit at the table and write letters. As night began to fall on this wet gray day, our tent platform still had a massive tree hanging over it, so the lab became our home, as well. We set up our tent in the lab which, in combination with Vonjy's and Rafidy's two tents, pretty much filled it up. There was barely room to get in and out of the tents.

I was miserable. Sleeping in a tent inside a rotting building, where rats come out at night and the air was stifling—ten degrees hotter even than the tropical air just outside—was not my idea of a good time. Just one night of this drove me to frustrated distraction, and I plotted how to escape the confines of the lab and regain the fresh air and privacy of our platform. If it was destroyed, as was likely, we would need an alternate plan, for sleeping in our tent in the lab was not a viable option.

Every morning just before dawn, I was up to go watch frogs. The morning after the tree fall, I woke, confused, wondering why my clock told me it was 4:55 A.M. even though there wasn't a hint of light yet. Slowly, the day before came back—the deafening crash, the endangered tent platform, sleeping in the lab. I got up and went out to survey the damage again, and decided that I would add little or nothing by standing around observing the progress made on the tree this morning. I decided to go into the field as usual, hoping that I would return midday to find a reprieve, and not disaster.

Around 10:30 that morning, I heard a crash, then whoops of yelling from the direction of camp. I was half a mile away, too far to discern meaning from the yells—were they triumphant, or despondent? I sat watching my focal frog do nothing in particular for a few more minutes, before becoming so impatient to know the outcome of the tree fall that I packed up and went back to camp. As you come into camp from the south, on the coastal trail, the first thing you see is our tent platform. This day, as I rounded the corner into camp, I came upon exactly the same scene I'd been returning to for months. Our tent platform. Still standing. Looking up, I saw no uprooted tree leaning precariously over the platform. I dropped my backpack and ran around the back of the platform, where I found Lebon, Augustin, and Bret, standing there looking dazed.

"Great job, men!" I enthused. I couldn't have been happier. That tent platform, which only twenty-four hours before had seemed stifling and small, representing all of the limits of life on this remote island, now evoked feelings of home, of privacy and comfort, of cool breezes off the bay and limitless opportunity. The area in back of the tent platform, which had once been scrubby secondary forest, was now flattened, the low vegetation having succumbed when the tree bore down on it. Apparently, the plan had worked. When the tree finally came down, after four sections had been cut from it, it had swung within inches of the platform before landing just feet away.

This was cause for celebration. Our home had been saved, disaster averted, and no team of men had been called in. With our own in-house team of men and "bring your own rope" plan, the tree fall was a thing of the past. How to celebrate?

Were we home, we might have gone out for a good dinner, indulged in some fine wine, had some friends over, seen a movie. Had we been home, though, we wouldn't have had to fix the problem ourselves—indeed, it would have been a mistake to try. Living in the developed world, with its insurance policies and experts around every corner, means living with liability. Caution is imperative, and fixing your own problems is frowned upon. If a tree had fallen over our house in Ann Arbor and been caught in the arms of another tree just overhead, the extent of our response would have been to use the phone to call the appropriate people into action.

The irony is this: In the States, there is less opportunity to solve your own problems, but far greater means to celebrate your victories. In Madagascar, particularly on this little island reserve, where our victories were real and of the moment, the opportunity to celebrate was extremely limited. We made ourselves some rice and beans, and broke out one of our cherished boxes of cookies for dessert. The forest spilled out onto the coarse sand beach, turning a rich, saturated green in the setting sun, while needlefish swam lazily in a small school in the shallow water. Sitting on the dock while the sun set over Madagascar, relishing luscious, rare European cookies with Bret and Glenn, knowing that I was going back to my tent platform to sleep that night, all was right with the world.

22

But They Are Wild

On our first trip to Madagascar, when we were in the dry south, Bret and I had wanted to see nature untamed. We had heard about a "private reserve" that promised snakes and forest and sifakas, so we signed up to go. Our guide, who had no ecological knowledge, was a glorified driver, and he took the two of us along an interminable stretch of road. We were watching the clock, thinking the road might be the extent of what we would see on this all-day "nature tour."

Spotting a troop of ring-tail lemurs playing in the spindly, spiny native plants—reminiscent of Dr. Seuss, like so much in Madagascar—we grew excited and asked the driver to stop.

"You don't want to get out here. This is forest!" he exclaimed.

"Yes," we agreed, confused at the implication. "And there are lemurs here. We want to see them."

The driver shook his head. "Not these lemurs. These are no good."

"Why?" we persisted. "There's a whole troop—look, a baby on its mother's stomach, and juveniles chasing one another. These are wonderful lemurs!"

"But they are wild," he said. We were silent. "I'm taking you to better lemurs, lemurs that know people and approach when you give them bananas."

So this, like other reserves we had been to and were now avoiding, was to be a small plot of disturbed forest where friendly lemurs approached banana-toting tourists. As we were to find over and over again, few people trying their hand at ecotourism in Madagascar understand that some of us want to be immersed in nature, not carefully shielded from its betrayals and surprises.

Conservation is a tricky issue, especially in the developing world. White outsiders want to preserve the environment they view as precious, often without regard for the equally native and natural people who live in it. Ecologists and other trained scientists gain personally by convincing themselves and grant-bestowing agencies that their work will benefit conservation efforts. Native peoples cannot fathom why the welfare of animals they might eat, or of trees, is more important than their own survival and traditions.

Why do we want to save the forests? Some would say because they are valuable as potential harborers of undiscovered medicinal compounds, which might benefit humanity if found. But if we need justify all scientific inquiry on the basis of what specific, practical, benefit it will serve, we are lost. Our culture cannot claim foresight, nor intelligence, nor even a grasp of history, if we pursue only that which can be currently justified as useful.

If not for practical reasons, then, why do we want to save the forests? In part, because humans do not have the right to destroy them, though we have already destroyed so many in the developed world. We did not make them—indeed, they preexisted us, helped shape us into our current form. The emotional argument is perhaps the strongest: Do we really want a planet without natural places? Are we content to lose all space that is free of human nattering and influence? As human culture homogenizes to a lowest common denominator across the globe, do we also want to eradicate what advertising and big business cannot get to? Nosy Mangabe has never been touched by Adidas or Nabisco or McDonald's. Even Madagascar is too small a market for them to be there yet. Coca-Cola is there, represented by drinks with names we don't have at home, but their influence is relatively small. In 1999, the theme song from *Titanic* blared from every speaker in Maroantsetra. Luckily, Maroantsetra has very few speakers. There are a few huts in town where you can go watch a video on a certain night every week, the name of the film written on a chalkboard in front of the house. There is no television in Maroantsetra yet. Still, our Western influence is coming, albeit under a different guise.

The new hotel, the grand hotel, the Relais, opened in Maroantsetra in

1997. At the time, Maroantsetra had one wheelbarrow to its name, and when Jessica and I tried to commission it to aid us in carrying our baggage and provisions to the boat, it had no wheel. Maroantsetra had, as its sole attraction for the *vazaha*, the proximity of Nosy Mangabe and the more isolated Masoala peninsula. And yet the hotel came to Maroantsetra.

It is debatable whether conservation should encourage tourism at all. It may be helpful to conservation efforts for interested laypeople with a fascination for nature to spread the word about the beauty and diversity of the world's ecosystems. But should it be a stated goal to attract Westerners to preserved areas in the developing world? I believe so, for the following reasons: Naturalist guides are required to show *vazaha* tourists the forest. In general, naturalist guides are locals, and these people, if they are good at what they do, will have an interest in the forest, even a passion for it. Furthermore, if their welfare depends on being hired by *vazaha* to be shown the forest, they will come to respect and help to protect the forest. They will speak of the forest with fondness and care, to their families and friends. It will become clear to the community that protecting the forest brings money into town, and not just for the naturalist guides.

In Maroantsetra, the food vendors in the marketplace benefit from tourism, as do the hotels and the restaurants. The weavers who make baskets and hats benefit from our presence, for we buy their products. And the charcoal sellers, who sit at the bottom of the economic ladder among the vendors in the *zoma*, they, too, benefit from us, for we must buy charcoal to cook our rice. Even the *vazaha* must eat. With tourists comes an infusion of money into the local economy. In all of these ways, ecotourists, who come to see the forest, bring an economic bloom to the town of Maroantsetra. The townspeople can see, even if they do not understand why, that the attraction is the forest, and that without the forest, the *vazaha* would stop flowing, and so would the money.

But the introduction of a hotel such as the Relais de Masoala changes all of this. The Relais charges rates that are an order of magnitude higher than the other hotels in town—$70 per night, to the Maroa's $7.50. If you stay at the Relais, their vehicle picks you up at the airport and ferries you through town without stopping—Maroantsetra passes by the window. You are delivered to their little haven, which has very little to do with Madagascar. All of the workers are dressed in specifically non-Malagasy costumes. No other villagers are allowed on the grounds.

Patrons of the Relais are discouraged from going into town. Why take that long, hot, dusty walk, where you might be obliged to interact with townspeople who share no life experiences with you, and may not even share a language. It will probably be frustrating, and perhaps even a little frightening, to have interactions so foreign to your expectations. The Relais successfully protects its patrons from ever realizing that Maroantsetra is filled with smiling, life-loving people. The Relais provides European meals, a full bar, hot showers, laundry service. And for an additional fee, it offers day trips to Nosy Mangabe.

At first, the Relais did not want to advertise Nosy Mangabe to its patrons. Access to Nosy Mangabe requires the acquisition of permits from government agencies, and hiring naturalist guides from their association at Projet Masoala. The Relais is otherwise free from such restrictions. Monique wanted to take tourists to her flat little deforested island, where the Metcalfs and I had spent Easter two years earlier, rather than to the lush rain forest of Nosy Mangabe. But her tourists were having none of it. So she made a bid to take over Nosy Mangabe. The Wildlife Conservation Society has the interests of the forest and the local people in mind. Were the new hotel to take over Nosy Mangabe, however, those interests would be turned on their head. It would, I am certain, be the end of the reserve. Monique's hotel is not a megacorporation. Because the new hotel is relatively small, it seems less dangerous. I believe it may be more so.

Before the Relais, the few tourists who came to northeastern Madagascar were ecotourists—people engaged with nature, wanting to see the results of millions of years of evolution in weird and fantastic forms, and willing to be somewhat uncomfortable in order to do so. The people Monique is attracting are wealthy tourists, adventurous enough to go off the beaten path to Madagascar, but unwilling to endure hardship to experience Madagascar as it really is. These people are probably aware that one of Madagascar's claims to fame is the extraordinary diversity and endemism of its biota. But these are not people awed by nature. They are tourists, not ecotourists, and by catering to their desires, while protecting them from interacting with the real people who live just outside the gates of the Relais, the hotel management ensures that their preconceptions about the developing world will remain.

The Relais would turn Nosy Mangabe into a beach resort for wealthy *vazaha*. I have seen this before, in Central America. A facade is erected to look like home. Tourists hand over large amounts of cash for the pleasure of visiting the facade, and little of the money ever trickles into the local economy. The money would probably be poured into a more functional and beautiful plumbing system; into a kitchen that could prepare meals without charcoal smoke or rice; into easy walking trails. The Relais would probably begin feeding lemurs, to ensure close encounters for the tourists, so that nobody would go home feeling they had not gotten their money's worth.

Money would not be expended for the services of the exquisite naturalist guides who have trained themselves so well in the ways of the forest, in languages, and in how to interact with *vazaha*. Already there were arguments over pay—the hotel did not want to pay the minimal rate the guides had agreed upon among themselves. Little of the money spent by tourists at the Relais has gone to the local economy. What value, then, does this new hotel have to local people?

If the new hotel administered Nosy Mangabe, the people of Maroantsetra would come to dislike the island, too. There would be no incentive to protect the forest once economic incentive vanished. Even the guides, even Felix, with the most naturalist in him of all, a man who loves to go into the forest even when his tourists do not, would have to find other work, or he and his young son Alpha would starve. Knowledge of the forest and its intricacies would die out in Maroantsetra. Ecotourists would no longer be attracted here, because the prices commanded at the Relais are too high for most. Having one or two researchers hanging about to explain some curious natural history revelations to fellow *vazaha* might be handy, and surely there are enough out-of-work Ph.D.s to take that job, demoralizing and, indeed, destructive as it is. For that job would take food and knowledge out of the mouths and minds of the local people.

Northeastern Madagascar, including the newly minted Masoala National Park, has more endemic species than do most countries. It is the largest remaining piece of lowland rain forest in Madagascar, and it is incomparable, irreplaceable. It is at risk, because decisions are being made that put greater emphasis on impressing the wealthy than on protecting the environment. It is a deal made with the devil, the devil being money hunger from the West. Bring rich *vazaha* here while exploiting their desires for comfort and there will be no returning. Pirates, a Dutch hospital, a Malagasy cemetery, Malagasy fisher people—all of these are part of this island's history, and all have left a mark, but none is indelible. The mark of Western money would never be erased.

Once the mark of comfort-driven consumption comes to a place, everyone believes that their lives, too, would be better *if only*. If only I had a tarp like hers. If only I had hiking boots like his. If only I had as much money as they do. Given their longings, and the increasing availability of consumer goods, we will turn them into us, with our lost communities, our clans spread thin. They will forget to value what they have, and care only for what they do not. And in all of that cultural change, while the generous and real people of Maroantsetra turn into Western wanna-bes like the rest of the world, the forest will disappear. It will go quietly. A few people will notice. Nobody will heed the cries of despair. And then, it will be gone.

The new hotel was not the only risk to Nosy Mangabe. Lebon and Fortune had grown complacent in their jobs, bored with their lives on the island, so that even their large incomes (by local standards) weren't incentive to actually protect the island they were being paid to protect. Before Rosalie left, she saw a sailor hunting lemurs with a spear. She had dissuaded the man, but when we alerted the conservation agents to the problem, we received only glassy stares in return.

The guides began reporting that *Uroplatus*—the magnificent camouflaged leaf-tailed geckos—were declining on the island. They had reason to believe that the cause of this decline was that someone in town was paying five thousand FMG for any that came their way—less than one dollar each for one of the most spectacular lizards on the planet. Probably they were being whisked to the First World, where a tropical herp enthusiast would pay in excess of one hundred dollars for that same animal, which had been ripped from its wild life. When we reported this probability to the conservation agents and their employees, again nothing was done. Several weeks later, a crate of *Uroplatus* was discovered being smuggled out of Maroantsetra on a plane.

For reasons I could never understand, when the guides generated plausible explanations for mysteries such as the dwindling *Uroplatus* population, they were not paid any heed. The guides, to a person, are tremendous—eager to learn, already possessing a good deal of knowledge, intuitive about humans and nature, amiable and fun to be with. By comparison, the conservation agents had become a hazard to the island, accepting kickbacks from sailors with spears.

Like Rosalie, the guides remained optimistic and intellectually curious in the face of an uncertain future. Augustin asked me to make a list of the frogs I had seen, so he and the other guides could learn them. When he was out on the island with Hungarian tourists one day and they wanted to play alone in the water with their snorkels (they just kept multiplying), Augustin went into the forest with a notepad. Felix, Emile, Armand, Jean, and Paul all asked me separately to teach them about the forest, about frogs, and about the process of scientific discovery. The work that I do is all particularly well suited to what ecotourists like to hear. I told the guides about the tiny, beautiful, social frogs who fight and court with such frequency that a tourist with an hour to spend, if taken to the right place, and weather permitting, would be likely to see a social interaction. Armed with the full narrative, the guides could try to find for their tourists some of the other players that round out this story—perhaps a *Plethodontohyla notostica* father frog taking care of his young in a well once used by *Mantella laevigata*, or the parasite that eats frog eggs.

The fact that the guides had both a passion for the forest and the wit to understand it seemed extraordinary, but it made sense that such motivated, savvy people should be naturalist guides. Doesn't it also make sense, though, that the people hired to protect the forest should have passion and wit enough to comprehend and care for it? Why this disconnect, where a connection is most critical?

Lebon and Fortune were slipping further into inaction, and with the bit of entropy they added to the system, the camp actually fell into disrepair faster when they were around. Twice more, they broke the pipe connection to the shower, and left it there, spilling hundreds of gallons of water into camp, until Bret or I fixed it. One morning, a group of sailors invaded my small research area, leaving a pile of fresh human feces before I arrived, and attacking me verbally once I was there. I asked them to stay outside the boundaries of my bamboo stand, which I had demarcated in bright flagging tape, but they just laughed. When I reported the incident to Lebon and Fortune, they told me, as they had before, "The beach is not protected."

"It is protected, and besides, my stand is not on the beach; it's in the forest," I objected. It was futile. There would be no conservation from the conservation agents that day.

Toward the end of that final field season, the conservation agents were replaced in stages. First, Lucien arrived. He was a slight, hardworking man with a perpetual smile on his face, who daily cleaned camp and walked the coastal trail, clearing the path and making his presence known to any unpermitted Malagasy who might come ashore. Two weeks later, Lucien left for a few days to be with his family in town, and he was replaced by two brothers, Joe and Vincent. The first thing Joe and Vincent did on arrival was to build gym equipment out of bamboo. A chin-up bar and parallel bars were sturdily erected in camp, so that Vincent might continue his passion for exercise while on Nosy Mangabe. The two brothers were indefatigable. After constructing their bamboo gym, they insisted on cleaning the spiders out of the lab. Besides not being their job, it was a losing battle. They cleared a tree fall that had been blocking a path for at least three months, perhaps longer. They actively watched for boats, and when three of them had to moor in our little bay during a storm, they made sure that the sailors came on land only to get drinking water.

When Lucien returned, he brought his family. His sweet, terrified wife couldn't make eye contact with the *vazaha*. His four exuberant children couldn't help but. The oldest, a lithe, long-limbed boy of nine or ten, was honing his skills at retrieving mangoes from trees. The two girls, the middle children, liked to stand on the dock and watch the waves, or dig in the sand for crabs to fish with. The littlest, but a toddler, was everyone's responsibility, and his siblings took just as keen an interest in his well-being as did his parents. I asked Lucien if he would allow me to take pictures of his family, both for me and for them, and he was pleased at the request. His wife was too timid to come out of hiding, but the children, who vaguely understood what a camera did but had not seen one previously, were natural hams. Maybe, I thought, if Lebon and Fortune had been encouraged to bring their families out to the island, they would have been more content, and therefore more productive, during their time there. Although I only saw the first four weeks of the new agents at work, their work ethics and personalities boded well for the future of Nosy Mangabe.

There is one trash can on Nosy Mangabe, half an old oil drum. It is not particularly large—about twice the size of an under-the-sink kitchen garbage can. A *programme* exists for its regular pickup and emptying in town and its return, but it is not adhered to. Probably, when there are no *vazaha* on the island, the trash can fills so slowly that it seems ludicrous to those who would be doing the work to cart a quarter- or third-full trash can into town twice a month.

When Bret, Glenn, and I arrived, the situation quickly became dire. We almost doubled the population of the island. But it was not our numbers that made the difference. Had three Malagasy researchers arrived—as, indeed, the two pig researchers did shortly before us—trash accumulation would have accelerated, but not by much. The Malagasy eat rice, smoke fish and cigarettes, and reuse every made or found object. As Westerners, we are consumers—this despite our personal environmentalism, which translates, in the United States, to buying in bulk, thus reducing consumption of packaging; recycling papers and glass and most plastics; reusing boxes and shopping with baskets or cloth bags. But these efforts are, by comparison with a simpler way of life, trivial.

We arrived on Nosy Mangabe with many baskets of rice, which would have comprised most of our purchases for the next four months had we been Malagasy. But the increased options in Maroantsetra meant that there was pasta to be had, imported Marie 22 crackers, tomato paste, soy sauce, mustard. There was even soy oil, prepackaged in plastic bottles. Previously, the only cooking oil available was coconut oil in dirty oil drums, with flies resting on the surface. An old ladle was used to dip into the drum and deposit some of the opaque oil, sediment and all, into a container you brought. We preferred the stuff that came with its own clean plastic skin, easily tossed when the contents were used.

We bought soap for cleaning clothes—which came in individual plastic packets—to augment the biodegradable CampSuds we had brought from home. We also found soap for personal use, a new kind that didn't stick to your skin for days after each use, as was true of the only soap you used to be able to buy in Madagascar—*Nosy* soap. It means "island soap." *Nosy* soap is still used by the locals for cleaning their dishes, their clothes, and themselves. It is sold as unwrapped bars and is cheap. The new soap, which appealed to our Western sensibilities because it came off when we rinsed, had a nicely comforting name—Lux—and came well packaged, wrapped in several layers of paper, with plastic on the outside, bearing a picture of a beautiful, smiling, immaculate white woman. We believed that we prefered it only because it did not leave the sticky residue that *Nosy* soap always did, but perhaps the name and packaging also attracted some deep-seated consumer in us. Perhaps it is precisely when I am sure that I am not the target audience for an advertisement that they have gotten into my head.

We bought more of these products every time we went into town. The Malagasy don't tend to—both because they cannot afford it and because it is not what they are used to. Rice comes without packaging in Madagascar. The diversity most Westerners expect in our diet requires that a great deal of food be moved around the planet, and with that food, its packaging. Our desires brought packaging to Nosy Mangabe. Packaging is just trash, an earlier life stage. We filled the trash can quickly.

To alleviate some of the trash problem, and to satisfy our composting urges, we suggested that a pit be dug for organic trash. At first glance, it seemed extremely odd that this had not been done before—wasn't composting a natural outgrowth of farming on poor soils such as these, a way to recycle what nutrients you could? Our suggestion was taken, and we watched with interest as the pit began to fill with uneaten rice, fruit peels, fish bones and heads. The trash can, now devoted to nonorganic material, remained empty. The Malagasy generated essentially no inorganic trash.

We drank perhaps a bottle of wine a week, and the empty bottles were of value to the Malagasy. They do not usually drink wine. The Lazan'i Betsileo vintage, made in the Fianar region of Madagascar, is not a fine wine, but it's drinkable, and a bargain at three dollars a bottle. Who here could afford a three-dollar bottle of wine when they could get *toka gasy*— the extremely strong local rotgut—for pennies? They understood neither our penchant for wine nor our willful indifference to the glass bottles that hold the wine. To contain the coconut oil they bought in bulk, a wine bottle did nicely.

The trash can never remained empty for long, as we dumped our inorganic trash into it and filled it. We generated plastic bottles with soy oil residue in them. And tomato paste cans. And the plastic wrapping from pasta, candles, malaria pills.

When you buy prepared food from street vendors in town—samosas or macaroons—it is handed to you on a piece of old paper. The paper tends to be from a long-since-irrelevant bureaucratic document in French, delineating the hierarchy of now-extinct personages in a particular government ministry. Everything is reused until it is gone. We would take those greasy pieces of paper and throw them away.

When we bought bouillon cubes in one store, they gave us a plastic bag to hold them. The bag was printed in Chinese, advertising tea strainers from a remote province in China. How many hands must it have passed through before reaching ours? Its journey ended with us. Once it was emptied of jumbo cubes, we threw it away. In a land of practically nothing, we still managed to generate trash—a tiny amount by American standards, but huge by those of the rest of the world.

The trash can on Nosy Mangabe overflowed with *vazaha* trash. I left our friends anything they found useful, but still the trash can overflowed. Ten years from now, one may still be able to find a plastic bag from Kmart or REI in Maroantsetra. As I happily roam farmer's markets in the States with my Maroantsetra-bought baskets, feeling virtuous, the rest of the world is sorting through my trash, making it valuable.

23

Cinema Maroantsetra

If our trash was valuable to the local people, the stuff we brought with us was even more so. I woke up to an unwelcome surprise on what was to be the final day of my female choice experiment. I had been robbed, again. The dry bag holding all of my frog song playback equipment—several hundred dollars' worth of scientific gear, including a tape player not designed to play music, though it could function in that regard—was gone. Some other items and cash had been taken as well, but the sound equipment was critical. Given my experimental design, that last day's data were critical—without it, I could use none of the data I had. I either had to get the gear back, or figure out a new way to record onto tapes the digitized frog calls that I had stored on the computer.

The theft sent me into a tailspin, not only because of the threat to my research. All of the details pointed to an inside job—the careful point of entry, the taking of an opaque bag that only people who were familiar with the lab would know contained sound-recording equipment. It wasn't anyone on the island, either—Lucien, the only conservation agent there at the time, was as trustworthy as they come. The fisher family down at the remote camp couldn't be thieves. I felt it in my gut.

Bret and I went into town as soon as we could—the radio was broken again, so we couldn't communicate with the mainland, and had to wait until a boat showed up the following day. We wanted to get the word out, try to retrieve the equipment (the cash, we assumed, was a lost cause), and figure out how to get the digitized frog calls onto tapes.

Those first few hours in town were riddled with doubt and suspicions. Edwige quickly went into action, took notes on what had happened, and put together a message in Malagasy to be read on the air from the radio station at noon. Later, because we still had to eat, we went searching for *le derniere fromage*—our final interface with European cuisine. We met with success, but before the woman behind the counter would sell us that last bit of cheese that Maroantsetra had, she asked if the radio announcement was about us. Had we been robbed? Wanting to know all the details, she asked probing questions that got to the heart of the matter.

"Who else was on the island?"

"Just the guardian, and a couple of fisher people."

"Are you sure it wasn't the guardian?"

"Yes, quite sure."

"But why? He easily could have done it."

"Yes, but he wouldn't. I can't explain. I'm just sure."

"How about the fishermen?"

"No, it wasn't them, either—we have a relationship, you see. We know each other, from two years ago. The man . . . " I paused. This was going to sound lame. I sighed, and continued. "The man, he used to bring me mangoes in the forest." She nodded, understanding.

"Were there any boats there?"

"No. No boats. And it was raining." She was asking all the right questions, but she was just going to end up as confused by the whole incident as I already was. We bought our cheese and left.

We went back to the Maroa. As we were sitting down to order tomato salads, Felix walked by. I told him about the robbery, and he sat thinking for a few moments.

"Sounds like an inside job," he said. Then he sighed. It was the first time I'd seen him look sad. "Maybe Rafidy did it," he suggested. I gaped at him.

"Rafidy? You don't think he is honest?"

"Oh, I think he is honest, but think about what happened, and what he knows. He knows the lab—he was living in it. He knows what you have—he was living with you, and your things. He is a fisherman, and he has a pirogue, so he had the means to get there."

I was stunned. All of what I had come to love about the people of

Madagascar and the interactions I had with them was suddenly in doubt. Were my instincts wholly wrong? Could Rafidy, the radio repairman for Maroantsetra and assistant to Vonjy, have done it? The same man who would fish the entire morning, then present us with fried fish as a supplement to whatever meal we were cooking for ourselves? The same man who had wanted to see a picture I received from my dearest friend of her family, and who had asked me about the details of her life?

My mind wouldn't let this one pass. I desperately wanted to be far away, not to have to wonder at every new interaction I had. Then reason kicked in. If it was a Malagasy we knew, it would be impossible not to be disappointed. But anger wouldn't be relevant. We were the *vazaha*, after all, with inconceivable amounts of money and resources at our disposal. We seemed to throw money around like it meant nothing to us—a whole dollar for four immense avocados, and another for more candles, when we already had some. Some of our friends there might have stolen from us, but only because they perceived that such theft couldn't possibly make much difference in our lives but would make a huge difference in theirs.

"It definitely sounds like it was done by someone who knows the place," Felix said, thoughtful. Then without much hurry, and with a laugh, he added, "But it wasn't me." The blood drained from my face.

"No, Felix, of course it wasn't you," I agreed. But in my new, post-theft world, perhaps his words should have set off alarm bells. I wouldn't let myself question Felix, though. It was all swirling in my head. I couldn't sort it out without more evidence, but there was no more evidence.

Lacking the ability to decipher the crime, we tried to fix some of the problems it had caused. We made arrangements to record my frog calls at the radio station. The station, we'd been told, was across from the bank, in a store next to the building where boat motors were repaired. Bret knew the repair shop, and there was only one store near it. There were five young Malagasy men sitting on the sagging stoop.

"Is this the radio station?" Bret asked in good French. The men looked confused. Bret tried again, with more gusto. They talked among themselves, then asked us in perfect French what it was, exactly, that we were looking for.

I repeated the question. The men resumed discussing among themselves. Two of them pointed down the street, back from where we had come. Two others literally scratched their heads, trying to figure out where this elusive radio station might be located. They grew animated, then stopped and asked Bret again what he had said.

"We are looking for the radio station. Do you know where it is?" he repeated.

"The what?"

"The radio station."

"You mean the radio station?" they asked.

"Ah, yes," Bret replied, "the radio station." The young men suddenly erupted in laughter and gestured to the steps under them.

"Ah, the radio station, of course. It is right here." They were sitting on the stoop of the radio station. And now that they understood, they found the whole thing very funny. They laughed at themselves for being thick-headed and stood up to let us go up the stairs.

Inside was the usual assortment of goods: Nosy soap, mosquito coils, crackers. The smiling woman behind the counter welcomed us and told us that Monsieur Philippe, the man who ran the radio station, would be back shortly. When he returned, I identified us as the *vazaha* about whom the radio announcement had been made, which he seemed to know already. I then explained the predicament this left us in—that we had everything we needed to make new tapes, except for a tape recorder. He was eager to help. He led us through the store, through a room containing bags of rice and a barrel of cooking oil with a slow leak, back to the room that was the radio station. Four stereo components, one of which was a fairly high-fidelity tape-to-tape deck, comprised the equipment. One wall was full of tapes, another half-full of CDs. A replay of the Peace Corps volunteer Angela's Friday night radio show in English was just finishing. The man unhooked the tape deck from the other components and brought it around to a table with two old microphones on it. Shortly, the DJ, a pretty young Malagasy woman, came in and began playing Malagasy pop. In the background, we recorded frog calls. Everything went smoothly, and within an hour, we were off, with many profuse thanks to Monsieur Philippe. Now Maroantsetra had two copies of tapes with male frogs, *deet-deet*ing endlessly. The thief, who had probably been hoping for American music, may have wondered at what strange music the *vazaha* listen to. But he must have continued listening, for we never did see the equipment again.

Later, Pascal showed up at our bungalows at the Maroa, looking for conversation. Bret and Glenn were on their way out to find crackers and kerosene, and Pascal accompanied me on my quest for small plastic cups to replace some I was using in an ongoing experiment. As dusk fell, we walked back to the Maroa. Bret, who wasn't yet back, had the key to our bungalow, so Pascal and I sat on the porch and talked. He asked me if there weren't frogs in the United States. I told him yes, but not so many, and not so interesting, and already quite well studied.

"Besides," I added, "part of the reason to do biological research, for me, is to experience different cultures and ways of living. Being in Madagascar is part of why I chose to work on Madagascar frogs." He was surprised at this assertion, just as Emile, Rosalie, and many others had been.

A beautiful young woman strutted by. She had on tight, skimpy black shorts and white platform shoes. As Pascal and I watched her pass, he said something to her in Malagasy, in a tone that sounded pejorative. She answered in French, and was gone.

"Why did she address you in French?" I asked Pascal. He sighed.

"She likes the *vazaha* and their ways very much. She is always going with the *vazaha*."

This seemed like my opening, so I pursued the subject. "When Malagasy women 'go' with *vazaha* men, do you, or do any Malagasy men, 'go' with them, as well?" He seemed to shudder at the very thought.

"No, no. Never."

"Why?" I asked him.

"Oh, hers is a dangerous life. Also, once they have been with the *vazaha*, all they want is money. Malagasy men can't offer them money the way the *vazaha* can."

"Why do they do it, then?"

"Because sometimes, very rarely, a *vazaha* marries a Malagasy woman, and then she is taken care of."

"But that doesn't happen very often, right?"

"No, hardly ever. And even if it does, the *vazaha* usually still has a family back in France, or wherever, and he is not here much of the time."

"So what happens to these women? What happens when they age and are not desired by the *vazaha* anymore?" I was asking questions that made him sad.

"They have a very difficult life," he said. "The *vazaha* give them money when they are here, but much of the time there are no *vazaha*. The women must eat every day. So the money disappears. And when the *vazaha* are no longer interested, because the woman is getting older, and her family does not help very much, because she has turned her back on them, she has difficulty finding enough to eat. Usually, these women die young." And then he said, in a tone that suggested that I might be surprised by the revelation,

"There are many different types of *vazaha*. Some are like you, curious about the Malagasy, and interested in talking with us. But many are rude, mean, and disrespectful. They come here with their money and expect to be able to do whatever they want. Often it's the French who act this way."

"You think the French are worse than the other *vazaha*?" I asked.

"We have a history with the French, you know. They colonized us, and they still think they own Madagascar. We threw them out almost forty years ago, but still they act like we are theirs. When they come here, they do not respect our culture or humanity."

We drifted through various topics. I asked him about his work, and whether he wasn't spending more time waiting now, since there were more people on Nosy Mangabe who needed to get back and forth. He said that yes, he waited for us, sometimes, but that he enjoyed the work and there was nothing he would rather be doing.

"Aren't you also waiting for other things? Like to get married?" I asked. Our earliest conversation had revealed that he had a *sipa* and that they were engaged to be married—next year, he hoped. Now he was more clear with me.

"No, I hope to get married someday, but I don't wait for it, because it will be a long time before it can happen. Until then, she and I live together, and we may start a family. I want only two children, because more is very expensive. But we cannot afford to get married now."

"What is the expense?"

"To get married, we must have all of our family with us. Much of my family is here in Maroantsetra, but hers is up north. Until we can afford to transport everyone here, we can't get married."

Pascal wasn't straining at the hurdles, at the time passing—he was a content, curious man with the love of a woman and the sea, and little else mattered.

"What are you waiting for?" he asked.

I thought about it. At that moment, there was nothing. I, too, was content to sit on our little porch, under a deepening night sky, and talk with Pascal. As long as I was in town, though, I did want to get some more vanilla.

"Vanilla, I guess," I said, and he laughed.

"I know a vanilla seller," he said, "a friend. I'll take you to him tomorrow."

And so the following day, we were led into another Maroantsetran's life, that of a vanilla merchant, who presented "only his finest beans" to us, huge piles on a big wooden table in his home. The whole place smelled rich and pungent. Pascal, standing in a corner watching our transaction, wrinkled his nose. Like most Malagasy, he didn't like the smell of vanilla.

Looking at Maroantsetra as an outsider, the economic reason for its existence seems primarily to be as the spice-growing epicenter of Madagascar. Most of the spices now grown in such profusion in Madagascar are not native, but this doesn't seem to have adversely affected their ability to be cultivated. Cinnamon, cloves, nutmeg, and vanilla are the primary exports, and the Masoala peninsula produces much of the world's supply. When the spice boats arrive in this small port town, everything smells of spice. After being in the region for a while, it's hard to tell by smell if a boat is carrying mainly cloves or mostly cinnamon, as the aromas begin to mingle in the head as well as in the air.

Sometimes spices are for sale in the stores, before the bulk of them get taken south to the larger port of Tamatave. In Maroantsetra, sweet and potent cinnamon is still in its freshest, natural form, thick pieces of tree bark, and costs five thousand FMG for half a kilo—about a dollar for more than a pound. One storekeeper invited me to taste her wares. It was like candy, and I realized I'd never known true cinnamon before. The same went for cloves, but they were even cheaper. So cheap, in fact, that I bought them by the kilo and distributed them among my clothes and shoes, as the persistent wet of the rain forest had begun to mold everything I had. The cloves didn't keep the rot away, but they helped cover the smell. After returning home, I found cloves for months, falling out of pockets, backpacks, field notebooks, every nook and cranny.

Vanilla wasn't for sale in the stores in town. To get vanilla in Maroantsetra, I had only to make my wishes known—to Solo, at Andranobe, or to Pascal, who knew someone in town. Everyone knew someone. If you are wondering what on earth I was buying vanilla for, you've never been close to this fantastic bean. Vanilla is pure luxury. There's a Gary Larson cartoon I had laughed at but never fully appreciated until I started going to Madagascar. The caption reads "Same planet, different worlds." The art is a split frame—a man in bed at the top, a woman in bed at the bottom. The man is thinking, "I wonder if she knows I exist. . . . Should I call her? Maybe she doesn't even know I exist? Well, maybe she does. . . . I'll call her. No, wait! . . . I'm not sure if she knows I exist. . . . Dang!" The woman is thinking, "You know, I think I really like vanilla." Well, I'm sure I really like vanilla.

Vanilla is extremely expensive in the developed world, so most things

labeled vanilla have such trace amounts that you can hardly detect any flavor. Foods proclaiming to be vanilla-flavored don't usually contain vanilla
at all, but synthetic attempts at vanilla that manifest as neutral, to which
you can add flavor. Americans use the word *vanilla* derisively, to suggest
blandness, ordinariness, an utter lack of intrigue. When I was a little girl,
I mocked my father for choosing vanilla ice cream—the real stuff, flecked
with tiny black seeds—and he would just smile and nod. How did he know
I would come to see the wisdom in choosing vanilla?

The edible vanilla bean is the reproductive product of a rare orchid, the
only species of orchid among more than thirty thousand that yields anything
edible. Native to the New World, it is produced in abundance in Mexico,
and has been introduced to Madagascar, as well as Indonesia. The pollinator
required to fertilize the orchid flower, a stingless bee, is found only in the
western hemisphere, in the native range of the vanilla orchid. Even where
it exists, the bee is quite rare, so vanilla farmers must hand-pollinate each
flower individually to produce a single bean. The bean, or seedpod, matures
on the plant for several months before being harvested, dried in the sun,
then cured for several more months. The beans have no odor when harvested, developing their signature scent only during the long curing process.

In the developed world, where vanilla isn't grown except by orchid en-
thusiasts, consumers usually buy vanilla in extract form—alcohol that has
been infused with vanilla beans, then strained. Beans are available at specialty stores, and increasingly at supermarkets, as well. They cost almost
two dollars each. If you want to make real vanilla ice cream, or better vanilla
extract than you'll ever find in a store, or just experience the wondrous
smell, the beans are the only way to go. I can say that. I pay less than ten
cents per bean when I'm in northeastern Madagascar, and I get enough
vanilla to keep me in raptures, the deep, faintly sticky beans exuding their
power for years.

Theft took us to the one-room radio station in town, and Pascal led me to
a vanilla merchant, whose house had deeply polished wood floors. Town, it
seemed, was full of items not immediately apparent to the outsider. When
dogs started showing up dead in great numbers, though, it was hard not to
notice.

Opération Chien had hit Maroantsetra. When we arrived in town for
our last provision run before leaving Nosy Mangabe for good, we found
dogs lying dead in the streets. First one, then two, now a pile of three over

behind that shack, another one under a palm tree. On every path we turned down, there were more dogs, motionless. It seemed at first that they were merely lying, perhaps sleeping, as many dogs do, stretched out and relaxed, but these dogs were different. Their eyes were open, and flies hung about their heads.

It was raining. As we approached the center of town, the carcasses grew more dense. The *zoma* was vibrant, rice and fish and vegetable vendors all set up in the rain, with people roaming about with children on their hips and umbrellas over their heads, nimbly avoiding the corpses of dogs that littered the marketplace. Chickens pecked at them. The dogs did not move.

In one of the outlying villages, there had been three cases of canine rabies identified. Maroantsetra responded by mounting an attack on stray dogs, which was probably a reasonable response. Dogs with a rare vaccination certificate for rabies were spared. Beginning the day before we had come to town, and for the following month, there was a human curfew from 11:00 P.M. to 3:00 A.M. During that time, the veterinarian and his crew would deliver poisoned meat to the streets of Maroantsetra. Dogs (or, presumably, any mammal) who ate this meat would die within minutes. We did not know what poison was so effective and quick at killing animals. We did know that the second, important part of the plan was not being put into quick action: There was no cleanup crew.

After the dogs were killed, they were left where they had died. That first morning, at 9:00 A.M., there were corpses littering all the streets of Maroantsetra. Rain fell onto the poisoned bodies and ran off into the streets, where the children ran barefoot, where the food in the marketplace sat, where the chickens, ducks, and geese drank, where it ultimately seeped into the water table. By 11:00 A.M. the dogs in the central marketplace had been cleaned up. By 3:00 A.M., we saw no more corpses anywhere in town. But that night, the killing began again. The next day, corpses again littered the market and streets of Maroantsetra.

On one level, it was clearly a great mistake on the part of the government of Maroantsetra to have allowed half of a gruesome plan to take place without carrying out the other half. But why was it so disturbing to witness this scene? The remaining dogs wandering about might be killed over the next few nights, and it was hard to look the survivors in the eyes. They saw other dogs dead in the streets. Did they have fear? And did we care for those who were still living, or were we primarily reacting to the vision of those that had been killed?

If it was primarily the latter, we must remember that in the United

States, such activity goes on much more often, but behind closed doors, quietly. Thousands upon thousands of dogs and cats are killed—one may say *euthanized* or *put to sleep*, but euphemisms do not change the facts—because we have no room for them in our streets. People do not want stray animals roaming the streets of America, for the same reason that people worked every night for a month to eliminate them from Maroantsetra. Dense populations of strays are a hazard to us. We in the United States refer to the agencies controling the animal population as "humane" societies, emphasizing our compassionate nature. The Maroantsetrans unrepentantly call their control effort Opération Chien, highlighting its true character: an attack on dogs, by people, initiated out of real and carefully calculated self-interest. Confronting dead dogs is nothing compared to facing rabid humans. We tell ourselves it is better for the animals, but of course it is not. It is better, perhaps, that they never were born, if only to be killed. But stray animals at risk of spreading a disease that may easily be passed to humans are a real threat, and no society will tolerate it. In the United States, we are perhaps more sanitary, and certainly more discreet. How much of our despair at seeing these corpses in Maroantsetra was hypocrisy, much like worrying over the death of cattle while salivating for a hamburger?

Other than Opération Chien, one of the strangest and most obvious facets of life in Maroantsetra is the movies. On several of the dusty streets near the middle of town, wood-framed chalkboards announce the movie that will play inside a nearby shack that night on the poorly working VCR and television. The videotapes are probably poor-quality bootlegs from Asia, but because there is no television reception, this is the only visual media most Maroantsetrans have ever been exposed to. In 1999, *Titanic* was the clear winner in terms of popularity, appearing on several of the ten or fifteen television sets. The rest were dedicated to typical Hollywood adventure schlock, or earlier movies of possibly higher quality. Usually a star or two was listed on the boards—Jackie Chan, Steven Seagal, Arnold Schwarzenneger. Sometimes the movie's name (translated into French) and star were so remote from my experience that my only clue to the gist of that night's promised entertainment was the genre, assigned by the author of the sign. *Actien Kung Fu. Aventure Dance suggestif* (for *Dirty Dancing*). And the much-maligned *Aventure Grand Monstre* (*Godzilla*).

It occurred to me that, in the States, we might better avoid films not targeted at us by careful application of the Maroantsetran "chalkboard-genre" system. There would be Alien Invasion Adventures, and Brilliant Lunacies (*Rain Man, π, Good Will Hunting*). Incomplete Voyage would attract several applicants, the subgenre Almost Incomplete Voyage attracting fewer (say, *Apollo 13*). For the geek biologists among us, Hollywood could sort films by evolutionary relationships. Birds, crocodiles, and dinosaurs are all closely related to one another, in a group called Archosauria. The diverse genre Archosauria might represent Hitchcock's *The Birds, Crocodile Dundee,* and *Jurassic Park*.

While I was trying to decipher a particularly complex chalkboard genre one day, two policemen in dainty pillbox hats bicycled past me, waving cheerily. It was mango season, and there were men hanging from trees all over town. Maybe the policemen were out making sure nobody had fallen, or erupted into fights over mango rights. On that long, lazy afternoon, Bret and I took a Frisbee out into one of the wide roads punctuated by large puddles and chickens but little else. Quickly, we attracted a crowd of thirty or forty children, who were intensely curious to see the *vazaha* flinging a plate at each other in the heat of the day. They retreated en masse when one of us threw them the Frisbee, moving like a wave, but after a few attempts at engaging them, some of the braver boys gave it a shot. On the island, we had been teaching Lucien to play Frisbee in the restricted space of camp, and we were amazed at his intuitive grasp of the physics involved. These children, too, caught on very quickly. They learned to catch the spinning disk almost immediately, although throwing took a bit longer. Their less intrepid friends were more than willing to howl with laughter at these early attempts, but every time a new child tried his hand, there was one fewer person to laugh at the rest.

Two little girls stood apart from the rest, one dressed in ancient black lace, a party dress from a different time and place, probably donated in Europe with the best intentions, now worn as the sole garment in a child's wardrobe. Unlike most of the children, and all the rest of the girls, these two did not hide and giggle when the Frisbee came near them. The participating boys tried to wrest incoming Frisbees from the two girls, but they stood their ground, and learned to throw, too. Perhaps we sparked a love of Frisbee in Maroantsetra that day. If so, I feel we did our country proud.

24

Frogs in Paradise

The beautiful little yellow-and-blue frogs that I had been tracking for so many months seemed largely oblivious to my presence. They did not yearn to be studied, or known. That desire lay wholly in me. When I went out on a hot, dry morning, or a torrentially wet morning, and could not find male Z7 hopping around the edges of the bamboo stand, looking for an opportunity, or female B4, swollen with eggs, even though I had seen her the day before, I was disappointed. When I did not go out on a pale blue morning after a night of rain, because I was in town getting provisions, even though I knew the weather was perfect for frogs, they were not disappointed. They did not need me.

And yet I put together their story—in pieces, with several reversals, in fits and starts. There are still holes in that story, to be sure, but there are threads of logical continuity connecting most of what I came to understand about these frogs, and these threads hold the narrative together in a cohesive mass. Before this work, science knew essentially nothing about these frogs. Now we have a set of ideas and hypotheses, some tested, some not. Hopefully, their behavior remains largely unchanged whether scientists have explained it or not. But, as physics has taught us, just the act of observation affects the outcome of any event. Nobody can know precisely what nature looks like when there's no one around to watch.

Mantella laevigata are social animals. Being brightly colored and poisonous, they're relatively free of predators, which allows them to be active during the day, when color-seeing, visually oriented predators, such as most birds, are awake and hunting. Jessica and I did see one predation by a zonosaur. We also saw an attempted predation on a *Mantella* by a boa. Two males were simultaneously trying to court a female. She was hopping away from them, when the snake lunged at her from under the leaf litter and grabbed her in its mouth. The males scattered. The boa held her in its mouth, sometimes appearing to chew, but after twenty minutes, it released her. The next day, the snake, which had lived in that spot for several weeks, was gone, never to return. The frog, on the other hand, though bloodied and bitten after the event, went on to care for her offspring.

Yes, these frogs give maternal care. There is so much complexity in their social system. I am describing here but a thin slice of what I know, and even what I know is probably but a sliver of what is true. Males call from territories they defend, the best of which contain wells—broken pieces of bamboo, tree holes. Other territories are only spots on the forest floor, but males fight over these spots, though they appear to be without value beyond their proximity to wells within other males' territories. These tiny frogs can fight for hours, wrestling with one another, tumbling, chasing, yelling, the same call over and over again: *Deet-deet deet-deet deet-deet*. *"And don't come back."*

When they are not engaged in these spectacular fights, males may call to establish their location, their ownership of a piece of territory, or to attract females. Females who are receptive—most are not, at any given moment in time—approach calling males. When a male sees a female approach, that interminable call changes, softens. Now emitting a single repeated note, spaced further apart, *Deet, deet, deet,* he approaches her and rests his chin on top of her head or back—"chinning," I called it. *Deet, deet, deet: "So glad you came. Please, let me show you a well you might be interested in."* Then he leads her, oh so slowly, returning to her often to chin her again, calling all the while. He takes her to a well.

When finally they do arrive, and climb the well, she explores it thoroughly. This, after all, is where her child will develop, if she agrees to mate with the courting male. She may reject the well. Perhaps it is too acid, or not acid enough (they actually prefer extremely acid wells, I found, to my surprise). Perhaps it is too dry, or too tall, or already contains a tadpole, which she tries to avoid. It will probably not contain other species of frogs, or the parasites that prey on *Mantella* eggs, for the male has already discriminated against such wells. Male and female alike are trying to find the best spot for their offspring to develop, although their interests are not entirely the same.

If the female rejects the well, the courtship begins again, with chinning and leading and calling. *Deet, deet, deet. "I have another. You'll like it better, really."* Often the courtship dissolves at this point, the female losing interest in a male who took her to a well she didn't like. Even more often, surprisingly, the male will abandon courtships to fight with other males, males who are sneaking into his territory. But sometimes, a courtship is successful.

The female may accept the well, then allow the male to enter it with her and amplex her—rest on top of her in the position assumed by almost all mating frogs. If they mate, but a single egg is laid. Most frogs lay hundreds, if not thousands, of eggs in a single mating, the long strings of eggs twisting in currents, easily spotted by hungry birds or fish. Not so *Mantella laevigata*. These eggs are laid in protected, isolated water bodies, tiny little wells, on the inside wall above the water. The parents know who their offspring are, simply because they know *where* they are. With this luxury comes the ability to care for offspring, and once you are caring for offspring, it no longer makes sense to produce thousands of them, for who has the energy to take care of so many? Fewer children tend to mean more care for each of them.

Parental care is relatively rare in frogs—less than 10 percent of frog species take any sort of care of their offspring. Most of that care is in the rather noninteractive form of egg attendance, in which one parent stays with the eggs until they hatch into tadpoles, presumably dissuading potential predators, sometimes keeping the eggs wet, or free of fungus. Male *Mantella* do engage in a sort of egg attendance, continuing to defend the territories in which their offspring are developing. But mothers do even more.

If the single egg hatches, and drops into the water as a tadpole, its needs change. As an egg, it needed to stay wet, and not get eaten, but it didn't have to find food. Eggs don't eat. Some species of tadpoles don't eat, either, but most need to in order to grow and metamorphose, to become frogs. *Mantella laevigata* tadpoles need to eat. And when they do, they eat the eggs of their own species. They are cannibals.

As a result, when a female is looking for a place to mate, she is careful not to accept a well that already has a tadpole in it, for any egg she lays in that well will probably get cannibalized by the preexisting tadpole. The male that courts her is probably the father of that tadpole, so he benefits from a courtship in that well regardless of the fate of the resultant egg. If the egg develops and hatches, as the female desires, he gains another offspring. If his tadpole eats the egg, and so gains strength and size, that tadpole has a better chance of survival. Either way, his offspring benefit. But a female that isn't the mother of the tadpole is unlikely to see it that way. And so there is conflict between male and female frogs.

Although there is, theoretically, conflict between mother and child, too, regarding how much care the child should receive, and for how long, the mother does want the child to survive. In this system, where tadpoles survive by cannibalizing eggs, but courting females are on the lookout for wells containing tadpoles, tadpoles may sometimes go hungry. Mothers return to wells containing their tadpoles, especially those wells that have not been the site of large numbers of courtships, and feed their young. Mothers deposit unfertilized eggs for their tadpoles to eat. And the voracious tadpoles inevitably eat these eggs, sometimes beginning even before the egg is entirely laid.

All of this activity focuses on and around the wells where eggs and tadpoles develop. Males fight over wells. Females investigate wells even before they are reproductively receptive, and do so again before mating. Males cruise wells, too, learning which ones have been usurped by predators, or competitors. Several other species of frogs use the same wells *Mantella* does. Two of these species have extended paternal care, the fathers staying with their brood as the eggs develop, and later, as the tadpoles grow as well. The larger competitor species, a flat brown frog with a pointy snout and attractive white designs on its back—*Plethodontohyla notostica*—not only stays with its young but actively dissuades anyone else from getting near them. When another frog, or a person, peers into a well containing one of these protective fathers and his young, the dad emits a sharp bark of amazing intensity. It's hard not to keep going back for more, following the same instinct that causes people to watch horror films and go on roller coasters. The frog, though, is not as amused, and if continually hassled, will climb the inside of the well and bark right at your face, unfazed by the fact that the primate causing all this grief is roughly five thousand times its size.

Frogs aren't the only animals that use these wells. Land crabs sometimes crawl into them and stay awhile. Mosquitoes lay their eggs on the filmy surface. And the snarled "worms" I had seen eating frogs eggs were actually crane-fly larvae that lived inside the wells. These wormlike larvae, which attract all the gunk of the well and tend to tangle themselves into writhing knots, will never be the poster child for any conservation scheme. Not only are they unpleasant to look at, they are voracious predators, quickly dispatching frog eggs unfortunate enough to share their space. But they are an integral part of this system.

These wells, used by so many members of this rich animal community, are rare. There aren't enough of them to go around. *Mantella laevigata* has specific requirements for these wells—no other frog species, no crane-fly larvae, full of water, high acidity . . . the list goes on and on. There aren't enough wells in the forest. When I added more, in an experiment to assess if such wells really were limiting for these frogs, the frogs moved in almost overnight. Adults have plenty of food. Calling perches, water, shelter—all of those resources are abundant in these lowland rain forests of northeastern Madagascar. But wells are in short supply.

When a female of any species is choosing among possible mates, she might try to assess which male will offer a better genetic contribution to her offspring, better resources, or better paternal care. But *Mantella* females are focused on a single thing: the quality of the well. The male can be highly successful, one that defends broad swaths of territory, or one that doesn't defend any territory at all, one who creeps in and sneaks matings when the territorial males aren't paying attention—it doesn't matter. If the well is up to her standards, she will mate with him.

It is thrilling to discover the previously unknown aspects of a distinct evolutionary lineage, a species of poison frogs that are beautiful even to those who usually find such things slimy or repulsive. True, some aspects of fieldwork are less stimulating than others—the laying of transects, the routine collection of water-chemistry data, the iterated experiments. But there is little dissatisfaction in the actual work. I go to Madagascar to watch frogs, and never when I wake up in my tent at five in the morning do I think, Damn, another day watching those animals doing the same things ceaselessly. I love watching animals behave, interpreting what they do, basing that interpretation on theory that has worked itself into my head.

This is not to say, however, that there are no risks. People hear that you're working in the tropics, and the first thing they want to know about is the snakes. How big are they? How poisonous? How aggressive? How many people die every year? How many did I see? Did I have to fight any off with sticks? Despite the fact that I did, in fact, once come face-to-face with a Costa Rican fer-de-lance, snakes don't tend to be a big risk for tropical biologists. Especially not in Madagascar, where there are no—count them, zero—poisonous snakes.

Disappointed by the lack of belligerent snakes, their fangs dripping with deadly poison, people begin asking about the predators. Were there any really large cats—jaguars, or perhaps lions—prowling about for their next big meal? Were the crocodiles voracious? Did anything with large teeth and a nasty attitude come my way? Anything at all?

The predominant risks are not what you think. Sure, things with sharp teeth kill people. But the abiotic forces, the water and the lightning and the vast distances that separate you from help—these are what you really have to watch out for.

On my first field season in the tropics, I was in Costa Rica with Bret, five other grad students, and the esteemed biologist John Vandermeer. John tired of hearing our excited discussions whenever we saw the tail of a snake disappear beneath the leaf litter.

"I'm not concerned about you getting killed by snakes," he told us. "It's the water that will get you." He was prescient. Part of the reason the snakes were a low risk was precisely because we were afraid of them and were thus careful not to walk around without high boots on, or reach our hands into holes in the ground without first investigating them thoroughly. Part of the reason the water was dangerous was because we had no idea what he meant. Water? A threat?

A few days after John alerted us to his fears, Bret and I were walking across the high, sturdy bridge that ran over the river near our field site. There was a lovely swimming hole, accessible from the other side of the river, and all of us had swum in it frequently. We were done with our work for the day, work that had been particularly muddy because of all the rains we had gotten in the night, and were looking forward to a refreshing dip. As we began to turn down the path to the water, a local man stopped us.

"Wait," he advised. "Look at what is coming." We didn't speak much Spanish at the time, so we weren't sure what he was saying. We thought it probable that he was just trying to make conversation, but we were eager to swim, so we smiled and kept going.

"No!" he urged, pointing upstream. "Look." We stood at the railing of the bridge, gazing across the wide, smooth, slow river, at the trees on either side, which were dripping with vines and epiphytes. It was a beautiful scene, but we had seen it before. What we really wanted to do was swim.

Then, before our eyes, the river began rising. In minutes, the water level came up ten feet, then more. The river became urgent, threatening. Swirling eddies formed in tight, deadly whirlpools, then disappeared again. The shores were completely submerged, the detritus from the hills rushing down into the floodplain. Whole trees—immense boles two, three feet in diameter—rushed by. Stuck in a whirlpool, they would spiral madly, then get sucked down, finally shooting out like a bullet far downstream. Even on the bridge, we were not completely safe. A bridge once thirty feet above the water was now less than half that, and the water continued to rise. Humbled, Bret gave our savior the only thing we had—literally, the shirt off his back—and we gazed at the awesome spectacle for a few more minutes before retreating to safety. We had come within minutes of being torn apart by a raging river in the throes of a flash flood, a river we thought we knew.

Later on the same trip, six of us, minus John, our leader, were in the dry forests of Guanacaste, in northwestern Costa Rica. Bret and I knew of a beautiful beach a day's hike down through the parched landscape. Here, the Pacific coast is not ragged and dangerous, but relatively calm, with long expanses of white sand beach, iguanas and raccoon-like coatis living at the margins of sea and forest.

We went swimming in the refreshingly cool water, but as the waves came up, everyone except for me retreated to the shore. Quickly, I found myself pulled by a riptide, being dragged ever farther out, unable to surmount the looming waves that formed just in back, then just ahead of me, the land growing ever more distant. Intellectually, I knew how to deal with a riptide—swim parallel to shore, or even let it take you out a little, until it weakens, then swim parallel to escape its grasp. But feeling the twin threats of a riptide and the frenzied waves growing in intensity around me, I was just scared. I was swallowing water, all the while growing less certain of my strength as a swimmer, less certain that I knew how to escape.

Finally, feeling myself losing both strength and reason, I dived down into the seething dark waters, swam as long as I could toward what I hoped was shore, then let myself be pushed by the churning water. I don't know how long I was under, out of view of my friends, distanced from my own sense of self, but it seemed forever, to them and to me. I emerged near shore, able now to stand in the frothy water that still churned around me. I was safe. I had survived the trial by water that John had alluded to. Never again would I assume I knew the risks of a place simply because I knew what dangerous animals lived there.

Lightning is another unexpected hazard in the tropics. Bret must have particularly unusual electromagnetic fields surrounding him, for too often he has found himself unnervingly close to the location of lightning strikes. Once, when he was working on a forested hilltop in Panama, a storm that had been on the horizon began moving toward him. He covered his equipment with a tarp, put down the large antenna he was using to radio-track bats—an antenna that would have been a perfect lightning rod—and huddled by a tree to let the storm pass. Soon the storm was upon him, lightning strikes growing nearer. In an instant, searing flash, there was an impossibly loud *crack*, the lightning striking so close that everything shook with the force and the entire forest lit up. He bolted, running down the hill toward the field station while, all around him, lightning continued to strike, intolerably close. It never quite got him.

All the inhabitants of the field station were standing in the lab, gazing up at the hill he had been on, when he raced in, drenched and shaking. The forest was getting pummeled over and over again by spears of intense, bone-melting energy. He had escaped, this time. But nature is a tenacious enemy, and there is no telling when or how quickly the next electrical storm would move in with such mighty force.

In Madagascar, where there are no large land predators or poisonous snakes to worry about, it is easier to concern yourself with the sea and the lightning, the tree falls that may result from lightning strikes, the diseases that can kill if left untended, the injuries that fester interminably in the hot, wet environment of the rain forest. The overarching risk, that which affects all decisions in northeastern Madagascar, is the sheer remoteness of the place.

You would be foolish to travel to such a place without emergency evacuation insurance, something that, in theory, guarantees an airlift out to medical facilities should the need arise. But this insurance doesn't really do you any good. At Andranobe, with no radio at all, or on Nosy Mangabe, with a radio that rarely works, there is simply no way to call for help. Even if you make it the four miles to a radio at Andranobe, or jerry-rig a communication at Nosy Mangabe, maybe there will be no boat working that can come retrieve you. If you did somehow manage to get on a boat and make it back to Maroantsetra, how would you notify anyone that now was the time to collect on the promise of an emergency helicopter? The phones in Maroantsetra rarely work, and then only to access Tana. During the floods of 1997, following the hurricane, the two helicopters that landed in town had to be donated by the French government. There are no helicopters to spare in this country. And though lives are certainly saved in Tana, and even in Maroantsetra, at the locally available medical facilities, many more people die than we Westerners are comfortable with. The nearest reliable emergency room is in Nairobi—itself a risk, the blood supply tainted with HIV. Most people try to get to Paris. Arranging for all of those legs of an impossibly long voyage while suffering from a health situation that puts you at risk of dying isn't particularly plausible. The time necessary to rescue you from an emergency situation and get you to safety is what will kill you.

Working in Madagascar, the research itself is rich and rewarding, the risks stranger and more hidden than you might expect, but the benefits of such a life aren't what you might think, either. Certainly my raison d'être in Madagascar was to study frogs, to understand a life-form not previously known. But this did not fully explain why I was there. It was an excuse to tweak my world, turn it on its head. It is so easy to grow complacent in the comforts of the developed world, to simultaneously grow dependent on and weary of the constant barrage of news, communication, and product. It is hard, when the comforts are close at hand, to remove yourself willingly from their reach, even for a day, much less a lifetime. And it is sometimes surprising to remember that most of the world's peoples live without these accoutrements for their entire lives. But strip yourself of the ability to *order in* or *dial up* or *buy now* or *turn it on*, and life is laid bare. The essentials become clear, as do the luxuries that bring particular joy to your life. I need to buy rice, find clean water to drink, wash my clothes, keep dry enough not to mold from the inside. I want to be able to read books, sit in a comfy chair, have time to think. Immersed in Western culture, it's easy to mistake want for need, and ease of acquisition for desire. Do I want to check my E-mail five times a day, or is it a strange compulsion that arises only when I can, and during those times when I'm searching for meaning in a life stripped of the urgency of cooking over a charcoal fire or taking advantage of a hot afternoon to dry out a tent?

Then there is the realization over and over again that people are the same everywhere. No matter the culture, there are good people and bad, and finding the good in another culture opens doors of understanding and goodwill. To find yourself being "other" in a society, when in your own you have always blended in, forces an investigation of the xenophobia in all of us. I can believe that all people, regardless of origin or skin color, are equally valid and valuable, but I can't have a clue what it feels like to live as an African-American in the United States until, perhaps, I have lived as *vazaha* in Madagascar. Some people there have accepted me, some people never will, and the vast group in the middle regard me with some skepticism regardless of what I do. As unprecedented and difficult as that has been for me, I have an out. When I am there, my life as other is finite, for I know I will be going home someday. I will never know what it feels like to have no choice in the matter.

My memories of Madagascar are a series of snapshots, frozen in time. Much of the hardship of daily life is erased from these, replaced with images of fisher people with mangoes, little boys curious about language, brightly colored frogs courting and singing. I remember the sweet smell of cloves wafting through camp, and standing under a waterfall stunning in its strength and glory, and listening to the forest wake up, the ruffed lemurs cackling as the sun warmed their furry bellies high in the trees. The frogs didn't care if I came or not, if I sat among them on my little three-legged stool and studied their every move. But I did. For in starry-eyed retrospect, wiping clean the frustrations and disappointments, these are frogs in paradise.

EPILOGUE

Leaving Madagascar in 1999, I didn't know when I might return. Our friends wanted to know if it might be next year, or the year after that. I couldn't say. I had scheduled our departure so that by the end of April, on my thirtieth birthday, I would be back home. This was my birthday present to myself. By the end of that trip, though, I had finally fallen in love with Madagascar, and as long as everything was going as planned, I didn't feel the predicted urgency to leave.

Then Air Mad decided not to send the plane that flew between Maroantsetra and Tana, a flight for which we had had tickets for months. The plane simply didn't arrive. Our international flight out of Tana would leave only seventy-two hours later. In the ensuing twenty-four-hour dash to get out of Maroantsetra, we tried hiring a boat, a *taxi-brousse*, and even tried to charter a plane. A fast boat, we had heard, existed in town, captained by the mayor's son, and perhaps he would take us. Heloise, the chauffeur, took us to the weird outskirts of town, an area where we had never been, dense with forest and broken-down shacks. Here the son, a corpulent man surrounded by fawning women, lived on a small estate. He agreed to take us to Tamatave on his boat, for the astounding price of 5 million FMG, almost one thousand dollars. I didn't have that kind of money with me. On the way back to town on the muddy rutted road, deep forest tangling in from both sides, we ran into one of the guides, who jumped into the Rover with us as we tore through town, trying to figure out what to do next. Perhaps we could hire a *taxi-brousse*.

There were no *brousses* equipped to make the long trip south, and besides, many of the roads were impassable at that time of year. We couldn't count on reaching Tana in three days, even if we had found a vehicle capable of the trip.

Two *vazaha* who were staying at the new hotel had also been put out by Air Mad's negligence, as they needed to get home for their wedding celebration. They had enough wealth to cover the fact that we didn't, and when they chartered a plane, they let us accompany them for far less than they were paying. It was due to arrive at six the next morning, and would take off immediately thereafter, so we had to be there early or miss our opportunity. That night, there were no rooms available at the Maroa, and our air mattress was packed away behind a locked door at Projet Masoala, so we spent a fitful, miserable night on the floor of the Projet Masoala building worried that we would somehow miss the flight and be out of options.

By morning, it was pouring, sheets of water peeling off the sky, turning the still-dark streets into pools. Heloise, who was going to take us and our stuff to the airport, was late. Very late. I went out to the main road in town, where he would be coming from, and looked vainly down the empty street. There were no signs of movement. I was wet, it was dark and several miles out of town a plane would be touching down shortly, then leaving again. Bret went off to find someone, anyone, awake or not, with a vehicle who could take us. He found a man with a *brousse*—his was a tarp-covered pickup truck. We had spoken to him the day before, and though he couldn't get us to Tana, the airport was within range. *Brousses* don't travel anywhere with just a driver, so shortly he and his two men arrived at Projet Masoala. We loaded the *brousse* up, and took off down the wet, rutted roads. Over the roar of the engine and the pounding of the rain, I thought I heard a plane engine. Was it coming, or going? As we pulled up to the airport, I leapt out of the back of the *brousse* where we were sitting, and ran around to the back of the airport, where the airstrip was. En route, I plunged into a hole, submerging my leg up to the knee in cold, murky water. I continued on. Rounding the corner of the building, I saw . . . nothing. No plane. No evidence of a plane. No other *vazaha*. It was seven o'clock now. Surely they had left without us. I stared in disbelief, frozen, until Bret and Glenn caught up with me.

"Where's the plane?" one of them asked. I couldn't speak. It was too tragic. We were never leaving, and I was destined to celebrate my thirtieth birthday on the floor of the Projet Masoala building, dirty and damp.